Docker

3 Books in 1 - "Docker: From Beginner to Pro - A Comprehensive Guide to Container Deployment "

Allan Finley

Table of Contents

BOOK 1 – Docker: *"A Beginner's Guide to Mastering Containerization and Virtualization"*

Introduction...9

Chapter One: Understanding Virtualization and Containerization 20

Chapter Two: Installing and Configuring Docker.30

Chapter Three: Docker Images and Containers 42

Chapter Four: Working with Docker Containers..53

Chapter Five: Docker Networking Basics..............64

Chapter Six: Docker Storage and Volumes...........76

Chapter Seven: Building Docker Images...............88

Chapter Eight: Docker Compose: Simplifying Multi-Container...99

Chapter Nine: Managing Application Data with Docker.. 110

Chapter Ten: Docker Security Fundamentals.......121

Chapter Eleven: Docker APIs and Ecosystem.......133

Chapter Twelve: Troubleshooting and Debugging Docker Containers...143

Chapter Thirteen: Preparing for More Advanced Docker Topics...156

Conclusion..167

BOOK 2 - Docker: *"A Middle-Level Guide to Optimizing Docker Workflows and Efficiency"*

Introduction 178

Chapter One: Advanced Docker Configuration 190

Chapter Two: Efficient Container Management.....203

Chapter Three: Streamlining Docker Images......... 216

Chapter Four: Docker Networking Deep Dive........228

Chapter Five: Docker Storage Solutions 241

Chapter Six: Scaling Docker Containers 253

Chapter Seven: Orchestrating Containers with Docker Swarm...266

Chapter Eight: Continuous Integration and Deployment with Docker 278

Chapter Nine: Monitoring and Logging Docker Environments 292

Chapter Ten: Docker Security Enhancement 306

Chapter Eleven: Docker APIs and SDKs 318

Chapter Twelve: Performance Tuning in Docker ... 331

Chapter Thirteen: Advanced Troubleshooting Techniques...344

Chapter Fourteen: The Docker Community and Future Trends 358

Conclusion 370

BOOK 3 - Docker: *"A Pro-Level Guide to Cutting-Edge Techniques in Docker Performance Tuning"*

Introduction 382

Chapter One: Advanced Container Architecture....394

Chapter Two: Deep Dive into Docker Engine 407

Chapter Three: High-Performance Networking.... 420

Chapter Four: High-Density Container Deployments 432

Chapter Five: Resource Management and Scheduling 444

Chapter Six: Performance Benchmarking and Testing 457

Chapter Seven: Scalability and Elasticity 472

Chapter Eight: Docker in Hybrid and Multi-Cloud Environments 485

Chapter Nine: Advanced Docker Security Practices 498

Chapter Ten: GPU and Hardware Acceleration......509

Chapter Eleven: Docker and Microservices Optimization 519

Chapter Twelve: Monitoring, Profiling, and Tracing 530

Chapter Thirteen: Performance Anti-Patterns and Common Pitfalls 543

Chapter Fourteen: Future Trends in Docker Performance 555

Chapter Fifteen: Automating Performance Optimization 567

Conclusion 580

Introduction

Overview of Docker and its importance in modern software development

Docker has significantly altered the field of modern software development by introducing the concept of containerization, which has changed how applications are developed, deployed, and maintained across various environments. Docker utilizes container technology—a method where applications are encapsulated along with their entire runtime environment, libraries, and dependencies in isolated packages called containers.

Docker's Core Technology

The essence of Docker lies in its ability to use containers to separate applications while sharing the host system's kernel. This setup allows developers to package their applications with all necessary components into a single deployable unit. This container ensures consistent performance across different computing environments, from development through to production.

Enhancing Development with Docker

Docker refines the development process by creating consistent environments for the entire development lifecycle. It eliminates common issues like discrepancies between different working environments that can lead to problems when moving from a local machine to a production environment. Docker's streamlined configurations allow developers to focus more on their code and less on setting up environments, thus speeding up the development cycle and reducing time to market.

Example: Simplifying Development Environments

Consider a development team working on a Python application that requires Redis for caching and PostgreSQL for databases. Traditionally, setting up these services on every developer's workstation can be tedious and error-prone. Docker solves this problem by using **Dockerfile** and **docker-compose.yml** files to codify the entire environment:

```yaml
version: '3.8'
services:
  web:
    build: .

    ports:
      - "5000:5000"
    volumes:
      - .:/code
    links:
      - redis
      - db
  redis:
    image: "redis:alpine"
  db:
    image: "postgres:13"
    environment:
      POSTGRES_USER: exampleuser
      POSTGRES_PASSWORD: examplepass
      POSTGRES_DB: exampledb
```

This setup specifies three services—web, Redis, and PostgreSQL—each running in its own container. With Docker Compose, launching these services is as simple as executing docker-compose up, which ensures environmental consistency across all developers' systems.

10

Facilitating Continuous Integration and Continuous Deployment (CI/CD)

Docker plays a critical role in CI/CD, helping teams deploy updates more rapidly and with greater assurance of consistency between development and production environments. Docker containers can be integrated seamlessly with CI/CD tools like Jenkins and GitLab CI, automating the processes for testing and deployment in a consistent and controlled manner.

Optimizing Resource Utilization

Docker's approach to containerization is more resource-efficient than traditional virtual machines that require a complete operating system. Containers leverage the host system's kernel and consume fewer resources, allowing for a higher density of applications per server, thereby maximizing hardware utility.

Enhancing Application Security

Docker improves application security through isolation. Each container operates with its own file system, provided by the Docker image, which is immutable once established. This containment helps safeguard against unauthorized code alterations. Docker further enhances security through built-in mechanisms such as namespaces and cgroups, which manage and limit the resources accessible to each container.

Conclusion

The advent of Docker and its containerization technology has become a cornerstone in software development, ensuring that applications deploy smoothly across any platform. It has streamlined development processes, maximized hardware efficiency, and strengthened security protocols. As more organizations move towards microservices architectures, and adopt DevOps and Agile practices, Docker's role in facilitating scalable, secure, and efficient software deployments continues to grow.

Benefits of using Docker for containerization and virtualization

Docker has fundamentally transformed the way software is developed, deployed, and managed, making it an indispensable tool for modern software development environments. Its innovative approach to containerization allows applications to be packaged with all necessary components—code, runtime environment, libraries, and dependencies—into a single deployable unit. This ensures consistent performance across various computing environments, from development through to production, fostering agility and efficiency.

Portability Across Diverse Environments

A standout feature of Docker is the seamless portability it provides. By encapsulating the application's entire runtime environment, Docker containers ensure that the application will operate uniformly, whether it is running on a developer's local machine, a test server, or a live production environment.

Docker Portability Example

Consider a setup where a developer needs to deploy a Node.js application with a MongoDB backend. The Docker configuration could include a **Dockerfile** for setting up the Node.js environment and a **docker-compose.yml** to orchestrate the application and database containers:

```
# Dockerfile for Node.js Application
FROM node:14
WORKDIR /app
COPY package.json package-lock.json ./
RUN npm install
COPY . .
EXPOSE 3000
CMD ["node", "server.js"]
```

```
# docker-compose.yml for Node.js and MongoDB
version: '3.1'
services:
  app:
    build: .
    ports:
      - "3000:3000"
    links:
      - db
  db:
    image: mongo
    environment:
      MONGO_INITDB_ROOT_USERNAME: admin
      MONGO_INITDB_ROOT_PASSWORD: secret
```

This setup defines a service for the application and another for MongoDB, with Docker Compose handling the orchestration. By using **docker-compose up**, the entire environment can be instantiated uniformly across any Docker-enabled system, thereby avoiding the common issue of inconsistent environments.

Resource Efficiency

Unlike virtual machines that require their own full-blown OS, Docker containers share the host OS's kernel. This shared approach means containers are lighter, require fewer resources, and can boot up much faster than VMs, allowing more applications to run simultaneously on the same hardware.

Boosting Developer Productivity

Docker enhances productivity by reducing setup times for development environments through the use of Docker images. These images are reproducible, version-controllable, and can be shared among team members, ensuring everyone works in a consistent environment. This homogeneity helps in minimizing the time spent on debugging environment-specific issues and speeds up the development cycle.

Streamlining Configuration Management

Docker's approach to using images as standalone, version-controlled entities simplifies configuration management. Images can be stored in registries and pulled as needed to maintain consistency across different stages of the deployment pipeline, which is particularly beneficial in microservices architectures where different services might have varied requirements.

Security Enhancements

Docker improves application security by isolating applications from one another and from the underlying infrastructure. Each container interacts with its own set of resources and is segregated from others, enhancing security. Docker also allows users to define security settings, controlling the degree of access containers have to underlying system resources.

Seamless CI/CD Integration

Docker's compatibility with continuous integration and deployment systems facilitates smoother workflows from development to production. Containers can be integrated into CI/CD pipelines, allowing the same container used for development or testing to be deployed in production, ensuring consistency across environments.

```
# Example snippet for a Jenkins pipeline integrating Docker
pipeline {
    agent any
    stages {
        stage('Build Docker Image') {
            steps {
                script {
                    docker.build("my-app:${env.BUILD_NUMBER}")
                }
            }
        }
```

```
        stage('Push to Registry') {
            steps {
                script {
                    docker.withRegistry('https://registry.mydomain.com', 'registry-creds') {
                        docker.image("my-app:${env.BUILD_NUMBER}").push()
                    }
                }
            }
        }
    }
}
```

Conclusion

Docker's introduction has brought a paradigm shift in how applications are developed and managed, simplifying the process while enhancing the performance and scalability of deployments. Its role in modernizing software development practices has made it a critical asset for any organization aiming to streamline and secure their application deployment processes. Docker not only accelerates the deployment cycle but also reduces operational overhead and improves the overall quality of software.

What to expect from this guide: from basics to proficient use

In this detailed guide to Docker, readers will embark on a journey that begins with the basics of Docker and container technology and advances to mastery of sophisticated Docker functionalities, blending foundational knowledge with practical application tips. This guide is structured to demystify Docker's core concepts, offering both a deep dive into the technical nuances and hands-on examples to cement understanding.

Introduction to Fundamental Concepts

At the heart of Docker lies its ability to simplify the creation, deployment, and running of applications by using containers. Containers package an application and all its dependencies into a single unit, ensuring that the application runs consistently across any computing platform. This guide starts by contrasting Docker's containerization approach with traditional virtualization—where the former shares the host system's kernel, leading to enhanced efficiency and speed.

```
# Ensuring Docker is properly installed on your system
docker --version
```

Installing and Configuring Docker

This guide provides a walkthrough on setting up Docker across various operating systems such as Windows, Mac, and popular Linux distributions. It includes detailed steps to install Docker, execute your first container, and explore basic Docker operations like pulling an image from Docker Hub or monitoring active containers.

```
# Example commands to pull an image and run a container
docker pull ubuntu
docker run -it ubuntu /bin/bash
```

Advanced Topics: Networking, Storage, and Security

Building on the basics, the guide delves into more intricate aspects like Docker networking, which facilitates communication between containers and the external world, and Docker volumes, which manage data persistence beyond container lifecycles. Additionally, it covers securing Docker containers and images, teaching best practices and utilizing Docker's built-in security tools like namespaces and cgroups to isolate and manage container resources securely.

```
# Commands for managing Docker networks and volumes
docker network create my-custom-network
docker run --network=my-custom-network alpine
docker run -v /my/persistent/data:/data alpine
```

Mastery with Docker Compose and Docker Swarm

For users ready to scale applications or manage complex multi-container deployments, the guide covers Docker Compose for service coordination and Docker Swarm for multi-host container orchestration. These tools simplify deploying applications across different environments, making them essential for efficient container management at scale.

```yaml
# Sample docker-compose.yml demonstrating basic service configuration
version: '3'
services:
  web:
    image: nginx
    ports:
      - "80:80"
  database:
    image: postgres
    environment:
      POSTGRES_DB: exampledb
      POSTGRES_USER: admin
      POSTGRES_PASSWORD: password
```

Advanced Use: Optimizing Performance, Monitoring, and CI/CD

Moving towards more advanced use, the guide explains how to optimize Docker setups for performance, monitor containers effectively, and integrate Docker workflows into CI/CD pipelines. This part aims to enhance proficiency in maintaining Docker environments, ensuring applications are both robust and responsive.

```
# Example of using Docker stats for monitoring and a Jenkins pipeline integration
docker stats

# Jenkins pipeline integration snippet for Docker
pipeline {
    agent any
    stages {
        stage('Build') {
            steps {
                sh 'docker build -t my-application-image .'
            }
        }
        stage('Test') {
            steps {
                sh 'docker run my-application-image ./tests'
            }
        }
```

```
        stage('Deploy') {
            steps {
                sh 'docker push my-application-image'
            }
        }
    }
}
```

Conclusion

This guide is crafted to equip both beginners and seasoned developers with the necessary skills to navigate and utilize Docker's ecosystem efficiently. From initial setup to advanced deployment strategies, this guide aims to provide a thorough understanding of Docker, preparing users for competent and professional use in diverse software development scenarios.

Chapter One

Understanding Virtualization and Containerization

Definitions and fundamental concepts

In today's technological landscape, Docker has become a seminal platform, transforming the management and deployment of software through its advanced containerization technique. This guide explores the essential concepts underpinning Docker's robust capabilities: containerization, Docker images, containers, registries, Dockerfiles, and Docker Compose. These foundational elements are indispensable for developers and IT professionals eager to fully exploit the benefits of Docker.

Containerization

Containerization is a lightweight form of virtualization that deploys applications within containers—self-sufficient units that operate using shared parts of the host operating system's kernel. This architecture contrasts sharply with traditional virtual machines that virtualize entire hardware systems, making containers quicker to launch and less resource-intensive.

Containers

Containers operate as discrete, isolated processes within their user spaces, each derived from Docker images. They are inherently temporary, with changes to their file systems being non-persistent unless explicitly saved outside the container. This characteristic is especially advantageous for stateless applications that require high scalability and reliability, as it simplifies data management and scaling.

Images

A Docker image is an immutable blueprint for creating containers, composed of layered adjustments as defined in a Dockerfile. These layers optimize data reuse and minimize storage requirements, which expedites the deployment process by leveraging cached layers.

```
# Example of building a Docker image from a Dockerfile
docker build -t myimage:latest .
```

Dockerfiles

A Dockerfile is a scripted set of directives that Docker uses to build images automatically. It contains various instructions such as **FROM**, which specifies the base image; **RUN**, which executes shell commands; **COPY** and **ADD** for adding files from the host into the image; and **CMD**, which sets the default command to run upon starting a container.

```
# A simple Dockerfile for a Python application
FROM python:3.8-slim
WORKDIR /app
COPY requirements.txt .
RUN pip install -r requirements.txt
COPY . .
CMD ["python", "app.py"]
```

Docker Registries

Docker images are stored and distributed through Docker registries, such as Docker Hub, which is the most common public registry. Users can also establish private registries to manage image distribution within their organizations. Registries are central to maintaining the version control of images and facilitating seamless sharing across teams.

```
# Retrieving an image from Docker Hub
docker pull nginx:latest
```

Docker Compose

Docker Compose is a tool that orchestrates the deployment of multi-container applications. It utilizes a YAML file to define multiple services, their configurations, and relationships, simplifying complex deployments into manageable operations.

```
# docker-compose.yml example for a basic web application
version: '3'
services:
  web:
    image: nginx
    ports:
      - "80:80"
```

```
backend:
  build: .
  depends_on:
    - db
db:
  image: postgres
  environment:
    POSTGRES_DB: sampledb
    POSTGRES_USER: user
    POSTGRES_PASSWORD: password
```

Conclusion

Understanding Docker's core concepts—containerization, Docker images, Dockerfiles, Docker registries, and Docker Compose—is crucial for harnessing Docker's full potential to enhance application deployment and management. These principles provide the tools necessary for developers to streamline processes, ensuring applications are both efficient and scalable across different environments. Mastery of these topics will equip IT professionals to implement more dynamic and responsive development practices.

Comparison of containers vs. virtual machines

In the dynamic arena of cloud computing and application deployment, distinguishing between containers and virtual machines (VMs) is essential for developers, system architects, and IT operations teams to make strategic decisions about their IT infrastructure. Both containers and VMs offer compelling solutions for application isolation and dependency management, but they do so through distinctly different technological approaches tailored to varying operational needs.

Fundamental Differences

Virtual Machines: VMs function at the hardware level, encapsulating an entire operating system along with a virtual copy of all the hardware that the OS requires to run. This setup results in a completely self-contained and independent operating environment for each VM, providing robustness and stability.

Containers: Conversely, containers operate at the OS level and share the host's kernel but run in isolated user spaces. They encapsulate only the application and its immediate dependencies, not the kernel or the OS, which results in a more lightweight and agile container than a VM.

Resource Utilization and Performance

Virtual Machines: VMs each run a full-fledged OS, requiring substantial system resources (CPU, memory, and storage), potentially leading to resource underutilization and higher operational costs, particularly in dense, dynamic environments like those needed for microservices.

Containers: Containers share the host's OS kernel and are more resource-efficient, requiring less CPU and memory than VMs. This efficiency enables higher application density and reduces infrastructure costs. Containers' minimalistic design allows for almost instantaneous startup times, favoring environments that demand rapid scaling.

Isolation and Security

Virtual Machines: The strong isolation provided by VMs, due to their separate OS environments, is advantageous for running diverse applications on the same server while keeping them completely isolated. This separation enhances security, limiting the potential for breaches to spread across environments.

Containers: Containers provide application isolation by segregating processes and deployments but share the host OS kernel, which can introduce risks if the kernel is compromised. Nevertheless, container security has seen significant improvements through the use of namespaces and control groups (cgroups), enhancing their viability in secure deployments.

Deployment and Scalability

Virtual Machines: VM deployment can be slow, often taking minutes, which may not be ideal for applications that require frequent, rapid scaling. Their larger size and slower boot times can hinder performance in environments that require quick responsiveness.

Containers: Due to their lightweight nature, containers can be deployed in seconds, making them particularly well-suited for applications that need to scale quickly and efficiently. This rapid deployment capability is critical in continuous integration and continuous deployment (CI/CD) scenarios and when employing horizontal scaling tactics to manage increased load.

Maintenance and Operations

Virtual Machines: Managing a fleet of VMs can be complex and labor-intensive. Each VM operates its own OS, which necessitates regular updates and patches, adding to the administrative burden, especially as the number of VMs scales up.

Containers: Containers streamline the update process and system maintenance due to their separation from the host OS. Individual containers can be updated, deployed, and managed without the need to overhaul the entire system, facilitating more consistent and manageable application deployments across various environments.

Conclusion

In conclusion, while VMs are ideal for applications that need full OS isolation, containers offer a more streamlined and resource-efficient solution perfect for applications that benefit from quick deployment and frequent scaling. The decision between using VMs or containers should be guided by specific application demands, security considerations, and overall infrastructure strategy. As container technologies continue to advance and mature, they are increasingly regarded as a practical alternative to VMs in many scenarios, aligning well with modern DevOps practices and offering substantial operational benefits.

History and evolution of Docker

Docker has emerged as a transformative force in software development and deployment, significantly shaping the landscape of application management. This guide traces Docker's evolution from its origins as a modest project within a startup to its status as a definitive technology in containerization.

The Genesis of Docker

Launched in March 2013 by Solomon Hykes and his company, originally named dotCloud, Docker debuted at the PyCon conference the same year. The project evolved from an initiative to improve application isolation using Linux Containers (LXC), a technology that allowed multiple isolated Linux systems on a single host. Docker was designed to simplify and enhance the usability of containers by providing a more accessible, higher-level API than LXC offered, which was often seen as too complex for routine development tasks.

Docker distinguished itself by packaging applications in containers that included all necessary dependencies, which streamlined development and deployment processes across any environment. This approach allowed developers to build and test applications locally and deploy them seamlessly in any Docker-supported environment.

Growth and Community Adoption

Docker quickly captured the attention of the developer community due to its user-friendly approach to container management. It simplified many of the operations associated with containers through straightforward CLI commands and Dockerfiles, which automated container creation through easy-to-understand scripts.

```
# Example of using Docker to run a simple nginx web server
docker run -d -p 80:80 --name webserver nginx
```

The ability of Docker containers to ensure consistent operation across diverse development, testing, and production environments contributed greatly to its popularity. This was particularly valuable in microservices architectures, which depend on multiple small, modular services that operate independently.

Development of the Docker Ecosystem

As Docker's user base grew, so did its ecosystem. Docker Hub was introduced as a centralized platform for developers to share and manage container images. This registry became a crucial tool for fostering an active Docker community, enabling developers to push updates and share applications easily.

Docker also expanded its toolset with Docker Compose, Docker Swarm, and Docker Machine, enhancing its offerings for orchestrating containers, managing clusters, and simplifying deployments across multiple machines, respectively. These tools addressed specific user needs around managing complex containerized applications and scaling them efficiently.

Standardization and Corporate Evolution

The success of Docker led to the rebranding of dotCloud to Docker, Inc., shifting the company's focus entirely to the development of Docker technology. The firm also spearheaded efforts to standardize container formats and runtimes through collaborations with the Open Container Initiative (OCI) and the Cloud Native Computing Foundation (CNCF), ensuring broader adoption and compatibility across the industry.

Docker Today and Its Future

Continuing to innovate, Docker has enhanced its offerings to better suit enterprise needs, particularly with Docker Enterprise Edition, which provides sophisticated security, management, and scalability features suitable for large-scale environments. Docker's support for multiple hardware architectures has also expanded, allowing it to accommodate a variety of infrastructures.

Docker's story is one of rapid growth and community-driven innovation, which has not only democratized container technology but also continuously leads the charge in cloud-native development practices. As Docker maintains its pivotal role in the DevOps field, its ongoing evolution promises further enhancements and broader applications in software deployment and management.

Chapter Two

Installing and Configuring Docker

Step-by-step installation on various operating systems (Windows, macOS, Linux)

Setting up Docker is an essential initial step for developers interested in leveraging the benefits of containerization. Docker can be installed on multiple operating systems, including Windows, macOS, and Linux, with specific installation processes tailored to each platform. This comprehensive guide will walk you through the installation of Docker, ensuring that you can quickly begin deploying and managing containerized applications on your chosen system.

Installing Docker on Windows

System Requirements:

- Windows 10 64-bit: Pro, Enterprise, or Education (Build 16299 or later).

- Both Hyper-V and Containers Windows features must be enabled.

Installation Procedure:

1. **Download Docker Desktop for Windows:**

   o Access Docker Hub, find the Docker Desktop section, and download the installer.

2. **Run the Installer:**

   o Launch the Docker Desktop Installer and follow the on-screen prompts. Make sure to select the option that enables Hyper-V Windows Features, as this is necessary for Docker to manage the required subsystems.

3. **Restart Your PC:**

   o After installation, restart your PC to allow the configurations to take effect.

4. **Open Docker Desktop:**

   o Find Docker Desktop in the Start menu and open it. The first time it runs, it may take a few minutes as it configures its settings.

5. **Test the Installation:**

   o To ensure Docker has been installed correctly, open a command prompt and execute **docker run hello-world**. This command pulls a test image from Docker Hub and runs it, which should print a confirmation message.

```
docker run hello-world
```

Installing Docker on macOS

System Requirements:

- Mac hardware from 2010 onwards.

- macOS Mojave 10.14 or later.

Installation Steps:

1. **Download Docker Desktop for macOS:**

   - Visit Docker Hub to download the Docker Desktop installer for macOS.

2. **Install Docker Desktop:**

   - Open the downloaded **.dmg** file and drag Docker into your Applications folder.

3. **Launch Docker:**

   - Open Docker from the Applications folder. During the initial launch, Docker may request your password to install necessary network components.

4. **Enable Necessary Permissions:**

   - If macOS prompts you, provide Docker with the required access permissions to files and notification privileges.

5. **Verify the Installation:**

   - Open a terminal and run **docker run hello-world** to confirm Docker is functioning properly.

```
docker run hello-world
```

Installing Docker on Linux

System Requirements:

- Compatible with various Linux distributions including Ubuntu, Debian, Fedora, and CentOS.

Installation Steps for Ubuntu:

1. **Update Your System:**

   o Use **sudo apt-get update** to refresh your package index.

2. **Install Prerequisites:**

   o Install necessary packages to allow the use of a repository over HTTPS:

```
sudo apt-get install \
    apt-transport-https \
    ca-certificates \
    curl \
    software-properties-common
```

3. **Add Docker's GPG Key:**

   o Securely add the official Docker GPG key to your system:

```
curl -fsSL https://download.docker.com/linux/ubuntu/gpg | sudo apt-key add -
```

4. **Setup the Docker Repository:**

   o Add the stable repository to get Docker packages:

```
sudo add-apt-repository \
  "deb [arch=amd64] https://download.docker.com/linux/ubuntu \
  $(lsb_release -cs) \
  stable"
```

5. **Install Docker Engine:**

   ○ Update your package listings and install Docker Engine:

```
sudo apt-get update
sudo apt-get install docker-ce
```

6. **Confirm Installation:**

   ○ Test Docker to verify it's installed correctly by running:

```
sudo docker run hello-world
```

This detailed setup guide ensures that you can install Docker smoothly on any major operating system and start utilizing Docker's powerful features for developing and deploying containerized applications. Each OS may have its own nuances during installation, but Docker's functionality remains consistent, providing a robust environment for development teams.

Configuring Docker settings for optimal performance

Optimizing Docker configurations is crucial for developers and system administrators to enhance both the performance and reliability of Docker environments. Proper configuration ensures efficient resource utilization and can prevent application downtime. This guide delves into several adjustments and best practices that can significantly improve how Docker performs in various deployment scenarios.

1. Resource Management

Controlling resource usage is fundamental to maintaining system stability and ensuring that Docker containers do not consume excessive system resources.

CPU Resources: Limiting CPU usage helps prevent a container from using too much of the host's CPU, which could impact other containers or host operations.

```
docker run -it --cpu-shares=512 --cpus=1.5 ubuntu:latest /bin/bash
```

The above command restricts the container to using up to 1.5 CPUs, assigning it a lower priority with 512 CPU shares.

Memory Resources: It's also important to restrict the memory usage of containers to prevent any single application from monopolizing system memory.

```
docker run -it --memory=1g ubuntu:latest /bin/bash
```

This command sets a limit, restricting the container to no more than 1 GB of memory.

2. Disk Utilization Strategies

Implementing Volumes for Persistent Storage: Using volumes instead of container layers for data storage enhances performance, especially for database storage or applications with high write requirements.

```
docker volume create myvolume
docker run -it --mount src=myvolume,dst=/data ubuntu /bin/bash
```

This configuration creates and mounts a volume, optimizing data persistence and performance.

Regular Cleanup: Removing unused data regularly helps in preventing Docker from slowing down due to clutter.

```
docker system prune -a
```

This command clears all unused containers, networks, and images, reclaiming disk space and resources.

3. Network Optimization

Adjust Network Configurations: For bandwidth-intensive applications, adjusting Docker's network settings can significantly improve throughput and reduce latency.

Host Networking Mode: Using the host networking mode eliminates the overhead of the default Docker bridge network.

```
docker run -it --network host ubuntu /bin/bash
```

This command runs the container using the host's network stack, which can enhance network performance.

4. Security and Runtime Efficiency

Minimize Capabilities: Limiting container capabilities to only those that are necessary can enhance security and reduce overhead.

```
docker run --cap-drop=all --cap-add=NET_BIND_SERVICE ubuntu:latest
```

This command drops all unnecessary capabilities except for the capability to bind to low-numbered ports.

Read-Only Containers: Configuring containers to run with read-only file systems where possible increases security and performance by preventing unnecessary write operations.

```
docker run --read-only ubuntu:latest
```

This setup prevents any modifications to the container's file system, enhancing its integrity and performance.

5. Efficient Logging and Monitoring

Opt for Efficient Logging Drivers: Choosing the right logging driver can prevent performance degradation due to excessive logging.

```
docker run -it --log-driver=syslog ubuntu /bin/bash
```

Using the syslog driver, as shown here, can offload logging duties from the container, improving its performance.

Utilize Monitoring Tools: Employ Docker's built-in tools like Docker stats or third-party monitoring solutions to keep track of resource usage and performance metrics.

Conclusion

Configuring Docker for optimal performance involves a holistic approach—from managing resources carefully and optimizing disk usage to tuning network settings and securing container operations. Regular updates to these configurations, based on ongoing monitoring and performance analysis, will ensure that Docker environments are both robust and efficient, supporting high-performance containerized applications.

Understanding Docker version updates

Keeping Docker updated is vital for ensuring that your containerized applications are secure, efficient, and stable. Docker regularly releases updates that include enhancements, new features, security patches, and bug fixes, crucial for maintaining the platform's robustness in the face of security threats and technological changes. This guide delves into the intricacies of Docker version updates, highlighting their significance, how they are structured, and effective update management strategies.

The Significance of Updating Docker

Security Enhancements: Regular updates are essential for security. Docker updates often address vulnerabilities that could be exploited by malicious entities, significantly mitigating potential security risks.

Feature Additions and Improvements: Updates frequently introduce new functionalities or enhance existing features, which can include upgrades to Docker's engine, command-line interface, networking capabilities, or system management features.

Performance Improvements: Each update can bring optimizations that make Docker more efficient, such as better resource allocation, faster container startups, and more effective scheduling.

Bug Fixes: Regular updates also fix known bugs that might impact the performance or stability of Docker, helping to ensure that container operations run smoothly without disruptions.

Docker Release Methodology

Docker adopts semantic versioning and schedules releases based on a time-based cycle, typically denoted as YY.MM (e.g., 19.03 or 20.10). This format helps users understand the timing of releases and anticipate the changes they bring.

Release Channels:

- **Stable Channel:** These releases are thoroughly tested and are suitable for production use due to their stability.

- **Edge Channel:** This channel suits users interested in the newest features and innovations, although these releases might be less stable and are generally not recommended for critical production environments.

Effective Docker Update Management

Checking Your Version: To determine which version of Docker is currently installed, you can use the following command:

```
docker version
```

This will provide detailed information about both your Docker client and server, including the API version and the server's operating system.

Updating Docker: Updating Docker varies based on your operating system. Desktop users can update through Docker Desktop's interface when notifications about new updates appear. For servers, Docker is typically updated using the host OS's package manager.

For example, on Ubuntu:

1. Refresh your package index with:

```
sudo apt-get update
```

2. Install the newest versions of Docker Engine and containerd:

```
sudo apt-get install docker-ce docker-ce-cli containerd.io
```

Update Best Practices:

- **Back Up Data:** Always back up important data before updating, including container states and data volumes.

- **Test Updates First:** Implement updates in a controlled staging environment before rolling them out in production to catch any potential issues early.

- **Monitor Post-Update:** After updating, keep a close watch on the Docker environment and running applications to ensure everything operates as expected.

Automating Docker Updates

For environments with multiple Docker systems, consider automating updates using tools like Ansible, Chef, or Puppet. These tools can help manage updates uniformly across various settings, ensuring compliance with your organization's update policies.

Conclusion

Regularly updating Docker is critical for maintaining a secure, efficient, and reliable container environment. By staying current with Docker updates, you take advantage of the latest features, performance enhancements, and crucial security patches. Effective update management, including thorough testing and strategic automation, is key to minimizing potential disruptions and maintaining the continuous operation of Docker deployments.

Chapter Three

Docker Images and Containers

Introduction to Docker images and containers

Docker has revolutionized the field of software deployment by introducing a standardized approach to containerization, a method that significantly simplifies the deployment and scaling of applications. An understanding of Docker images and containers is essential for effectively utilizing this technology. This introduction clarifies these fundamental Docker components, explaining how they operate and interact within both development and operational settings.

Understanding Docker Images

A Docker image serves as a blueprint for creating containers, containing everything necessary to run an application: the application's code, a runtime environment, libraries, environment variables, and configuration files. Each image is built up from a series of layers that encapsulate changes or updates made to the image. This layered structure facilitates efficient storage and execution, as only changed layers need to be updated or saved during image updates.

Characteristics of Docker Images:

- **Immutability:** Once created, an image remains unchanged. Modifications lead to new layers being added on top of the original image.

- **Layered Storage:** Docker employs a union file system that layers images in a way that maximizes reusability and efficiency. During image builds, Docker caches these layers and reuses them if unchanged, which accelerates the build process.

- **Registry Hosting:** Images are often stored and shared through registries such as Docker Hub or private organizational registries, enabling easy distribution and version control.

Creating and Managing Docker Images: Docker images are typically defined and constructed using a Dockerfile—a plaintext file that specifies the commands for building the image. Below is an example Dockerfile that illustrates creating a basic Ubuntu-based image with Python installed:

```
# Base image
FROM ubuntu:latest

# Install Python
RUN apt-get update && apt-get install -y python3

# Copy application code
COPY . /app

# Set the working directory
WORKDIR /app

# Default command
CMD ["python3", "script.py"]
```

This Dockerfile can be used to build an image with:

```
docker build -t my-python-app .
```

Understanding Docker Containers

A Docker container is essentially a runtime instance of an image, encapsulating the application and its environment in a complete filesystem. Containers provide an isolated environment for applications, running consistently across different computing platforms.

Features of Docker Containers:

- **Portability:** A container includes the complete runtime environment: an application, plus all its dependencies, libraries, and binaries, without external dependencies.

- **Isolation:** Each container operates independently of others and the host system, with its own filesystem and computing resources, secured via Linux namespaces and cgroups.

- **Efficiency:** Containers share the host OS kernel, rather than requiring one OS per application, which minimizes resource usage and overhead.

Running and Managing Containers: You can launch a container using a Docker image with commands like:

```
docker run --name my-running-app my-python-app
```

This command starts a container named "my-running-app" from the "my-python-app" image. Containers can be easily managed with Docker CLI commands designed to handle their lifecycle, from starting and stopping to removing instances.

Conclusion

Docker images and containers are integral to Docker's functionality, providing the mechanisms through which applications are containerized and managed. Images offer the templates from which containers are instantiated, while containers execute these templates in isolated and controlled environments. This ensures that applications deployed with Docker behave consistently and predictably across all environments, thereby simplifying development cycles and deployment operations. Mastery of Docker images and containers is essential for developers and system administrators seeking to leverage Docker's capabilities to enhance application deployment and management.

How to find, pull, and use images from Docker Hub

Docker Hub stands as the principal repository for Docker images, offering a vast collection of both public and private images contributed by software vendors, open-source projects, and individual developers. This guide explains how to navigate Docker Hub to find, download, and use these images effectively to streamline Docker operations.

Navigating Docker Hub

Docker Hub functions as a centralized registry service that facilitates the finding and sharing of Docker images. It plays an integral role in the Docker ecosystem by providing access to a multitude of images that can simplify and accelerate application deployment.

Locating Images on Docker Hub

The process of finding the right Docker images for your needs involves searching through Docker Hub, either via its website or directly using the Docker command-line interface (CLI).

Using the Docker Hub Website:

1. Go to **Docker Hub**.

2. Utilize the search bar to type keywords related to the image you need, such as "postgres", "alpine", or "python".

3. Explore the list of images that appear. Select any image to view its detailed documentation, available tags, and instructions for use.

Searching with the Docker CLI: Alternatively, you can find images directly from your command line:

```
docker search postgres
```

This command searches Docker Hub for images related to PostgreSQL and displays a summary list of available images.

Pulling Images from Docker Hub

After identifying an appropriate image on Docker Hub, the next step is to pull it to your local environment, making it ready for use.

Downloading an Image Using the Docker CLI: Pull the desired image by specifying its name and tag. If you omit the tag, Docker will default to the "latest" version.

```
docker pull ubuntu:18.04
```

This command retrieves the Ubuntu image tagged with 18.04 from Docker Hub.

Utilizing Docker Images

With the image downloaded, you can now use it to start a container. For example, to use the Ubuntu image you downloaded:

```
docker run --name my-ubuntu-container -it ubuntu:18.04
```

This command creates and starts a container named "my-ubuntu-container" from the Ubuntu 18.04 image in interactive mode.

Managing Local Docker Images

Viewing Downloaded Images: To list all Docker images stored on your local machine:

```
docker images
```

This command displays a list of all images, along with their tags and sizes.

Removing Unused Images: If you wish to delete an image, perhaps to clear space or update to a newer version, you can do so with:

```
docker rmi ubuntu:18.04
```

This removes the specified image from your local storage. Ensure no running containers are using the image before removal.

Conclusion

Understanding how to search for, pull, and deploy images from Docker Hub is essential for efficiently managing Docker workflows. Docker Hub's extensive repository offers valuable resources that can significantly reduce setup times and ensure that your applications run on well-supported and secure environments. By learning to navigate this resource effectively, developers can better harness Docker's power for application development and deployment, making the most of Docker Hub's expansive offerings.

Managing images and containers

Mastering the management of Docker images and containers is essential for optimizing the performance and efficiency of your Docker environment. Whether you're developing on your local machine or managing a suite of production services, understanding how to handle Docker's key elements can significantly improve your operational workflow and resource management. This detailed guide offers insights into best practices for managing Docker images and containers, equipped with practical command examples and strategic tips.

Management of Docker Images

Identifying and Understanding Images: Effective image management starts with the ability to identify and analyze images to comprehend their structure and metadata. Docker provides several CLI commands that help in listing all available images, inspecting specific images for detailed information, and searching for images on Docker Hub or other registries.

- **List Images:**

```
docker images
```

This command displays all images stored locally, showing their repository tags and sizes.

- **Inspect an Image:**

```
docker inspect <image>
```

Replace **<image>** with the image name or ID to get JSON-formatted details about the image, including its configuration and layer information.

Deleting Images: To manage disk space or eliminate outdated or unnecessary images, you can remove them using the Docker CLI.

- **Remove an Image:**

```
docker rmi <image>
```

This command deletes the specified image from local storage. If the image is currently used by any containers, it will need to be removed with the force option or after the containers are deleted.

Cleaning Up Unused Images: To maintain a clean system, Docker allows for the removal of unused images that are not tied to any containers.

- **Prune Unused Images:**

```
docker image prune
```

Execute this command to remove all dangling images. For removing all unused images, append the **-a** option.

Management of Docker Containers

Lifecycle Management: Handling the start and stop processes of Docker containers is crucial for effective container management.

- **Start a Container:**

```
docker start <container>
```

- **Stop a Container:**

```
docker stop <container>
```

These commands help in managing the running state of containers, identified by their names or IDs.

Monitoring Containers: Monitoring the performance and logs of containers is essential, especially in a production setting.

- **List Active Containers:**

```
docker ps
```

This command lists all active containers, providing insights into their current state.

- **Access Container Logs:**

```
docker logs <container>
```

Use this command to view the output logs of a specified container, crucial for debugging and monitoring application behavior.

Container Removal: Similar to image management, removing containers helps in freeing up resources and decluttering your environment.

- **Remove a Container:**

```
docker rm <container>
```

- **Prune Stopped Containers:**

```
docker container prune
```

These commands are used to remove individual or all stopped containers from the system.

Resource Limitation

Setting Resource Constraints: Docker allows the limitation of CPU and memory resources per container to prevent any single container from consuming disproportionate system resources.

- **Limit Resources on Container Creation:**

```
docker run -d --name <container_name> --memory 500m --cpus 1.0 <image>
```

This setup initializes a container with specified memory and CPU limits, promoting balanced resource usage across all active containers.

Automating Container Behavior

Automatic Container Restart: Docker can be configured to automatically restart containers that stop due to errors or system reboots, ensuring high availability.

- **Configure Restart Policies:**

```
docker run --restart=always <image>
```

This command ensures that the container restarts automatically under any circumstances, maintaining service continuity.

Conclusion

Efficiently managing Docker images and containers is foundational to running a streamlined, resource-optimized Docker environment. Utilizing Docker's CLI commands to manage lifecycle events, resource allocation, and cleanup processes ensures that your Docker deployments are both robust and efficient. These practices are integral for anyone looking to maximize their productivity and operational effectiveness with Docker, from local development to large-scale production environments.

Chapter Four

Working with Docker Containers

Running, stopping, and managing containers

Effective Docker container management is crucial for optimizing the functionality and reliability of applications within Docker environments. This involves proficiently handling the start, stop, and overall management of Docker containers. This article will outline the essential practices for managing the lifecycle of Docker containers, including tips and commands to enhance efficiency for developers and system administrators.

Starting Docker Containers

Launching a Container: To initiate a Docker container, you must specify an image that will act as the template. This image includes the necessary components such as software, libraries, and default configurations.

```
docker run -d --name example_container -p 80:80 nginx
```

This command:

- **-d** runs the container in detached mode, meaning it continues to run in the background.

- **--name** allows you to assign a more memorable name to your container for easier reference.

- **-p 80:80** maps port 80 of the container to port 80 on the host, which is typical for a web server.

- **nginx** specifies the image from which the container is created.

Interactive Container Sessions: For tasks that require active interaction with the container, such as shell access, the container can be started in interactive mode.

```
docker run -it ubuntu /bin/bash
```

The **-it** option attaches an interactive terminal session, allowing you to execute commands directly within the container.

Stopping Docker Containers

Graceful Shutdown: To stop a container while allowing it to terminate gracefully:

```
docker stop example_container
```

This command attempts to stop the container by sending a SIGTERM, allowing processes to terminate cleanly before shutting down the container.

Immediate Termination: If a container is unresponsive, you can force it to stop:

```
docker kill example_container
```

docker kill sends a SIGKILL to forcefully terminate the container, bypassing the graceful shutdown process.

Managing Container Lifecycle

Restarting Containers: To reset a container's state or apply updates:

```
docker restart example_container
```

This command is useful for quickly rebooting a container without manually stopping and starting it.

Configuring Auto-Restart: To ensure containers automatically restart after crashes or server reboots, use the **--restart** flag:

```
docker run -d --restart=always example_container
```

This setup configures the container to restart automatically under any failure conditions.

Overseeing Running Containers

Listing Active Containers: To view currently active containers:

```
docker ps
```

And to include inactive containers in the list:

```
docker ps -a
```

Inspecting Container Details: For a deep dive into a container's specific configuration and state:

```
docker inspect example_container
```

This command provides a comprehensive JSON-formatted output detailing the container's properties.

Monitoring Container Logs: To access the operational logs of a container, useful for troubleshooting:

```
docker logs example_container
```

Logs can provide real-time insights into the application processes within the container.

Setting Resource Limits: To prevent a container from monopolizing system resources:

```
docker run -d --name limited_container --memory 512m --cpus 1 nginx
```

This command restricts the container to specific resource limits, such as memory and CPU usage.

Conclusion

Managing Docker containers involves more than just starting and stopping them. It requires continuous monitoring and adjustment to ensure they run efficiently and securely. Proficiently managing containers includes setting up auto-restarts, configuring resource limitations, and maintaining detailed logs and inspections. By implementing these management practices, you ensure your Dockerized applications are stable, secure, and scalable, maintaining optimal performance across your deployments.

Executing commands inside a container

Mastering the execution of commands within Docker containers is a critical skill for those managing and interacting with Dockerized environments. This ability enables direct engagement with running containers for various tasks, including software updates, debugging, and dynamic adjustments to the environment. This comprehensive guide will detail the methods for running commands inside Docker containers, offering practical examples to illustrate these processes.

Accessing Active Containers

The **docker exec** command is pivotal for running commands in active containers. It provides a pathway to engage with a container without needing to restart or disrupt its operations.

Basic Command Execution: To execute commands, you must identify the container using its name or ID, which you can obtain by listing all active containers with **docker ps**.

For example, to access a terminal session inside a container:

```
docker exec -it my_container /bin/bash
```

This command opens a bash shell within **my_container**. The **-it** flags ensure that the session is interactive and that a tty device is attached.

Executing Single Commands

Executing a single command is straightforward with **docker exec**, ideal for quick operations within the container.

Example: Updating Package Lists: To update packages in an Ubuntu-based container:

```
docker exec my_container apt-get update
```

This command efficiently updates the package list inside **my_container**.

Administering Container Tasks

Admin tasks, such as installing software or altering configurations, can be performed directly using **docker exec**.

Example: Software Installation: Here's how to install a package inside a container without an interactive session:

```
docker exec my_container apt-get install -y curl
```

This installs curl by directly invoking the package manager inside the container.

Running Scripts Within Containers

For executing longer or more complex scripts within a container, you might need to transfer scripts from the host to the container and then execute them.

Running Host Scripts Inside Containers: First, transfer the script using **docker cp**, then execute it:

```
# Transfer the script
docker cp script.sh my_container:/tmp/script.sh

# Run the script
docker exec my_container bash /tmp/script.sh
```

This method allows you to perform detailed operations or maintenance tasks by running scripts directly within the container environment.

Database Interactions Inside Containers

Managing database operations within containers is often necessary for data manipulation or maintenance tasks.

Example: Interacting with MySQL: To open a MySQL command-line interface in a running MySQL container:

```
docker exec -it my_mysql_container mysql -uroot -p
```

This starts an interactive MySQL session, allowing for direct database commands and queries.

Debugging Container Applications

Utilizing **docker exec** for debugging can provide insights into running applications and their environments.

Example: Viewing Container Environment Variables: To display the environment variables set within a container:

```
docker exec my_container env
```

This lists the environment variables, aiding in troubleshooting configuration or environment-specific issues.

Conclusion

Running commands within Docker containers is a versatile function that significantly enhances management capabilities within Docker environments. From simple command execution to more complex interactions like database management or script execution, the ability to directly interact with containers streamlines processes and enhances the flexibility of container management. The **docker exec** command is integral to performing these tasks, providing essential functionalities for anyone involved in Docker operations to maintain, update, and troubleshoot containers effectively.

Exploring logs and container monitoring

Effective log management and container monitoring are critical components of maintaining Docker container health and performance. These practices provide crucial insights into container behavior, aiding in troubleshooting and enhancing the operational efficiency of applications hosted within Docker environments. This guide focuses on techniques for accessing logs and monitoring the performance of Docker containers, along with recommended tools and commands that facilitate these processes.

Docker Logging Mechanisms

Docker supports various mechanisms for managing and storing the logs generated by containers. These logs are essential for understanding the operational dynamics and outputs of containerized applications.

Logging Drivers in Docker: Docker allows configuration with different logging drivers which dictate how logs are handled and stored. The default **json-file** driver saves logs in a JSON-formatted file. Alternatively, Docker supports other drivers like **syslog**, **journald**, and **gelf**, which can integrate with broader logging infrastructure for enhanced log management.

To configure a logging driver when starting a container, use:

```
docker run -d --name example_app --log-driver=syslog my_image
```

This command initiates a container that uses the **syslog** driver, routing its logs to the host system's syslog service.

Accessing Logs from Containers

To review logs for a specific container directly, Docker provides the **docker logs** command, ideal for immediate troubleshooting:

```
docker logs example_app
```

This command outputs the logs from the **example_app** container. It supports several options like **--follow** for live tailing of logs, **--since** to filter logs starting from a specific time, and **--tail** to display only the most recent log entries.

Monitoring Containers

Basic monitoring of Docker containers is possible using Docker's built-in command:

```
docker stats
```

This command displays live statistics including CPU usage, memory consumption, I/O metrics, and network usage for all active containers.

For a more detailed and analytical approach to monitoring, incorporating third-party tools such as Prometheus and Grafana can provide comprehensive monitoring capabilities.

Implementing Prometheus and Grafana for Monitoring

Prometheus is a widely-used open-source monitoring solution that can scrape and store metrics from Docker containers. **Grafana** is a visualization tool that pairs with Prometheus to offer visual insights into those metrics.

To integrate these tools:

1. **Deploy Prometheus in a Docker container:**

```
docker run -p 9090:9090 -v /path/to/prometheus.yml:/etc/prometheus/prometheus.yml prom
    /prometheus
```

This sets up Prometheus with a specified configuration file.

2. **Deploy Grafana to visualize metrics:**

```
docker run -d -p 3000:3000 grafana/grafana
```

Grafana will be accessible at **http://localhost:3000**, where you can configure it to pull data from Prometheus and set up dashboards.

3. **Configure Grafana:** Add Prometheus as a data source in Grafana's web interface and build dashboards based on the metrics Prometheus collects from Docker containers.

Advanced Monitoring and Logging

In more complex scenarios, such as when Docker is part of Kubernetes, Docker's native tools might be insufficient. Kubernetes offers its own monitoring tools like **Kube-State-Metrics**, and integrates well with the **Elastic Stack** for comprehensive logging and monitoring solutions that scale with larger deployments.

Conclusion

Monitoring the performance and managing the logs of Docker containers are indispensable for ensuring that your applications run smoothly and efficiently. By leveraging Docker's native functionalities and integrating sophisticated third-party monitoring solutions, administrators can gain deep operational insights and effectively maintain container health. Whether using built-in Docker commands or advanced tools like Prometheus and Grafana, adopting robust logging and monitoring strategies is fundamental for any production-level Docker environment, ensuring continuous operational excellence.

Chapter Five

Docker Networking Basics

Understanding Docker's networking capabilities

Docker's networking capabilities form a crucial component of its functionality, enabling containers to effectively communicate within the same host or across different hosts. This overview will delve into how Docker handles networking, the variety of available network drivers, and practical applications of these features to optimize and secure container communication.

Overview of Docker Networking

Docker incorporates a flexible networking system that can be customized using different network drivers, each tailored to specific operational needs. These drivers manage the networking capabilities for containers, facilitating various levels of communication, isolation, and external access.

- **bridge:** Default network type when you run a container. It provides a private internal network on the host and isolates containers on different bridge networks from each other.

- **host:** This driver removes the isolation between Docker containers and the Docker host, sharing the host's networking namespace.

- **overlay:** Designed for Docker Swarm usage, it connects multiple Docker daemons and enables swarm services to communicate with each other.

- **macvlan:** Makes a container appear as a physical device on the network by assigning it a MAC address, useful for specific network configurations where containers need to appear as physical hosts.

- **none:** Provides no networking capabilities to containers, used for complete network isolation.

Setting Up Docker Networks

Configuring networks in Docker involves selecting an appropriate driver and defining network characteristics suited to your application requirements.

Creating a Custom Network: Here's how to establish a custom bridge network for enhanced container isolation:

```
docker network create --driver bridge custom_bridge
```

This command creates a bridge network named **custom_bridge**. You can connect containers to this network by specifying **--network=custom_bridge** when launching them.

Inspecting Network Details: To obtain information about a specific network or view all networks:

```
docker network inspect custom_bridge
```

This provides a detailed view of the network configuration, including which containers are connected.

Connecting Containers to Networks: Link containers to a network when they are run:

```
docker run -d --name nginx_container --network custom_bridge nginx
```

This starts an Nginx container and connects it to **custom_bridge**, allowing for networked interactions with other containers on the same network.

Communication Between Containers

Docker's network configuration simplifies the process of enabling containers to communicate with each other. Containers on the same network can address each other using container names, functioning as hostnames.

Enhancing Network Security and Isolation

Network isolation is a vital feature of Docker networking that enhances security by segregating container traffic. For instance, separation of frontend and backend containers ensures that only designated containers can communicate with database services, minimizing potential attack vectors.

Managing External Container Access

External access to containers is managed through port mapping, which binds ports on the container to ports on the Docker host:

```
docker run -d --name public_webserver -p 80:80 nginx
```

This maps port 80 of the container to port 80 on the host, allowing external traffic to access the service running in the container.

Docker Swarm Networking

For applications deployed using Docker Swarm, the overlay network enables containers across multiple nodes to communicate as if they were on the same physical network, essential for large-scale deployments.

Diagnosing Network Issues

Troubleshooting Docker networking involves checking container network configurations, verifying connections and communications between containers, and ensuring the correct operation of network drivers. Tools like **docker network inspect** are useful for these purposes.

Conclusion

Docker's comprehensive networking capabilities provide powerful tools for managing how containers communicate internally and with the outside world. By leveraging appropriate network drivers and configurations, users can achieve optimal security, efficiency, and scalability in their containerized applications. Understanding and effectively implementing Docker's networking features are crucial for anyone looking to deploy containers in a robust and secure manner.

Configuring and troubleshooting Docker networks

Mastering the setup and maintenance of Docker networks is crucial for ensuring efficient communication between Docker containers and the external world. Proper configuration of

Docker networks enhances application performance, while effective troubleshooting helps maintain system stability. This article provides a detailed walkthrough of how to configure Docker networks, tailor network settings, and address common networking issues.

Setting Up Docker Networks

Docker's versatile networking capabilities support various drivers to accommodate different networking needs, from simple isolated networks to complex, multi-host configurations.

Key Network Drivers:

- **Bridge:** Default network setting suitable for containers that need to communicate on the same Docker host.

- **Host:** Useful for cases where containers require direct access to the host's network, without isolation.

- **Overlay:** Ideal for Docker Swarm setups, enabling containers across multiple hosts to communicate.

- **Macvlan:** Assigns a MAC address to containers, making them appear as physical devices on the network.

- **None:** Completely disables networking for a container, providing maximum security.

Creating a Network: To establish a custom network in Docker, use:

```
docker network create --driver bridge my_custom_network
```

This command creates a bridge network named **my_custom_network**, allowing any containers connected to it to communicate internally while remaining isolated from external networks.

Inspecting Network Details: Gaining insights into a network's configuration can be crucial, especially when troubleshooting issues:

```
docker network inspect my_custom_network
```

This command returns detailed information about the network in JSON format, including settings, connected containers, and their IP addresses.

Connecting Containers to Networks

Assigning containers to specific networks can be managed at creation or by modifying existing containers.

Starting a Container on a Network: Launch a container and attach it to a predefined network with:

```
docker run -d --name nginx_server --network my_custom_network nginx
```

Connecting an Existing Container to Another Network: If you need to add a container to an additional network post-creation:

```
docker network connect second_network nginx_server
```

This facilitates the container's interaction with other containers on **second_network**.

Docker Network Troubleshooting

Addressing network problems involves identifying and resolving issues like connectivity errors, incorrect port mappings, or IP conflicts.

Typical Network Challenges and Resolutions:

- **Connectivity Checks:** Confirm the container's network attachments with **docker network inspect** and verify IP assignments.

- **Port Mapping Verification:** Check exposed ports and their mappings to the host using **docker ps** to ensure they match expected configurations.

- **Addressing IP or Subnet Conflicts:** Modify network settings to prevent overlapping subnets, especially in complex environments:

```
docker network create --driver bridge --subnet 192.168.50.0/24 --gateway 192.168.50.1
    another_custom_network
```

This specifies a unique subnet and gateway, mitigating potential IP conflicts.

Advanced Networking Strategies

For environments requiring sophisticated network setups, Docker's capabilities extend to detailed DNS configurations and enhanced security policies.

DNS Configuration and Service Discovery: Docker's built-in DNS service aids in resolving container names to their respective IP addresses, crucial for inter-container communication within user-defined networks.

Implementing Network Policies: Establishing network security policies restricts traffic to and from containers based on predefined rules, fortifying the application environment.

Conclusion

Effectively configuring and troubleshooting Docker networks is vital for managing a stable and secure container environment. By understanding Docker's networking options, correctly setting up and connecting containers to networks, and adeptly handling common network issues, administrators can ensure optimal network performance. Advanced network settings and consistent management practices further contribute to the robustness and scalability of Dockerized applications, making network knowledge indispensable for Docker users.

Connecting containers within and across hosts

Effective communication between Docker containers, whether housed on the same server or spread across multiple machines, is pivotal for the seamless operation of distributed applications. This guide delves into Docker's networking functionalities, explaining how to configure internal and cross-host container communications.

Introduction to Docker Networking

Docker's network subsystem is engineered to support isolated and secure container communication. By default, Docker uses a **bridge** network for intra-host communications but supports more complex configurations such as **overlay** networks for setups spanning multiple hosts.

Bridge Networks: A bridge network creates a private network within the host, allowing containers connected to this network to interact while maintaining isolation from others on different bridge networks.

Overlay Networks: For environments requiring containers to communicate across several hosts, such as those managed by Docker Swarm, overlay networks provide the necessary connectivity by simulating a single, continuous network.

Setting Up Bridge Networks

To establish a bridge network for containers on the same Docker host:

```
docker network create --driver bridge custom_bridge
```

This command creates a new bridge network named **custom_bridge**. Containers can be connected to this network during their creation, enabling them to communicate internally:

```
docker run -d --network=custom_bridge --name web_container nginx
docker run -d --network=custom_bridge --name db_container nginx
```

web_container and **db_container** are now capable of communicating using Docker's internal DNS service, which resolves container names to their respective IP addresses.

Implementing Overlay Networks

Overlay networks are essential for inter-host container communication within a Docker Swarm setup:

1. Initialize Docker Swarm:

```
docker swarm init
```

2. Create an Overlay Network:

```
docker network create --driver overlay global_overlay
```

3. **Deploy Services on the Network:** Services deployed to this network can communicate across different Docker hosts:

```
docker service create --name global_service --network global_overlay nginx
```

Overlay networks facilitate seamless connectivity for containers distributed across multiple Swarm nodes.

Facilitating Inter-Container Communication

Containers within the same network can seamlessly communicate using DNS names assigned by Docker. For instance, a container can connect to another using simple network commands:

```
docker exec web_container ping db_container
```

This command demonstrates how **web_container** can resolve and communicate with **db_container** through internal networking.

Cross-Host Container Connections

For Docker environments not using Swarm, connecting containers across hosts typically requires additional networking configurations or third-party tools. However, with Swarm, the overlay network simplifies this process by managing inter-container communications across hosts automatically.

Ensuring Network Security and Isolation

While setting up network connections between containers, it's crucial to consider security and isolation. Docker allows for stringent network isolation policies and integrates with external firewall solutions to regulate container communications.

Troubleshooting Network Issues

Common challenges in Docker networking include misconfigurations, DNS problems, or driver errors. To troubleshoot these issues:

```
docker network inspect specific_network
```

This command provides a detailed view of the **specific_network** configuration, helping to identify and resolve connectivity problems.

Conclusion

Configuring and managing Docker networks effectively is crucial for the performance and scalability of container-based applications. Whether employing bridge networks for local container communication or overlay networks for comprehensive multi-host environments, Docker offers robust networking tools designed to facilitate complex container setups. Proper network setup, combined with ongoing management and troubleshooting, ensures that containers operate smoothly and securely across various deployment scenarios.

Chapter Six

Docker Storage and Volumes

Overview of Docker storage options

Docker offers a variety of storage solutions designed to accommodate the data persistence needs of containerized applications. As containers themselves do not maintain state once stopped or deleted, it's critical to understand Docker's storage capabilities to effectively manage application data. This guide will explore Docker's primary storage options—volumes, bind mounts, and tmpfs mounts—and provide guidance on their usage and management.

Overview of Docker Storage Options

Docker's storage strategies are constructed to ensure data persists across container restarts and deletions, supporting applications that require reliable data storage.

1. **Volumes**: These are the most robust and preferred method for persisting data in Docker. Managed by Docker and isolated from the core functionalities of the host machine, volumes are stored in a designated directory on the host.

2. **Bind Mounts**: This option involves mapping a host file or directory to a container, allowing for data persistence and sharing between the host and the

container. Bind mounts are dependent on the host's filesystem.

3. **tmpfs Mounts**: For data that should not be stored permanently on disk, **tmpfs** mounts are used to store data in the host system's memory only, making it ideal for sensitive information or temporary data that requires quick access.

Implementing Docker Volumes

Volumes are highly versatile and can be used with both Linux and Windows containers. They are not tied to the lifespan of a container and can be more securely shared between containers.

Creating and Using Volumes: To create a volume:

```
docker volume create my_volume
```

This sets up a new volume that can be attached to a container, ensuring data persistence beyond the life of the container:

```
docker run -d --name devtest --mount source=my_volume,target=/app nginx
```

This command mounts the newly created **my_volume** inside the **devtest** container at **/app**.

Utilizing Bind Mounts

Bind mounts can be useful for specific use cases where precise control over the storage location is required, such as development environments where code on the host needs to be tested in a container environment.

Setting Up Bind Mounts: You can specify a bind mount at container run time:

```
docker run -d --name devtest --mount type=bind,source=/path/on/host,target=/app nginx
```

This command attaches the host directory **/path/on/host** directly into the container at **/app**, allowing for real-time synchronization of data between the host and the container.

Managing tmpfs Mounts

tmpfs mounts are useful for temporary data that does not need to be saved to disk, providing a fast and secure method to handle information within containers.

Creating tmpfs Mounts: To deploy a container with **tmpfs** storage:

```
docker run -d --name tmptest --mount type=tmpfs,destination=/app,tmpfs-size=1000000 nginx
```

This mounts a temporary file system inside the container at **/app**, with a specified size limit.

Docker Storage Best Practices

- **Regular Backups**: It's crucial to regularly back up important data, especially when using bind mounts, to prevent accidental data loss.

- **Utilizing Volume Plugins**: For advanced storage needs, such as distributed storage systems or cloud storage integrations, Docker volume plugins extend functionality beyond local storage management.

- **Security Practices**: Protect sensitive data using **tmpfs** mounts for ephemeral data storage or encrypted volumes to secure data at rest, adhering to best security practices.

Troubleshooting Storage Challenges

Common issues with Docker storage typically revolve around configuration errors, insufficient permissions, or disk space problems:

- **Inspect Volumes**: Use **docker volume inspect** to verify configurations and diagnose issues.

- **Check Disk Utilization**: Monitor and manage disk usage to prevent capacity limits from impacting container performance.

- **Permissions Management**: Ensure appropriate permissions are set for Docker to access and write to volumes or bind mounts.

Conclusion

Docker's storage capabilities are foundational to the successful deployment of stateful applications in containers. Understanding how to properly use and manage volumes, bind mounts, and tmpfs mounts allows for flexible, secure, and efficient data storage solutions. By leveraging these options appropriately, you can ensure your Docker environments are optimized for both performance and data integrity.

Using and managing volumes

Docker volumes are essential for ensuring data persists beyond the life of containers, making them invaluable for applications that require data retention, sharing, or frequent updates. This guide delves into how to effectively utilize and oversee Docker volumes, providing key insights into their creation, management, and integration with containers.

Fundamentals of Docker Volumes

Volumes in Docker are designated storage spaces that exist independently of containers, allowing data to persist even when containers are destroyed or recreated. Managed by Docker, volumes are typically stored within the host filesystem at **/var/lib/docker/volumes/**. This method of data storage offers several advantages over other options like bind mounts.

Benefits of Volumes:

- **Durability**: Volumes ensure that data persists across container restarts and deletions.

- **Flexibility**: Easily migrate or back up data associated with Docker containers.

- **Performance**: Optimal for write-heavy applications and databases as they can operate faster than other storage options due to their direct connection to the host filesystem.

- **Security**: Data isolation can be improved as volumes do not require a container to stay active.

Creating and Administering Volumes

Volume Creation: You can create a Docker volume with a simple command, which prepares it for attachment to any container:

```
docker volume create my_volume
```

This command results in a new volume named **my_volume** under Docker's management.

Volume Inspection: To view detailed information about a specific volume:

```
docker volume inspect my_volume
```

This command outputs detailed data in JSON format, showing the volume's configuration and other metadata, such as its mount point on the host.

Attaching Volumes to Containers

Mounting Volumes: When launching a container, you can attach a previously created volume using the **--mount** flag:

```
docker run -d --name app_container --mount source=my_volume,target=/app nginx
```

This mounts **my_volume** to the **/app** directory inside the container. Any data written to **/app** will be stored on **my_volume**, allowing it to persist beyond the life of the container.

Sharing Volumes Across Containers: Volumes can be shared between multiple containers, facilitating data sharing and consistency:

```
docker run -d --name another_container --mount source=my_volume,target=/app nginx
```

This additional container, **another_container**, can now access the same **/app** directory on **my_volume**, demonstrating the volume's ability to serve multiple containers simultaneously.

Volume Backup and Recovery

Backing Up Volumes: To safeguard data, you can back up a volume to a local path:

```
docker run --rm --volumes-from app_container -v $(pwd):/backup ubuntu tar cvf /backup
    /backup.tar /app
```

This command employs an Ubuntu container to create a backup tarball of the data within **/app**.

Restoring Data from Backup: Restoring data to a volume involves reversing the backup process:

```
docker run --rm --volumes-from app_container -v $(pwd):/backup ubuntu tar xvf /backup
    /backup.tar -C /
```

This restores the contents of the backup tarball to the volume mounted to **app_container**.

Managing Volume Lifecycles

Since volumes are independent of container lifecycles, managing unused volumes is crucial for optimal storage utilization.

Removing Inactive Volumes: You can remove volumes that are not in use by any container to free up space:

```
docker volume prune
```

This command deletes all volumes that are not attached to any containers.

Conclusion

Utilizing Docker volumes effectively is key to managing persistent data in containerized environments. By mastering the creation, management, and application of Docker volumes, you can enhance your applications' flexibility, performance, and reliability. Properly leveraging Docker volumes ensures that critical data is preserved, easily accessible, and securely stored, regardless of container states.

Best practices for data persistence

Ensuring data persistence is crucial for the stability and functionality of applications, particularly in distributed and cloud environments where data must be accessible and consistent. This guide will delve into the best practices for managing data persistence, highlighting methods to protect, access, and manage data effectively.

Key Concepts in Data Persistence

Data persistence ensures that data remains available beyond the lifespan of the process that generated it. In systems designed to operate without maintaining state, robust data persistence mechanisms are essential for maintaining continuity and statefulness across operations.

Selecting Optimal Storage Options

Choosing the correct storage solution is crucial and depends on the application's specific needs for performance, scalability, and data structure:

1. **Relational Databases**: These are suited for applications with complex transaction requirements and structured data, ensuring integrity with ACID properties.

2. **NoSQL Databases**: Ideal for handling large volumes of unstructured data, offering flexibility and performance enhancements for scalable applications.

3. **File Storage Solutions**: Best for storing large files such as images and videos, with services like Amazon S3 providing scalable and resilient options.

4. **Block Storage**: Typically used for environments that require frequent data access, offering robust performance.

5. **Caching Solutions**: Improving application performance by storing temporary data, tools like Redis and Memcached reduce load times and database query demands.

Implementing Data Redundancy

Data redundancy ensures data is not lost and remains accessible, even during partial system failures:

- **Data Replication**: Spread data across multiple physical locations to guard against regional failures and enhance accessibility.

- **Automated Data Backups**: Establish regular backup protocols to prevent data loss due to unforeseen events.

```
# Command to create a backup of a SQL database
mysqldump -u username -p database_name > backup_filename.sql
```

Partitioning and Sharding Data

Managing large data sets efficiently may require partitioning and sharding:

- **Horizontal Partitioning (Sharding)**: Distributes data rows across several storage environments, enhancing performance and manageability.

- **Vertical Partitioning**: Divides data into smaller subsets, typically distributing them based on feature sets across different databases or tables.

Maintaining Data Integrity

Accurate and reliable data is mandatory for operational effectiveness:

- **Database Transactions**: Utilize transactions to ensure data operations are executed reliably.

- **Data Validation**: Rigorous checks at both the application and database levels are crucial to prevent corruption and ensure data remains valid and intact.

Data Security Strategies

Protecting data from unauthorized access is essential:

- **Encryption Methods**: Secure data using encryption at rest and in transit, with protocols like TLS for transmissions and AES for stored data.

- **Access Control Mechanisms**: Implement comprehensive access controls to restrict data access to authorized users only.

Continuous Monitoring and Auditing

Ongoing monitoring and auditing are vital for ensuring that data systems function correctly and securely:

- **Performance Monitoring**: Regularly monitor storage systems to promptly identify and resolve potential issues.

- **Audit Logs**: Maintain comprehensive logs of all data access and modifications to support security analyses and regulatory compliance.

```
# Enabling query logging in MySQL for monitoring
SET global general_log = 1;
SET global log_output = 'table';
```

Conclusion

Effective data persistence strategies are foundational for applications operating in modern architectures, particularly those in distributed or cloud-based environments. By carefully selecting appropriate storage solutions, ensuring data redundancy, safeguarding data integrity, implementing robust security measures, and maintaining vigilant monitoring and auditing, organizations can ensure their data ecosystems are both resilient and efficient. These practices provide a structured approach to managing data persistence, crucial for any organization aiming to leverage data as a strategic asset.

Chapter Seven

Building Docker Images

Writing Dockerfiles

Dockerfiles serve as the blueprint for building Docker images, automating the process to ensure consistency and repeatability in Docker environments. This guide discusses the key components and best practices for crafting Dockerfiles to optimize container creation and maintenance.

Essentials of Dockerfile

A Dockerfile is a scripted set of instructions that Docker follows to build images automatically. It transforms a base image into a new customized image that includes your applications and configurations.

Anatomy of a Dockerfile

1. Selecting a Base Image: Use the **FROM** instruction to define the base image of your Dockerfile. Choosing the right base image (e.g., Ubuntu, Alpine) depends on the needs of the application and its dependencies.

```
FROM alpine:latest
```

2. Labeling the Image: The **LABEL** instruction adds metadata to the image, such as the maintainer's contact, version, or description of the image.

```
LABEL maintainer="name@example.com"
```

3. Executing Commands: The **RUN** instruction allows you to execute commands within the container. This is often used to install packages or make configurations.

```
RUN apk add --update python3
```

4. Copying Files: The **COPY** and **ADD** instructions transfer files from the local directory into the container. **COPY** is straightforward, while **ADD** has the capability to handle remote URLs and unpack compressed files.

```
COPY . /app
```

5. Setting the Working Directory: The **WORKDIR** instruction sets the directory in which command instructions are run.

```
WORKDIR /app
```

6. Exposing Network Ports: The **EXPOSE** instruction indicates which ports the container listens on at runtime.

```
EXPOSE 8080
```

7. Specifying Execution Commands: The **CMD** instruction sets the default command to run when the container starts. Only one **CMD** instruction should be used in a Dockerfile.

```
CMD ["python3", "app.py"]
```

Dockerfile Writing Best Practices

Reduce Layers: Minimize the number of layers in your Docker image by combining related commands into single **RUN** instructions.

```
RUN apk add --update python3 && rm -rf /var/cache/apk/*
```

Optimize Use of Cache: Arrange Dockerfile instructions to maximize the use of Docker's caching mechanism. Place instructions that change less frequently towards the top of the Dockerfile to avoid unnecessary rebuilds.

Exclude Unwanted Files: Utilize a **.dockerignore** file to exclude files not relevant to the build, such as logs, development tools, and temporary files.

Implement Multi-Stage Builds: Multi-stage builds allow you to selectively copy artifacts from one stage to another, minimizing the size of the final image. This is particularly useful for compiled languages.

```
# Builder stage
FROM node:12 as builder
WORKDIR /usr/src/app
COPY package*.json ./
RUN npm install
COPY . .
RUN npm run build

# Final stage
FROM nginx:alpine
COPY --from=builder /usr/src/app/build /usr/share/nginx/html
```

Conclusion

Crafting efficient Dockerfiles is a fundamental skill for developers working with Docker, allowing for the streamlined creation of lightweight, manageable Docker images. By adhering to best practices such as minimizing layers, utilizing build caching, excluding unnecessary files, and leveraging multi-stage builds, you can ensure your Docker images are optimized for performance, security, and size. These strategies enhance the deployment process and contribute to a more efficient development workflow in Dockerized environments.

Best practices for building efficient images

Creating efficient Docker images is essential for optimizing the deployment, operation, and scaling of containerized applications. This guide outlines crucial strategies for crafting Docker images that are lightweight, performant, and secure, focusing on everything from selecting the appropriate base image to optimizing the Dockerfile.

Selecting an Appropriate Base Image

The choice of base image is foundational to building an efficient Docker image. It affects the image size, security vulnerabilities, and maintenance overhead.

- **Opt for Minimal Base Images**: Use smaller base images, like Alpine Linux, which offers a minimal footprint compared to larger images like Ubuntu. This reduces the overall image size and the attack surface.

```
FROM alpine:latest
```

- **Prefer Official Images**: Stick to official images from Docker Hub whenever possible, as they are well-maintained, regularly updated, and optimized for security and performance.

Managing Layers Effectively

Since each instruction in a Dockerfile adds a new layer to the image, efficient layer management is key to building streamlined Docker images.

- **Consolidate Commands**: Group related commands into single **RUN** instructions to reduce the number of layers, which can decrease the image size and simplify updates.

```
RUN apt-get update && \
    apt-get install -y curl && \
    rm -rf /var/lib/apt/lists/*
```

- **Maximize Cache Utilization**: Docker builds images using a layer caching mechanism. Arrange Dockerfile instructions to exploit this feature by placing less frequently changed instructions at the top.

Optimizing the Build Context

The build context can significantly affect the performance of the Docker build process if not properly managed.

- **Implement .dockerignore**: Use a **.dockerignore** file to exclude unnecessary files from the build context, like temporary files or version control directories.

92

```
# .dockerignore example
.git
.gitignore
node_modules
npm-debug.log
```

Reducing Image Size

Smaller Docker images are faster to upload, download, and deploy, which also improves security by reducing potential attack vectors.

- **Utilize Multi-Stage Builds**: Separate the build environment from the runtime environment using multi-stage builds. This allows you to use a larger image for building the application and a smaller image for running it.

```
# Builder stage
FROM node:14 AS builder
WORKDIR /app
COPY . .
RUN npm install && npm run build

# Production stage
FROM alpine:latest
WORKDIR /app
COPY --from=builder /app/build .
CMD ["./my-app"]
```

Security Considerations

Enhancing the security of your Docker images is as critical as improving their efficiency.

- **Non-Root User**: Minimize security risks by running applications as a non-root user whenever possible.

```
RUN adduser -D myuser
USER myuser
```

- **Secure Build Stages**: In multi-stage builds, ensure that only the necessary components are included in the final image to keep it secure from unnecessary vulnerabilities.

Continuous Updates and Image Management

Regular maintenance is vital for keeping Docker images secure and efficient.

- **Update Base Images Regularly**: Rebuild your images frequently to incorporate the latest patches and updates from base images.

- **Label Your Images**: Use labels to manage and document your images effectively, tracking versions and configurations.

```
LABEL version="1.0" description="Optimized Docker Image"
```

Conclusion

Developing efficient Docker images is crucial for managing scalable, secure, and robust containerized applications. By carefully choosing base images, managing Dockerfile instructions and layers, minimizing the build context, and employing best practices in security and maintenance, developers can ensure that their Docker environments are optimized for performance and manageability. These strategies facilitate not only improved deployment but also enhance operational efficiency during runtime.

Building, tagging, and managing custom images

Custom Docker images are integral to ensuring consistency and reliability across various environments in software development. This guide explores how to build, tag, and manage these images effectively, providing essential practices for developers and DevOps professionals to optimize their Docker workflows.

Building Custom Docker Images

The construction of a Docker image starts with defining a Dockerfile, which outlines all the steps necessary to assemble the image based on your application's requirements.

1. Crafting a Dockerfile: Start by creating a Dockerfile that designates the base image and details the steps to install your application along with its dependencies.

```
# Starting with a lightweight Python base image
FROM python:3.8-slim

# Set the working directory to /app
WORKDIR /app

# Copy the local directory contents to the container
COPY . /app

# Install dependencies from requirements.txt
RUN pip install --trusted-host pypi.python.org -r requirements.txt

# Expose port 80 for external access
EXPOSE 80

# Set an environment variable
ENV NAME World

# Specify the command to run on container start
CMD ["python", "app.py"]
```

2. Image Building Process: Use the **docker build** command to compile your image, tagging it appropriately to facilitate version control and identification.

```
docker build -t my-python-app .
```

This command creates the image with the name **my-python-app**, where **.** indicates that Docker should use the current directory as the build context.

Tagging Docker Images

Properly tagging Docker images is vital for managing versions and maintaining order within your image repository.

1. Applying Tags to Images: Tags can be added to existing images to help differentiate versions or configurations.

```
docker tag my-python-app my-python-app:v1.0
```

This example shows how to assign a **v1.0** tag to your **my-python-app** image, which is useful for tracking and deployment purposes.

Managing Docker Images

Efficient image management is key to keeping your Docker environment clean and organized, ensuring that only useful and updated images are retained.

1. Viewing Images: You can list all images stored locally by using the **docker images** command.

```
docker images
```

This lists each image along with details such as the repository, tag, image ID, when it was created, and its size.

2. Deleting Images: To free up disk space and eliminate clutter, old or unused images can be removed with the **docker rmi** command.

```
docker rmi my-python-app:v1.0
```

This command deletes the **v1.0** version of the **my-python-app** from your Docker setup.

3. Utilizing Docker Registries: For broader sharing or deployment, images can be pushed to Docker registries such as Docker Hub or private registries.

```
docker push my-python-app:v1.0
```

This pushes the specified image to the registry, making it available for further use.

Recommended Practices

- **Reduce Image Size:** Aim for multi-stage builds and clear out unnecessary content post-installation to minimize the image size.

- **Enhance Security:** Keep your images secure by regularly updating the base images and installed packages, and scan for vulnerabilities using security tools.

- **Use Immutable Tags:** Prefer version-specific tags over mutable ones like **latest** to ensure precise control and easier rollback capabilities.

Conclusion

Mastering the building, tagging, and management of Docker images streamlines development cycles and enhances deployment consistency. By adopting best practices such as maintaining slim image profiles, using clear tagging strategies, and managing images judiciously, developers can fully leverage Docker's capabilities to improve application delivery and performance.

Chapter Eight

Docker Compose: Simplifying Multi-Container Applications

Introduction to Docker Compose

Docker Compose is a vital tool for developers and systems administrators working with Docker, particularly when handling applications that rely on multiple containers. It streamlines the setup, orchestration, and management of Docker containers using a single, comprehensive YAML configuration file. This guide introduces Docker Compose, detailing its purpose, features, how to install it, and demonstrates its usage through a straightforward example.

What is Docker Compose?

Docker Compose is a tool designed to simplify the deployment and management of multi-container Docker applications. By defining an application's services, networks, and volumes in a YAML file, Docker Compose enables users to launch and manage all related services collectively with a few commands. It is compatible across various Docker environments, including both development and production stages.

Primary Features of Docker Compose

- **Unified Service Configuration**: Docker Compose allows for detailed configuration of all application services in a single document.

- **Resource Isolation**: It ensures that each service operates within its own container, maintaining isolation from others.

- **Configuration Ease**: Inter-service relationships and shared resources are easily managed through Docker Compose, reducing manual configuration efforts.

- **Scalability**: Services can be scaled up or down easily with Docker Compose based on the application demands.

Installing Docker Compose

Docker Compose is included with Docker Desktop on Windows and Mac but requires manual installation on Linux systems.

Linux Installation Steps:

1. Download the latest version of Docker Compose from its official GitHub repository:

```
sudo curl -L "https://github.com/docker/compose/releases/download/1.29.2/docker
  -compose-$(uname -s)-$(uname -m)" -o /usr/local/bin/docker-compose
```

2. Set the downloaded script to be executable:

```
sudo chmod +x /usr/local/bin/docker-compose
```

3. Optionally, install Bash command completion:

```
sudo curl -L https://raw.githubusercontent.com/docker/compose/1.29.2/contrib
  /completion/bash/docker-compose -o /etc/bash_completion.d/docker-compose
```

Verify the installation by checking the Docker Compose version:

```
docker-compose --version
```

Crafting a Docker Compose File

Docker Compose relies on a **docker-compose.yml** file to define the specifics of your application. Below is an example Docker Compose file for a simple Python and Redis-based web application:

```yaml
version: '3'
services:
  web:
    build: .
    ports:
      - "5000:5000"
    volumes:
      - .:/code
    depends_on:
      - redis
  redis:
    image: "redis:alpine"
```

This configuration sets up two services, **web** and **redis**. It builds the **web** service using a Dockerfile in the current directory, maps port 5000, and links it to the Redis service.

Executing Docker Compose

To run the application described in your **docker-compose.yml**, use the following command:

```
docker-compose up
```

This starts all services defined in the Docker Compose file in detached mode, running them in the background. To stop the application and remove all its services, use:

```
docker-compose down
```

Conclusion

Docker Compose is an essential development tool that facilitates the easy configuration and management of multi-container Docker applications. It allows for streamlined command-line operations to control complex container setups, making Docker Compose indispensable for efficient Docker container management. By effectively using Docker Compose, development teams can ensure their applications are easily scalable, maintainable, and deployable across any environment.

Writing and managing Compose files

Docker Compose files are instrumental in orchestrating and managing containerized applications with precision. This guide explores essential strategies for crafting and maintaining Docker Compose files, ensuring your container setups are both efficient and straightforward to manage.

Fundamentals of Docker Compose Files

A Docker Compose file, generally named **docker-compose.yml**, is a YAML-formatted document where services, networks, and volumes are defined for Docker applications. It acts as a blueprint that Docker Compose uses to deploy containers according to specified requirements.

Core Elements of Docker Compose Files

Services: These are the primary focus of the Docker Compose file, detailing the containers to run, their configurations, images, and other parameters like exposed ports and volume mappings.

Networks: Docker Compose facilitates the creation of custom networks that enhance container-to-container communication, offering a more nuanced configuration similar to traditional networking setups.

Volumes: These are defined to ensure data persistence across container lifecycles, securing data even when containers are terminated or restarted.

Additional Configurations: Depending on your application's complexity, you might also define environment variables and deployment preferences directly in the Compose file.

Writing Docker Compose Files Effectively

1. Maintain Simplicity and Clarity: Compose files should be straightforward and annotated. Use comments to clarify why certain configurations are necessary, which enhances maintainability and understanding.

```yaml
version: '3.8'
services:
  web:
    image: "webapp:latest"
    ports:
      - "80:80"  # Expose port 80 on the container to port 80 on the host
    volumes:
      - type: bind
        source: ./html
        target: /var/www/html
```

```
    networks:
      - webnet
  db:
    image: "postgres:latest"
    volumes:
      - data:/var/lib/postgresql/data
    networks:
      - webnet
networks:
  webnet:
    driver: bridge
volumes:
  data:
    driver: local
```

2. Employ Environment Variables: Use environment variables for configurations that vary between environments (like development, staging, and production), enhancing both security and flexibility.

```
services:
  web:
    environment:
      - DEBUG=0
      - DATABASE_URL=${DB_URL}
```

3. Organize with .env Files: Keep environment-specific configurations in an **.env** file alongside your Docker Compose file. This keeps environmental settings centralized and the Compose file uncluttered.

4. Optimize with YAML Anchors and Aliases: Reduce repetition in your Docker Compose files using YAML anchors and aliases to reference common configurations.

```
x-common-env: &common-env
  environment:
    - DEBUG=0
    - NODE_ENV=production


services:
  web:
    <<: *common-env
  worker:
    <<: *common-env
```

5. Utilize Multiple Compose Files: For intricate setups, split your Docker Compose configuration across several files, merging them during runtime for different environments or specific tasks.

6. Version Control: Always keep your Docker Compose files in a version control system. This tracks changes and facilitates rollback when needed.

Managing Docker Compose Files

Version Specificity: Always specify exact versions for your Docker images and Compose file format to prevent unexpected behavior due to updates.

Integrate with CI/CD: Incorporate Docker Compose into your continuous integration and deployment pipelines to ensure deployments are automated and repeatable.

Keep Dependencies Updated: Regularly update Docker, Docker Compose, and the images used in your files. Regular testing against these updates will ensure compatibility and security.

Conclusion

Effectively managing Docker Compose files is essential for deploying robust and scalable container-based applications efficiently. By adhering to best practices such as simplifying configurations, leveraging environment variables, using version control, and integrating into CI/CD workflows, developers can ensure that Docker Compose serves as a powerful tool for development and operations teams. These approaches not only streamline development processes but also bolster deployment practices, ensuring applications are both reliable and easy to manage.

Running multi-container applications with Docker Compose

Docker Compose stands out as an essential utility for orchestrating multi-container Docker applications, enabling developers to streamline container setup and coordination through a single YAML configuration file. This guide delves into the effective operation of multi-container setups using Docker Compose, discussing configuration tips, execution steps, and best practices for maintaining operational efficiency.

Overview of Docker Compose

Docker Compose facilitates the management of multi-container Docker applications by allowing developers to define their applications' services, networks, and volumes within one YAML file. This approach simplifies tasks such as launching, stopping, and rebuilding containerized applications.

Installing Docker Compose

For users on Docker Desktop for Windows and Mac, Docker Compose is already integrated. Linux users, however, will need to install Docker Compose separately. This can typically be accomplished with a series of straightforward commands that download the binary and set the necessary permissions.

Crafting a Docker Compose File

The cornerstone of Docker Compose is the **docker-compose.yml** file. This file specifies how Docker containers should interact, how they're built, and their dependencies. Below is a simple example for a web application using Flask and Redis:

```yaml
version: '3.8'
services:
  web:
    build: .
    command: flask run --host=0.0.0.0
    volumes:
      - .:/code
    ports:
      - "5000:5000"
    depends_on:
      - redis
  redis:
    image: redis:alpine
volumes:
  data_volume:
```

This file describes:

- **Services**: Two services are defined (**web** and **redis**). The **web** service builds from the Dockerfile in the current directory, while **redis** uses a lightweight Redis image.

107

- **Volumes**: Utilized to ensure data persistence for Redis.

- **Ports**: Maps port 5000 on the host to port 5000 on the Flask application, facilitating local access.

- **Environment**: Manages settings like database user and password as environment variables for security.

Executing Docker Compose

To launch the application from the **docker-compose.yml** file, simply run:

```
docker-compose up
```

This command starts up all the defined services in a linked fashion based on the configurations specified. For background execution, append **-d** to run the services in detached mode.

To stop the application and clean up the containers, networks, and volumes created by Docker Compose, execute:

```
docker-compose down
```

Docker Compose Best Practices

- **Explicit Network Definitions**: For enhanced control and isolation, define networks explicitly in the Docker Compose file to manage how containers communicate.

- **Managing Service Dependencies**: Utilize the **depends_on** attribute to specify dependencies between services, ensuring they launch in the correct sequence.

- **Secure Configuration Handling**: Avoid hardcoding sensitive configuration details directly in the Docker Compose file. Instead, use environment variables or **.env** files to manage sensitive information securely.

- **Scaling Services**: Docker Compose supports the scaling of services to multiple instances, which can be achieved with the **--scale** option during service launch.

Conclusion

Docker Compose simplifies the deployment and scaling of multi-container Docker applications, making it a vital tool for developers. By defining all aspects of an application's containers in a single declarative file, Docker Compose allows for streamlined management and operation of complex applications. Following established best practices in Docker Compose file construction and execution can lead to more efficient development workflows and robust deployment scenarios, ensuring applications perform optimally across different environments.

Chapter Nine

Managing Application Data with Docker

Strategies for database management in containers

Database management within containerized environments demands strategies that marry the ephemeral nature of containers with the persistent demands of database systems. This article explores essential methods to ensure data persistence, optimize performance, enhance scalability, and secure databases when operated inside containers.

Key Considerations for Database Management in Containers

1. Appropriate Database Selection: Not every database is well-suited for operation within containers. Databases such as PostgreSQL, MySQL, and MongoDB are commonly used because they are supported by robust communities and are optimized for container deployment.

2. Container Orchestration Tools: Orchestration platforms like Kubernetes and Docker Swarm provide comprehensive features that facilitate the deployment, scaling, and management of containerized databases. Kubernetes, for instance, offers constructs like StatefulSets and Persistent Volumes that are particularly beneficial for managing stateful applications such as databases.

Ensuring Data Persistence

Maintaining data beyond the life of a container is a fundamental requirement for databases. There are multiple approaches to ensure data persists:

1. Persistent Storage: Utilizing external storage solutions that outlive the containers is a common strategy. Docker enables the creation of persistent volumes that containers can mount, thus ensuring data survives container restarts.

```
volumes:
  db-data:
    driver: local
```

In Docker Compose, this volume would be configured as follows:

```
services:
  db:
    image: postgres:latest
    volumes:
      - db-data:/var/lib/postgresql/data
```

2. Regular Backups: Automated backup solutions are vital for data integrity and recovery. Tools specific to databases, such as **mysqldump** for MySQL or **pg_dump** for PostgreSQL, are typically used. Storing backups offsite, like in cloud storage, ensures data can be restored following any container or host failures.

Optimizing Database Performance

Performance in containerized databases is critical and can be addressed through several practices:

1. Resource Management: Provision appropriate CPU, memory, and disk resources to your database containers. Kubernetes allows setting specific resource requests and limits to manage these allocations.

2. Clustering and High Availability: Use database features like replication or clustering to distribute data across multiple containers, enhancing both performance and data availability.

3. Proactive Monitoring: Utilize monitoring tools such as Prometheus, integrated with Grafana, to keep track of database performance and health, facilitating timely optimizations.

Security Enhancements

Securing containerized databases involves multiple layers of protection:

1. Controlled Network Access: Limit access to database containers using network policies in Kubernetes or Docker networking features, restricting connectivity to trusted applications.

2. Robust Access Management: Secure access to databases using strong authentication practices. Store sensitive access credentials using Kubernetes Secrets or other secure vault solutions like HashiCorp Vault.

3. Update Management: Regularly update your database containers with the latest security patches. Automate this process in Kubernetes with image pull policies to ensure containers are always up-to-date.

Practical Example: PostgreSQL on Kubernetes

Here's an example demonstrating how to deploy PostgreSQL in Kubernetes using a StatefulSet, which is designed for applications requiring persistent storage and unique identifiers.

```yaml
apiVersion: apps/v1
kind: StatefulSet
metadata:
  name: postgres
spec:
  serviceName: "postgres"
  replicas: 3
  selector:
    matchLabels:
      app: postgres
  template:
    metadata:
      labels:
        app: postgres
```

```yaml
    spec:
      containers:
      - name: postgres
        image: postgres:latest
        ports:
        - containerPort: 5432
        volumeMounts:
        - name: postgres-storage
          mountPath: /var/lib/postgresql/data
  volumeClaimTemplates:
  - metadata:
      name: postgres-storage
    spec:
      accessModes: ["ReadWriteOnce"]
      resources:
        requests:
          storage: 1Gi
```

This configuration sets up PostgreSQL as a robust, scalable StatefulSet with persistent storage, ensuring that each instance has its own stable storage that persists across pod rescheduling.

Conclusion

Effectively managing databases in containerized settings involves a strategic approach to integrate the best of both databases and container technology. By focusing on data persistence, performance optimization, security, and using advanced orchestration features, you can create a resilient, scalable, and efficient database management system within a containerized architecture.

Using Docker for stateless and stateful applications

Docker is a key player in the realm of software deployment, enabling consistent operational environments by encapsulating essential application components into containers. This guide explores the deployment methodologies for both stateless and stateful applications within Docker, outlining distinct strategies and highlighting best practices for each.

Distinction Between Stateless and Stateful Applications

Stateless Applications operate without storing user data from one session to another. These applications treat each interaction as standalone, making them ideal for Docker's transient container model due to their inherent adaptability and scalability.

Stateful Applications preserve user data across sessions, relying on persistent storage mechanisms to maintain continuity. Managing these applications within Docker requires specialized strategies to ensure data persistence, given the inherently ephemeral nature of containers.

Docker Management of Stateless Applications

The stateless nature of these applications aligns perfectly with Docker's capabilities, allowing for straightforward scalability and management.

Scalability Approaches: For stateless applications, scaling involves increasing the number of containers. Docker facilitates this process efficiently through simple commands.

```
docker-compose up -d --scale service-name=6
```

This command enables Docker Compose to scale a service up to six instances, effectively handling increased load across multiple containers.

Load Balancing Configurations: Implementing a load balancer such as Nginx helps efficiently distribute incoming traffic across several instances, optimizing resource use and enhancing responsiveness.

```
services:
  nginx:
    image: nginx:latest
    ports:
      - "80:80"
    volumes:
      - ./nginx.conf:/etc/nginx/nginx.conf
```

115

This setup configures Nginx to act as a reverse proxy, balancing the load among various instances of a web application, as directed by the specified **nginx.conf**.

Docker Strategies for Stateful Applications

Managing stateful applications in Docker focuses on data durability and availability.

Persistent Storage Solutions: Docker volumes are essential for maintaining data across container life cycles, crucial for stateful applications where data continuity is required.

```
services:
  mongodb:
    image: mongo:latest
    volumes:
      - mongo-data:/data/db
volumes:
  mongo-data:
```

This configuration attaches a persistent volume, **mongo-data**, to a MongoDB service, ensuring that database information persists beyond the container's lifespan.

Reliable Data Backup Methods: Regular data backups are vital to safeguard against data loss. Docker can facilitate these backups through specific commands.

```
docker exec mongo_container mongodump --out /data/backup/
```

This command initiates a MongoDB dump within the container, backing up the database effectively.

High Availability Setups: For stateful applications requiring high uptime and reliability, Docker can be used in conjunction with orchestration platforms like Kubernetes, which supports automatic replication and failover to ensure service continuity.

General Recommendations

- **Immutable Container Philosophy:** View containers as immutable; instead of altering an existing container, deploy a new one for each update.

- **Distinct Development Stages:** Use separate environments for development, testing, and production to enhance stability and minimize interference.

- **Comprehensive Monitoring and Logging:** Deploy monitoring tools such as Prometheus to track system metrics and employ logging solutions like the ELK Stack to manage and analyze logs, maintaining insight into operations and performance.

Conclusion

Docker's capacity to support both stateless and stateful applications underscores its robustness and flexibility in handling diverse software deployment needs. Stateless applications enjoy the simplicity and scalability of Docker, while stateful applications benefit from strategies that ensure data persistence and system resilience. By understanding and implementing the right approaches, organizations can leverage Docker to optimize application deployment and ensure effective, reliable operations.

Backup and restore techniques for Dockerized applications

Effective backup and restoration strategies are essential for maintaining the reliability and data integrity of applications deployed in Docker environments. This guide details practical methods for ensuring robust data backups and swift recovery for Dockerized applications, emphasizing the importance of these processes in container-based architectures.

Importance of Backup in Docker Environments

Docker's ephemeral nature underscores the need for diligent management of persistent data. Comprehensive backup strategies should encompass not only the data stored within volumes but also the application configurations and settings typically housed in Dockerfiles or Docker Compose files.

Techniques for Backing Up Dockerized Applications

1. Backing Up Data Volumes: Persistent data in Docker is often managed using volumes. To safeguard this data, you can perform backups by creating a tarball of the volume contents.

Example Using Docker Commands: For a MySQL database container, you might use the following command to backup its volume:

```
docker run --rm --volumes-from mydbcontainer -v $(pwd):/backup ubuntu tar cvf
    /backup/backup.tar /var/lib/mysql
```

This command utilizes an Ubuntu container to access the volume from **mydbcontainer** and tar the contents into a backup file located in the current directory.

2. Automated Backup Tools: Leverage tools like Duplicity or Rsync for automated and regular backups. These tools can be set up to perform incremental backups to external storage solutions, such as cloud storage, providing an off-site backup option.

3. Configuration File Backup: Backup your Docker configurations, which include Dockerfiles, Docker Compose files, and other related scripts. These should be version controlled and regularly backed up along with your application code.

Techniques for Restoring Dockerized Applications

Restoring data in Docker involves applying the reverse process of the backup to ensure the data aligns with application demands.

1. Restoring Data Volumes: To restore a database from a backup, you might use:

```
docker run --rm -v mydbdata:/var/lib/mysql -v $(pwd):/backup ubuntu bash -c "cd
    /var/lib/mysql && tar xvf /backup/backup.tar --strip 1"
```

This command reconstructs the data volume **mydbdata** from a backup by extracting the tar file directly into the volume mounted at **/var/lib/mysql**.

2. Full Disaster Recovery: In scenarios where a complete recovery is necessary, re-deploying the Docker containers using Docker Compose and then restoring the data from backups is essential. Your disaster recovery plan should include detailed procedures for redeploying the services and networks outlined in your Docker Compose configuration.

Best Practices for Backup and Restoration

1. Test Backups Regularly: Conduct routine tests by restoring from backups to a test environment to ensure data integrity and the effectiveness of the backup process.

2. Secure Storage of Backups: Keep backups in a secure location with controlled access. If backups are stored in the cloud, consider additional security measures such as encryption to protect data at rest and in transit.

3. Multi-Region Backup Storage: For critical data, utilize cloud storage services that offer multi-region replication to mitigate risks associated with regional outages.

4. Documentation: Maintain up-to-date documentation of your backup and restoration procedures, detailing the backup intervals, the nature of the data stored, storage locations, and explicit recovery instructions.

Conclusion

Establishing and maintaining effective backup and restoration practices are crucial for Dockerized applications to ensure data persistence, operational continuity, and minimal downtime. By adopting a structured approach to data backups, implementing regular testing, securing backup storage, and clearly documenting processes, organizations can enhance the resilience and reliability of their Docker deployments. These strategies not only protect data but also support the operational stability of containerized applications across diverse environments.

Chapter Ten

Docker Security Fundamentals

Basic security practices for Docker installations

Docker, known for its efficient application deployment capabilities through containerization, also necessitates stringent security measures to protect against unauthorized access and potential threats. This guide covers fundamental security practices for safeguarding Docker installations, highlighting essential steps to fortify Docker environments.

Regular Updates to Docker

One of the simplest yet most effective security measures is to keep Docker updated. Regular updates ensure that security patches and enhanced features are applied, mitigating vulnerabilities found in previous versions.

Update Command Example:

```
sudo apt-get update && sudo apt-get install docker-ce docker-ce-cli containerd.io
```

This command will update Docker on systems that use the apt package manager, ensuring the latest security patches are in place.

Control Access to Docker Daemon

The Docker daemon operates with high-level privileges, which makes securing its access paramount.

Security Tips:

- Employ TLS for secure, authenticated connections to the Docker daemon.

- If network exposure of the Docker daemon is necessary, secure it with TLS and strict firewall rules to prevent unauthorized access.

Enable User Namespaces

User namespaces enhance security by segregating the user IDs between the host and the containers, limiting the potential for privilege escalation.

Configuring User Namespaces: Add or modify the **/etc/docker/daemon.json** file to include:

```
{
    "userns-remap": "default"
}
```

Restart the Docker daemon to apply:

```
sudo systemctl restart docker
```

This adjustment maps the container's root user to a non-privileged user on the host, minimizing the capabilities of processes running inside containers.

Establish Robust Logging and Monitoring

Maintaining detailed logs and implementing a robust monitoring strategy are critical for detecting and managing security incidents.

Configure Docker Logging: Docker can use various logging drivers. Here's how to set up syslog as the logging driver:

```
{
  "log-driver": "syslog",
  "log-opts": {
    "syslog-address": "tcp://192.168.1.1:514"
  }
}
```

This configuration sends Docker logs to a remote syslog server, which can be monitored to detect unusual activities or security breaches.

Secure Docker Networking

Docker's default network settings may not suffice for security purposes and usually require customization.

Networking Best Practices:

- Avoid the default bridge network by setting up custom networks.

- Implement firewall rules to control traffic flow to and from containers.

- Use network segmentation to minimize the risk of lateral movements in case of a compromise.

Restrict Container Privileges

Running Docker containers with minimal privileges necessary for their operation is crucial for security.

Example Using AppArmor: You can specify a security profile for your containers to limit their capabilities:

```
docker run --security-opt apparmor=your_profile_name your_image
```

This command enforces an AppArmor security profile that restricts the operations that the container can perform.

Vulnerability Scanning for Images

Regularly scanning Docker images for vulnerabilities is crucial for maintaining container security.

Using Trivy for Scanning:

```
trivy image your_image_name
```

Trivy is an open-source tool that scans for vulnerabilities in Docker images, providing detailed reports to help remediate security issues.

Utilize Trusted Base Images

Opt for official or verified base images to construct your Docker containers. These images are maintained by trusted entities and are regularly updated to address security vulnerabilities.

Conclusion

Securing Docker installations is multifaceted, requiring diligent updates, controlled access, secure configurations, and continuous monitoring. Implementing these foundational security practices will greatly enhance the protection of your Docker environments, ensuring that your containerized applications are not only efficient but also secure against evolving threats. These strategies are crucial for maintaining the integrity and resilience of Docker deployments.

Securing Docker containers and images

Implementing robust security measures for Docker containers and images is critical to safeguarding applications in Dockerized environments. This guide outlines essential strategies to secure Docker installations, emphasizing the importance of comprehensive security from the image creation phase through to container runtime.

Best Practices for Docker Image Security

1. Utilize Reputable Base Images: Starting with secure, official, or well-maintained base images from trusted registries like Docker Hub or private, secure registries is crucial. These images are routinely updated to address security vulnerabilities and compliance standards.

```
# Selecting a secure, minimal official base image
FROM python:3.9-slim
```

2. Reduce the Attack Surface: Minimizing the contents of your Docker images to only what is necessary reduces potential security risks. Employ multi-stage builds in your Dockerfiles to ensure that only essential components are included in the final production image.

```
# Implementing a multi-stage build to minimize the final image
FROM node:14 AS builder
WORKDIR /app
COPY . .
RUN npm install && npm run build

FROM nginx:alpine
COPY --from=builder /app/build /usr/share/nginx/html
```

In this Dockerfile, the final image contains only the built application served by Nginx, excluding the Node.js environment and source code.

3. Continuously Update and Scan for Vulnerabilities: Regularly updating images and scanning them with tools such as Trivy, Clair, or Docker Scan ensures any known vulnerabilities are identified and addressed promptly.

```
# Using Trivy to scan an image for vulnerabilities
trivy image your-image-name
```

Strengthening Docker Container Security

1. Implement Resource Restrictions: Setting resource constraints on containers can help prevent resource abuse, which could lead to Denial-of-Service (DoS) attacks.

```
services:
  app:
    image: my-app:latest
    deploy:
      resources:
        limits:
          cpus: '0.5'
          memory: 50M
```

2. Apply Runtime Security Measures: Leverage Docker's security mechanisms like AppArmor, SELinux, Seccomp, and capabilities to tightly control container permissions.

```
# Starting a container with security options
docker run --rm -it \
    --security-opt apparmor=your_apparmor_profile \
    --cap-drop all \
    --cap-add NET_BIND_SERVICE \
    your-image-name
```

3. Enforce Read-Only Filesystems: Configuring containers to use read-only filesystems where possible will prevent unauthorized changes to the filesystem.

```
# Running a container with a read-only filesystem
docker run --read-only -d your-image-name
```

4. Configure Network Segmentation: Properly segmenting container networks can reduce the risk of inter-container attacks and restrict containers to minimum necessary communications.

```
# Establishing isolated Docker networks
docker network create private-net
docker run --network=private-net -d app-image
```

5. Securely Manage Secrets: Avoid embedding secrets in Dockerfiles or source code. Utilize Docker Secrets or integrate a secrets management tool like HashiCorp Vault for managing sensitive information.

```
# Creating a Docker secret
echo "your_secret_data" | docker secret create my_secret -
```

6. Implement Logging and Monitoring Systems: Set up tools such as Prometheus, Grafana, and Fluentd to monitor container activity, ensuring all actions are logged and anomalies are quickly detected.

Conclusion

Securing Docker containers and images involves a layered security approach, addressing potential vulnerabilities from the build stage to deployment and runtime. By employing secure base images, minimizing build contents, restricting runtime capabilities, and vigilant monitoring, the security of Dockerized applications can be significantly enhanced. These practices not only protect against external threats but also fortify the infrastructure from within, ensuring operational security and compliance.

Understanding and using Docker security tools

Docker is integral to the modern deployment and management of containerized applications, but ensuring robust security within Docker environments is crucial for protecting against threats and vulnerabilities. This guide delves into Docker's essential security tools and outlines how to utilize them effectively to bolster the security of Docker containers and images.

Key Docker Security Tools and Features

1. Docker Bench for Security: Docker Bench for Security, a comprehensive tool that assesses Docker installations against best practices, is crucial for identifying potential security improvements. It evaluates your Docker configurations and provides recommendations based on industry standards.

How to Run Docker Bench for Security:

```
docker run --net host --pid host --cap-add audit_control \
    -e DOCKER_CONTENT_TRUST=$DOCKER_CONTENT_TRUST \
    -v /var/lib:/var/lib \
    -v /var/run/docker.sock:/var/run/docker.sock \
    -v /usr/lib/systemd:/usr/lib/systemd \
    -v /etc:/etc --label docker_bench_security \
    docker/docker-bench-security
```

This command executes Docker Bench for Security in a container that accesses various host resources to conduct a thorough evaluation of the Docker environment.

2. Docker Content Trust: Docker Content Trust offers a security layer that uses digital signatures to secure the data transferred between Docker registries and your environment, ensuring the authenticity and integrity of Docker images.

Activating Docker Content Trust: Set an environmental variable to enable it:

```
export DOCKER_CONTENT_TRUST=1
```

When enabled, Docker operations like pull, push, or build will require images to be signed, verifying the source's credibility.

3. User Namespace Support: User namespaces enhance security by isolating container privileges. This prevents container processes from gaining host privileges, crucial for mitigating the risks associated with potential container breaches.

Enabling User Namespaces: Modify the Docker daemon's configuration to activate this feature:

```
{
    "userns-remap": "default"
}
```

This configuration remaps container user IDs to less privileged user IDs on the host system, enhancing security by limiting the potential damage from compromised containers.

Advanced Network Security Configurations

1. Custom Network Bridges: Creating user-defined networks rather than relying on Docker's default bridge network can significantly improve the isolation and security between containers.

Create a Custom Network:

```
docker network create --driver bridge isolated_nw
```

This command sets up a custom bridge network, allowing for controlled inter-container communication and better overall security management.

2. Implementing Network Policies: In Docker environments orchestrated with Kubernetes, defining network policies can restrict the traffic between pods based on designated security requirements.

Sample Network Policy:

```yaml
kind: NetworkPolicy
apiVersion: networking.k8s.io/v1
metadata:
  name: example-network-policy
spec:
  podSelector:
    matchLabels:
      role: db
  policyTypes:
  - Ingress
  - Egress
  ingress:
  - from:
    - podSelector:
        matchLabels:
          role: frontend
```

```yaml
  egress:
  - to:
    - podSelector:
        matchLabels:
          role: backup
```

This policy limits connections to and from a database pod, permitting traffic only from certain frontend pods and to backup pods, enforcing strict traffic flow guidelines.

Secure Management of Secrets

Docker Secrets: A native Docker tool for managing sensitive data such as passwords and tokens securely, Docker Secrets is especially useful in Docker Swarm environments.

Creating a Secret:

```
echo "SensitiveData" | docker secret create my_secret -
```

This command securely stores a secret within Docker Swarm, preventing sensitive information from being exposed in Dockerfiles or source code.

Conclusion

Utilizing Docker's built-in security tools and features is vital for securing container environments. By implementing Docker Bench for Security, Docker Content Trust, user namespaces, custom network configurations, and Docker Secrets, developers and system administrators can significantly enhance the security of their Docker deployments. These tools provide critical defenses and practices necessary for maintaining secure, reliable, and robust Docker-based applications.

Chapter Eleven

Docker APIs and Ecosystem

Exploring Docker APIs for automation and integration

Docker's widespread adoption in software deployment is largely attributable to its powerful API, which enables detailed automation and seamless integration of Docker functionalities into broader application ecosystems. This guide delves into how the Docker API can be harnessed to automate processes and integrate with various systems, enhancing operational efficiency and scalability.

Overview of the Docker API

The Docker API is a RESTful service that allows direct interaction with the Docker daemon, enabling programmatic management of Docker resources such as containers, images, networks, and volumes. It mirrors the capabilities available in the Docker CLI, providing a comprehensive set of endpoints for detailed control.

API Versioning and Endpoint Configuration

To maintain consistency and compatibility, the Docker API is versioned. Specifying an API version in requests is critical to ensuring that applications interact with Docker in an expected manner without being affected by changes in API behavior across different Docker versions.

Typical API Request Format:

```
/v1.xx/containers/json
```

In this format, **v1.xx** represents the API version, and the path delineates the targeted Docker resource and the action required.

Initial Setup and Security for Docker API

Accessing the Docker API securely requires careful configuration, especially when enabling remote access over the network.

1. **Modify the Docker service configuration:** Open the Docker service file found typically at **/lib/systemd/system/docker.service**.

2. **Adjust the Docker daemon start command:** Add or change the line to include TCP and Unix socket options:

```
ExecStart=/usr/bin/dockerd -H tcp://0.0.0.0:2376 -H unix:///var/run/docker.sock
```

3. **Apply changes and restart Docker:** Reload the Docker daemon settings and restart the service to apply the new configuration:

```
sudo systemctl daemon-reload
sudo systemctl restart docker
```

4. **Secure with TLS:** When exposing the Docker API over TCP, it's crucial to secure it using TLS to prevent unauthorized access.

Docker API for Automation

The Docker API can be utilized to automate numerous Docker operations efficiently using simple commands. Below are examples using the **curl** command to interact with the API:

List all containers:

```
curl -s --unix-socket /var/run/docker.sock http:/v1.40/containers/json
```

Start a container:

```
curl -X POST --unix-socket /var/run/docker.sock http:/v1.40/containers/container_id/start
```

Stop a container:

```
curl -X POST --unix-socket /var/run/docker.sock http:/v1.40/containers/container_id/stop
```

Docker API in CI/CD Pipelines

Integrating the Docker API into CI/CD pipelines allows for the automation of container builds, testing, and deployment workflows, ensuring that each integration or code change is automatically reflected in Docker containers.

Automating image builds:

```
curl -X POST --unix-socket /var/run/docker.sock -H "Content-Type: application/json" \
    -d '{"t": "my-image:tag", "remote": "https://github.com/my/repo.git"}' \
    http:/v1.40/build
```

This command triggers the Docker daemon to build an image from a Git repository and tag it, all based on configurations specified in the POST request.

Conclusion

Utilizing the Docker API effectively allows developers to embed Docker functionalities into their development workflows, automating tasks and integrating with other platforms. This not only streamlines operations but also enhances the potential for scale and efficiency within development teams. With appropriate security measures, the Docker API is a powerful tool for modern DevOps, facilitating extensive automation and robust integration capabilities.

Tools and services that enhance Docker workflows

Docker has revolutionized the deployment of software by encapsulating applications in containers, streamlining their delivery and operation. Enhancing Docker's native capabilities are several tools and services that facilitate more effective orchestration, integration, monitoring, and security management. This exploration highlights critical tools and services that boost Docker workflows.

Utilizing Docker Compose

Docker Compose is pivotal for simplifying the management of Docker environments that run multiple containers. It allows developers to configure entire applications using a single YAML file, initiating complex multi-container setups with ease.

Docker Compose Example:

```yaml
version: '3'
services:
  web:
    build: .
    ports:
      - "5000:5000"
  redis:
    image: "redis:alpine"
```

This Docker Compose file illustrates setting up a basic application with web and Redis services, delineating how multiple services are managed seamlessly.

Kubernetes

Kubernetes is a sophisticated container orchestration tool that extends Docker's capabilities, particularly useful for managing large-scale container setups. It automates various tasks such as deployment, scaling, and network management across clusters of containers.

Docker Swarm

Docker Swarm integrates closely with Docker's own ecosystem to manage clusters of Docker engines. It's noted for its simplicity and ease of use, making it an attractive option for those seeking straightforward orchestration solutions within Docker.

Portainer

Portainer is an administrative tool that provides a graphical interface for managing Docker environments. It facilitates easier oversight and management of containers, images, and networks, particularly enhancing usability for those who prefer visual management over command-line interactions.

Jenkins

Jenkins is widely recognized for its robust automation capabilities, particularly in continuous integration and continuous deployment (CI/CD) processes. It integrates smoothly with Docker to automate the lifecycle of containerized applications.

Jenkins Pipeline Example:

```
pipeline {
    agent any
    stages {
        stage('Build') {
            steps {
                sh 'docker build -t my-app .'
            }
        }
        stage('Deploy') {
            steps {
                sh 'docker run -d -p 5000:5000 my-app'
            }
        }
    }
}
```

This script demonstrates how Jenkins can be configured to automate Docker operations, from building images to deploying containers.

Prometheus & Grafana

Prometheus paired with **Grafana** offers sophisticated monitoring solutions for Docker environments. Prometheus collects metrics from containers, and Grafana provides a powerful visualization interface, enhancing the ability to monitor and react to application and environment status.

Trivy

Trivy is a security tool that scans container images for vulnerabilities. It's designed to be simple yet effective, providing essential security assessments to ensure container images are free from known vulnerabilities.

Conclusion

Supplementing Docker with these advanced tools and services not only enhances Docker's core functionalities but also solidifies the security, efficiency, and scalability of containerized applications. From orchestrating complex environments with Kubernetes to simplifying container management with Docker Compose, and securing deployments using Trivy, these integrations are indispensable for maximizing the potential of Docker deployments in robust, scalable environments.

An overview of Docker's ecosystem and community

Since its launch in 2013, Docker has fundamentally transformed software development with its innovative containerization technology, enabling developers to efficiently package, deploy, and manage applications consistently across different environments. Docker's ecosystem extends well beyond the software itself, encompassing a broad suite of tools, services, and an active community that collectively enrich the Docker user experience.

The Components of Docker's Ecosystem

1. Docker Engine: Central to the ecosystem, the Docker Engine is a powerful runtime that manages containers. These containers provide isolated environments for applications, ensuring they run uniformly regardless of the deployment environment.

2. Docker Hub: Docker Hub serves as the public repository for Docker images, offering a vast collection of pre-configured containers that developers can use to speed up setup and deployment. It acts as a pivotal platform for sharing and collaboration within the Docker community.

3. Docker Compose: Docker Compose facilitates the management of multi-container applications through simple YAML scripts. Developers can define all aspects of their application—services, networks, and volumes—and deploy the entire stack with just one command, streamlining development processes considerably.

4. Docker Swarm: Docker Swarm provides native clustering functionality that allows multiple Docker engines to work together as a single virtual Docker engine. This is crucial for managing container replication and orchestrating multiple containers across different hosts.

5. Docker Desktop: Available for both MacOS and Windows, Docker Desktop is an application that lets developers build and share containerized applications easily. It integrates seamlessly with Kubernetes and comes equipped with several developer tools to enhance productivity.

Additional Tools and Services in the Docker Ecosystem

The Docker ecosystem includes numerous tools and services designed to extend Docker's capabilities:

Docker Enterprise: This subscription-based offering delivers an enterprise-grade platform for container management across diverse infrastructures, integrating advanced security features and supporting multi-OS environments.

Docker Trusted Registry: Included with Docker Enterprise, this tool offers a secure, private repository for Docker images, featuring capabilities like image signing and scanning to bolster security.

Portainer: Though not a native Docker product, Portainer is an open-source project that enhances Docker's environment by providing a graphical interface to manage Docker setups. It supports both Docker Swarm and Kubernetes, offering detailed management features for containers.

Docker's Vibrant Community

Docker's community is a dynamic aspect of its ecosystem, comprising developers, enthusiasts, and contributors who engage through various forums and events:

Docker Forums: These forums are bustling with discussions ranging from beginner queries to expert advice, facilitating a collaborative environment for sharing Docker strategies and solutions.

DockerCon: As Docker's official conference, DockerCon attracts thousands from the global Docker community to network, share insights, and learn about the latest in Docker technology and containerization.

GitHub Repositories: The open-source nature of Docker is evident in its public GitHub repositories, where the community actively contributes to its ongoing development by addressing issues and proposing enhancements.

Local Meetups: Globally, numerous Docker Meetups bring together local members of the community to exchange knowledge, discuss Docker projects, and share experiences in a collaborative setting.

Conclusion

Docker's rich ecosystem and community offer an extensive range of tools and services that make it a powerful platform for modern software development. From simplifying deployments with Docker Compose to fostering community engagement through DockerCon and GitHub, Docker provides a comprehensive infrastructure that supports the development, deployment, and scaling of applications in containers. This robust support system not only enhances technical processes but also cultivates a thriving network of collaboration and innovation among developers around the world.

Chapter Twelve

Troubleshooting and Debugging Docker Containers

Common Docker problems and how to solve them

Docker revolutionizes software deployment with its containerization technology, but navigating through its challenges requires understanding and strategy. This guide provides insights into common Docker-related problems and offers effective solutions to enhance your Docker experience.

1. Managing Complex Container Deployments

Problem: Handling an expanding suite of containers across various environments can become unwieldy.

Solution: Implement robust orchestration tools like Kubernetes, Docker Swarm, or Apache Mesos. These frameworks automate the management, scaling, and networking of containerized applications, simplifying operations for complex deployments.

Example: Initialize Docker Swarm mode with:

```
docker swarm init
```

2. Ensuring Environment Consistency

Problem: Containers may operate differently across various stages of development due to discrepancies in environment setups.

Solution: Standardize configurations across all environments using Docker Compose, which allows you to specify and run multi-container Docker applications with a YAML script.

Example: A basic **docker-compose.yml** might look like:

```
version: '3'
services:
  web:
    image: webapp:latest
    ports:
      - "5000:5000"
```

```
  db:
    image: postgres:latest
    volumes:
      - data:/var/lib/postgresql
volumes:
  data:
```

3. Data Persistence Issues

Problem: Data stored in containers can be lost when containers are destroyed, as they are inherently ephemeral.

Solution: Use Docker volumes or bind mounts to ensure data persists beyond the life of individual containers.

Example: To create and use a Docker volume:

```
docker volume create myvolume
docker run -v myvolume:/data app
```

4. Network Configuration Difficulties

Problem: Configuring networking for Docker containers to communicate effectively can be complex.

Solution: Employ Docker's networking features to establish isolated or interconnected networks among containers or configure them to appear as physical devices using the Macvlan driver.

Example: Create a user-defined network:

```
docker network create --driver bridge my-bridge
```

5. Reducing Image Size

Problem: Bulky Docker images are slow to upload and download, consuming excessive storage and bandwidth.

Solution: Optimize Dockerfiles to reduce image sizes through multi-stage builds, using smaller base images, and consolidating layer-creating commands.

Example: Here's how you can use a multi-stage build to minimize image size:

```
# Build stage
FROM golang:1.14 AS builder
WORKDIR /app
COPY . .
RUN go build -o myapp .

# Final stage
FROM alpine:latest
WORKDIR /root/
COPY --from=builder /app/myapp .
CMD ["./myapp"]
```

6. Addressing Security Concerns

Problem: Default container configurations and outdated images may pose security risks.

Solution: Regularly scan containers for vulnerabilities with tools like Trivy, enforce non-root user operation, and utilize Docker Bench for Security to audit against security standards.

Example: Scan a Docker image for vulnerabilities:

```
trivy image myapp:latest
```

7. Limiting Resource Consumption

Problem: Containers without resource limits can monopolize system resources, impacting overall performance.

Solution: Set explicit CPU and memory limits on containers to prevent resource hogging.

Example: Restrict resources for a container:

```
docker run -it --cpus="1.5" --memory="1g" ubuntu:latest
```

Conclusion

While Docker simplifies application deployment, managing its ecosystem effectively requires tackling inherent challenges with strategic measures. By understanding common issues—from orchestration complexities and environment consistency to security and resource management—and implementing targeted solutions, Docker users can optimize their containerized environments for better performance and security.

Tools and techniques for troubleshooting

Troubleshooting in intricate IT landscapes is an essential capability, encompassing a comprehensive understanding of diverse tools and strategies to efficiently pinpoint and address system malfunctions. This competency is crucial in various settings, from corporate systems and networks to software development projects. This discussion highlights an assortment of critical troubleshooting tools and methodologies that facilitate effective problem resolution.

Critical Troubleshooting Tools

1. **Logging Tools**:

   o **Overview**: Logs are invaluable for recording sequences of events within systems, providing the first clues in troubleshooting endeavors.

   o **Tools**: Sophisticated logging platforms such as the ELK Stack (Elasticsearch, Logstash, Kibana), Splunk, and Graylog enable the systematic organization and analysis of log data from multiple sources.

   o **Implementation**: Ensuring systems and applications log important operational data is crucial. Employing comprehensive log management solutions can streamline the process of sifting through logs to quickly identify anomalies and issues.

2. **Monitoring Tools**:

- o **Overview**: These tools play a vital role in observing system operations continuously, alerting technicians to deviations and potential issues as they arise.

- o **Tools**: Prometheus, Nagios, and New Relic are equipped with extensive monitoring capabilities, which include collecting detailed metrics and visualizing this data effectively.

- o **Setup**: Deploy monitoring agents on servers or containers to gather metrics. Configure dashboards and set alerts to notify of critical conditions or performance dips.

3. **Debugging Tools**:

- o **Overview**: Debuggers provide deep insights into application execution, allowing developers to trace through code execution and inspect variables.

- o **Tools**: Debuggers such as GDB for C/C++, PDB for Python, and those integrated in IDEs like Visual Studio or IntelliJ IDEA are widely used.

- o **Application**: Utilizing debugging involves running applications in debug mode, setting breakpoints, and stepping through code to explore and resolve issues.

4. **Network Diagnostics Tools**:

   o **Overview**: Ensuring network functionality is paramount, and diagnostic tools can help identify issues like poor connectivity or bandwidth problems.

   o **Tools**: Wireshark for traffic analysis, Ping for testing connectivity, and Traceroute for determining data paths are critical for network troubleshooting.

   o **Usage**: Analyzing network traffic with Wireshark helps identify configuration errors or congestion, while Ping and Traceroute are fundamental for assessing network paths and connectivity issues.

Proven Troubleshooting Methods

1. **Issue Replication**:

   o **Approach**: Consistently reproducing a problem can greatly simplify the diagnosis process.

   o **Method**: Strive to replicate the issue under controlled conditions to accurately pinpoint triggers and contributing factors.

2. **Incremental Isolation**:

   o **Approach**: Narrowing down potential causes by systematically isolating system segments is key in identifying the root of a problem.

- Method: Start with broad system evaluations and gradually focus on specific segments or components to localize the issue.

3. **Root Cause Analysis (RCA)**:

    - **Approach**: This analytical method seeks to discover the fundamental reasons for a problem beyond its immediate symptoms.

    - **Method**: Employ iterative questioning, such as the "Five Whys" technique, to delve deeper into each layer of a problem until the primary cause is revealed.

4. **Comparative Analysis**:

    - **Approach**: Comparing the operation of a malfunctioning system to one that functions correctly can illuminate discrepancies.

    - **Method**: Analyze settings, active processes, and performance metrics against those of a functioning system to detect variances that may be causing issues.

5. **Change Management Review**:

    - **Approach**: Modifications in system configurations or updates often precipitate technical issues.

    - **Method**: Log and review all recent system changes to determine if they correlate with the emergence of the problem. Reversing these changes may mitigate the issue.

Conclusion

Effective troubleshooting necessitates not only a solid grasp of diagnostic tools but also an organized approach to applying these resources efficiently. By integrating advanced monitoring systems, precise log analysis, and targeted troubleshooting strategies, IT professionals can adeptly resolve issues, ensuring system stability and optimal performance. This comprehensive approach to troubleshooting is indispensable for maintaining robust and efficient technological infrastructures.

Best practices for maintaining Docker environments

To ensure Docker environments are managed effectively, a set of optimized practices is essential. These practices span from efficient image construction and rigorous security measures to meticulous resource management and diligent monitoring. Applying these best practices elevates the functionality and security of Docker deployments. This guide provides an overview of essential strategies for maintaining robust Docker environments.

Streamlined Image Construction

1. **Adopt Minimal Base Images**: Using lean base images like Alpine Linux helps minimize Docker image

sizes and reduces potential attack vectors, providing a secure and efficient base for applications.

Example:

```
FROM alpine:3.12
RUN apk add --no-cache nginx
```

2. **Implement Multi-Stage Builds**: Multi-stage builds in Dockerfiles help segregate the build environment from the runtime environment. This approach only carries over the essential components needed for the final image, reducing its size and surface area for security vulnerabilities.

Example:

```
# Build stage
FROM golang:1.15 AS builder
WORKDIR /application
COPY . .
RUN go build -o app .

# Final stage
FROM alpine:3.12
COPY --from=builder /application/app .
CMD ["./app"]
```

Security Practices

1. **Conduct Regular Security Scans**: Employing scanning tools such as Trivy or Clair to routinely check Docker images for vulnerabilities can preemptively address security issues.

Example:

```
trivy image your-image-name
```

2. **Restrict Container Privileges**: Limiting container privileges by running them under non-root users can significantly mitigate risks associated with privilege escalation.

Example:

```
FROM node:14
WORKDIR /app
COPY . .
RUN npm install && chown -R node:node /app
USER node
CMD ["node", "app.js"]
```

Resource Optimization

1. **Set Explicit Resource Constraints**: Defining specific resource limits for containers helps prevent any individual container from consuming excessive CPU and memory, promoting stable operations across the system.

Example:

```
docker run -d --name optimized-app --memory=500m --cpus="1.0" my-app:latest
```

2. **Utilize Docker Compose for Configuration Management**: Docker Compose facilitates the configuration and management of multi-container applications, streamlining development and testing phases.

Example:

```
version: '3.8'
services:
  webapp:
    build: .
    ports:
      - "8080:8080"
  database:
    image: postgres
    environment:
      POSTGRES_PASSWORD: example
```

Monitoring and Log Management

1. **Implement Centralized Logging**: Centralizing logs using tools like Fluentd or ELK Stack (Elasticsearch, Logstash, Kibana) provides a cohesive view of all logs, aiding in swift troubleshooting and monitoring.

Example:

```
docker run -d --name fluentd fluent/fluentd
```

2. **Set Up Routine Health Checks**: Configuring health checks in Docker ensures that containers are functioning as intended and helps quickly identify failing services.

Example:

```
HEALTHCHECK --interval=1m --timeout=10s \
  CMD curl -f http://localhost/ || exit 1
```

154

Regular Maintenance and Updates

Keep Software Up-to-Date: Regular updates to Docker, containerized applications, and base images are vital to maintain security and efficiency, preventing vulnerabilities and performance issues.

Conclusion

Adopting a comprehensive approach that includes refined image management, stringent security protocols, strategic resource handling, and proactive monitoring will significantly enhance the maintenance of Docker environments. These best practices ensure Docker deployments are not only performant but also secure and reliable, enabling organizations to fully leverage the advantages of containerization.

Chapter Thirteen

Preparing for More Advanced Docker Topics

Preview of intermediate Docker concepts (e.g., orchestration with Docker Swarm)

As Docker solidifies its role in modern software deployment, understanding intermediate Docker concepts, especially in the realm of orchestration, is crucial for those aiming to enhance operational efficiencies and scalability. Docker Swarm, Docker's native clustering and orchestration tool, is central to these advanced operational needs. This detailed overview explores Docker Swarm, shedding light on its capabilities and demonstrating how it facilitates the management of containerized applications across a cluster of machines.

Docker Orchestration Explained

Orchestration automates the management of container lifecycles within dynamic environments. Effective orchestration improves application scalability, deployment speeds, and overall reliability by automating tasks such as provisioning, deployment, scaling, and networking. Docker Swarm integrates with Docker's API, making it a seamless and powerful tool for users familiar with Docker's command-line interface.

Key Features of Docker Swarm

Docker Swarm transforms a pool of Docker hosts into a single, virtual Docker host, streamlining the management of container clusters. It's designed for ease of use without sacrificing the power needed to manage complex container topologies.

Core Capabilities of Docker Swarm:

- **High Availability:** Docker Swarm ensures there are always containers running as specified, even if some nodes fail, thus eliminating single points of failure.

- **Load Balancing:** The tool automatically distributes tasks across the cluster, balancing the load and optimizing resource utilization.

- **Decentralized Approach:** Swarm operates with a decentralized architecture, which improves system resilience and scalability.

- **Scalability:** Users can scale their applications up or down with simple commands, adapting to changes in demand.

Deploying Docker Swarm

Setting up Docker Swarm involves a few straightforward steps:

1. **Initialize the Swarm:** Begin by setting up the Swarm on a Docker Engine designated as the manager node.

```
docker swarm init --advertise-addr <MANAGER-IP>
```

2. **Join Nodes to the Swarm:** Other Docker Engines can join the Swarm as worker nodes by using a token from the manager node.

```
docker swarm join --token <TOKEN> <MANAGER-IP>:2377
```

3. **Deploy Services:** You can then deploy services to the Swarm, which are definitions of the tasks to execute.

```
docker service create --replicas 3 -p 80:80 --name webservice nginx
```

This command starts a service named **webservice** with 3 replicas running nginx across the cluster.

Advanced Docker Swarm Features

- **Rolling Updates:** Docker Swarm supports rolling updates to deploy updates with minimal downtime, allowing parameters such as update delays and parallelism to be set.

```
docker service update --image nginx:latest --update-delay 10s --update-parallelism 2
    webservice
```

- **Networking Options:** Swarm also provides overlay networks for containers on different Docker hosts to communicate securely.

```
docker network create --driver overlay --subnet 10.0.9.0/24 my-overlay-network
```

- **Secret Management:** Secure handling of sensitive information is achievable using Docker secrets within the Swarm.

```
echo "secure_data" | docker secret create example_secret -
```

Conclusion

Docker Swarm is a robust solution for Docker orchestration, offering simplicity alongside powerful orchestration capabilities. By mastering Docker Swarm, organizations can greatly enhance their container management processes, ensuring that applications are not only deployed efficiently but also maintained with high availability and resilience. For any team looking to leverage Docker to its fullest, understanding and utilizing Docker Swarm is an essential step forward in their DevOps practices.

Resources for further learning and deep dives

In today's rapidly changing technology landscape, ongoing education is crucial for professionals seeking to enhance their skills and keep pace with new developments. There is a vast array of learning resources available that cater to different learning preferences and levels of expertise, aimed at deepening individuals' understanding of complex technical subjects. This guide outlines various key resources for advanced learning, including books, online platforms, interactive environments, and community forums.

Books

Books offer a solid foundation for learning, providing detailed explorations of subjects from basic concepts to advanced applications.

- **Technical Books**: For in-depth coverage of specific technologies or programming techniques, books like

"Clean Code" by Robert C. Martin or "Designing Data-Intensive Applications" by Martin Kleppmann are invaluable, offering insights and practical advice.

- **E-books**: With their regular updates, e-books are a great way to stay current on technological trends. Many authors and companies offer e-books, sometimes for free, that cover a wide range of technical topics.

Online Courses and Tutorials

Online educational platforms provide courses ranging from beginner to expert levels, incorporating interactive elements such as hands-on projects and community forums, often led by industry experts or academics.

- **MOOCs (Massive Open Online Courses)**: Platforms like Coursera, edX, and Udacity offer a diverse range of courses in collaboration with leading universities and technology companies, spanning areas from artificial intelligence to computer science.

- **Targeted Learning Platforms**: For those focused on specific technologies, platforms such as Pluralsight, LinkedIn Learning, and Codecademy provide specialized courses designed to enhance proficiency in particular tools or programming languages.

Interactive Learning Platforms

Hands-on learning is especially beneficial for disciplines like programming, where applying theoretical knowledge through coding is crucial.

- **Coding Practice Sites**: Platforms such as LeetCode, HackerRank, and Codewars offer coding challenges that improve coding skills through practical engagement and competition.

- **Browser-Based Coding Environments**: Tools like Repl.it and Jupyter Notebooks provide a real-time coding environment in the browser, allowing for instant experimentation and learning.

Webinars and Workshops

Interactive sessions like webinars and workshops offer opportunities to engage directly with experts and learn about the latest trends and technologies.

- **Tech Conferences**: Many tech conferences now offer virtual access options, featuring a variety of sessions and the opportunity to interact directly with thought leaders.

- **Tech Company Webinars**: Many technology companies regularly host webinars that feature their engineers or guest experts who discuss specialized technologies or demonstrate new solutions.

Community and Peer Learning

Engaging with a community of peers can significantly enhance the learning experience by providing support, motivation, and a wealth of shared knowledge.

- **Online Forums and Discussion Groups**: Digital platforms such as Stack Overflow, Reddit, and specific technology-focused forums offer a vibrant community for discussion, advice, and knowledge exchange.

- **Meetups and User Groups**: Meeting with local or virtual groups focused on specific technology interests can offer valuable networking opportunities, insights, and shared experiences.

Research Papers and Articles

For those on the cutting edge of technology, staying informed through research papers and industry articles is essential.

- **Academic Journals**: Journals like IEEE Transactions or ACM Transactions on Computer Systems publish research articles that detail the latest discoveries and innovations in technology.

- **Technology Blogs and Company Blogs**: Many technology firms maintain blogs where they explore challenges, discuss new technologies they are implementing, and share industry best practices.

Conclusion

The range of available resources for further learning allows individuals to explore technical topics thoroughly, enhancing both knowledge and practical skills. From detailed books and interactive courses to engaging with community forums and keeping abreast of the latest research, these educational tools are crucial for anyone looking to advance their technological expertise and remain competitive in the field.

Community and support structures for Docker users

Docker's widespread adoption as a leading containerization platform is supported by a vibrant community and a comprehensive array of support structures that enrich user experience. These resources are essential for Docker users ranging from beginners to seasoned professionals to learn, solve problems, and enhance their Docker implementations. This discussion outlines the various community and support avenues available to Docker users, highlighting how these resources promote a collaborative and supportive ecosystem.

Online Forums and Community Engagement

Docker Community Forums: The Docker Community Forums act as a central hub for users to seek advice, share experiences, and address Docker-related issues. The forums are segmented into different categories like Docker Hub, Docker Desktop, and more, which aids in easy navigation and finding pertinent discussions.

Stack Overflow: A pivotal resource for more technical Docker inquiries, Stack Overflow allows users to post questions tagged with 'docker' to attract solutions from other developers and Docker experts. This platform is crucial for exchanging best practices and tackling programming challenges.

GitHub: Beyond hosting Docker's open-source projects, GitHub facilitates user involvement through bug reporting, feature suggestions, and direct contributions to the codebase, encouraging active collaboration within the Docker community.

Social Media and Real-Time Communication

Twitter: Docker's active engagement on Twitter (@Docker) offers a direct channel for updates, tips, and community interaction, helping users stay up-to-date with the latest Docker news.

Reddit: The Docker subreddit (r/docker) hosts a thriving community for Docker discussions, where users share articles, discuss Docker trends, and seek peer advice.

Slack/Discord Channels: Docker's Slack community, along with various Docker-centric Discord servers, provide spaces for real-time discussions, support, and community interaction concerning Docker topics.

Official Docker Learning Resources

Docker Documentation: The comprehensive resource for all things Docker, the official documentation (docs.docker.com), covers everything from basic tutorials to advanced functionalities, with regular updates that mirror the latest Docker developments.

Docker Official Blog: This blog is an essential resource for insights into Docker's advancements, featuring articles from Docker authorities and community experts, discussing new features, use cases, and best practices.

DockerCon: As Docker's flagship conference, DockerCon brings together the Docker community to share innovations, experiences, and expand their Docker knowledge through workshops, talks, and networking opportunities.

Training and Professional Development

Docker Training: Docker's official training sessions provide structured learning paths to help users at various proficiency levels deepen their understanding of Docker technologies.

Docker Certification: The Docker Certified Associate (DCA) certification is designed to validate professional expertise with Docker environments, offering recognition for skills in a competitive job market.

Localized Events and Community Programs

Local Meetups: Local Docker meetups and user groups facilitate in-person interactions, allowing users to network, share ideas, and gain insights into practical Docker implementations.

Docker Captains Program: This program acknowledges distinguished Docker experts who contribute significantly to the community by sharing knowledge, developing Docker-based projects, and leading community events.

Conclusion

The Docker community, supported by its extensive support resources, plays a crucial role in the platform's ongoing success and user satisfaction. These resources equip Docker users with the necessary tools and knowledge to efficiently manage Docker solutions. Through forums, social media, official guides, certification programs, and community events, Docker ensures that its users have access to a supportive and informative network. This dynamic community not only assists users in leveraging Docker technology effectively but also drives continuous innovation within the Docker ecosystem.

Conclusion

Recap of what has been learned in the book

In this comprehensive exploration of Docker, we have journeyed from the foundational elements to the more complex capabilities of this pivotal containerization technology. The book aimed to equip both newcomers and experienced professionals with a deep understanding and practical skills necessary for leveraging Docker to streamline and enhance the deployment and management of applications. This summary recaps the essential topics and key learnings presented throughout the book, consolidating your understanding and encouraging further exploration and application.

Introduction to Docker and Its Core Components

We began with an introduction to Docker, explaining its critical role in contemporary software development and deployment ecosystems. We detailed Docker's core components, including Docker Engine, Docker Images, Docker Containers, and Docker Registries. This foundation set the stage for understanding how Docker packages applications into containers to ensure consistency across different computing environments.

- **Docker Images and Containers**: The discussion on Docker images as immutable templates from which containers are created provided insights into how applications are prepared and managed in Docker environments.

Essential Docker Commands and Operations

We delved into essential Docker commands, providing a hands-on tutorial on how to manage and interact with containers. Key commands like **docker run**, **docker pull**, and **docker ps** were covered, alongside advanced commands such as **docker exec** and **docker logs**. These sections included code snippets to demonstrate typical Docker operations, helping readers to start containers, inspect their state, and manage container logs effectively.

```
docker run -d --name my_app nginx
docker exec -it my_app /bin/bash
```

Docker Networking and Persistent Data Management

An in-depth look at Docker networking explained how containers communicate on the same host and with external entities. We discussed the setup of default and custom networks, and the role of Docker's embedded DNS in service discovery. The book also tackled persistent data management strategies involving volumes, bind mounts, and tmpfs mounts, essential for running stateful applications in Docker:

```
docker volume create data_volume
docker run -d --name my_database -v data_volume:/var/lib/mysql mysql
```

Advanced Docker Features: Docker Compose, Docker Swarm, and Security

Progressing to more complex scenarios, we introduced Docker Compose as a tool for defining and managing multi-container Docker applications using **docker-compose.yml**. This simplifies configuration and deployment processes:

168

```
version: '3'
services:
  web:
    build: .
    ports:
      - "5000:5000"
  database:
    image: postgres
    volumes:
      - persistent_data:/var/lib/postgresql/data
volumes:
  persistent_data:
```

Docker Swarm was explored as a native clustering and orchestration solution, and we emphasized the importance of security practices in Docker usage, such as implementing non-root user configurations and ensuring regular updates.

Docker in Production Environments

The final chapters focused on deploying Docker in production settings, discussing logging, monitoring, and performance optimization. Tools like Prometheus for monitoring and ELK Stack for logging were highlighted. We also emphasized the significance of establishing a CI/CD pipeline integrating Jenkins or GitLab CI to automate Docker tasks from development through deployment.

Conclusion

This book has provided a thorough grounding in Docker, covering a wide array of topics from basic concepts to sophisticated production deployment strategies. It is designed to prepare readers to effectively tackle real-world challenges, enhance operational workflows, and fully utilize Docker's capabilities to expedite development cycles and improve application delivery. Readers are encouraged to keep exploring and practicing, staying abreast of Docker's ongoing developments and expanding their expertise in containerization technology.

The transition to the next level: What to expect in the middle-level guide

As learners progress from the foundational aspects discussed in the introductory Docker guide, the intermediate-level guide is designed to broaden this knowledge base, introducing more complex functionalities and applications of Docker. This next guide will delve deeper into Docker's capabilities, preparing readers to handle more sophisticated environments and refine their Docker deployment strategies. Here's an outline of what can be expected in the intermediate guide to Docker, focusing on expanding expertise and tackling advanced Docker functionalities.

Enhanced Docker Configurations and Networking

The intermediate guide will explore intricate Docker configurations, teaching readers how to tailor Docker setups for specific operational requirements. The guide will provide insights into advanced Docker daemon configurations, in-depth management of Docker networks, and strategies to enhance the security of Docker containers and networks.

- **Advanced Daemon Configuration**: Learn how to modify Docker's daemon settings to improve system performance and manage resources more effectively.

- **Sophisticated Networking Solutions**: Understand the setup of complex Docker networking scenarios, including creating overlay networks for distributed applications and defining network policies for enhanced security.

Deep Dive into Docker Compose

Building upon the introductory coverage of Docker Compose, the intermediate guide will cover more nuanced uses and configurations, focusing on optimizing Docker Compose for both development and production scenarios.

- **Advanced Service Setup**: Detailed explanations on configuring services in docker-compose.yml, such as setting service-specific conditions, incorporating environment variables, and managing service dependencies.

- **Handling Multiple Environments**: Strategies for deploying Docker Compose across different environments (development, testing, production), including environment-specific configurations and secret management.

```yaml
version: '3.8'
services:
  app:
    build: .
    environment:
      - NODE_ENV=production
    depends_on:
      - db
  db:
    image: postgres
    volumes:
      - data:/var/lib/postgresql/data
volumes:
  data:
```

Orchestrating with Docker Swarm

Introducing Docker Swarm in detail, the guide will cover how to orchestrate and manage multi-container deployments across clusters using Docker's native orchestration tool.

- **Swarm Management**: Guidance on establishing a Docker Swarm, adding nodes, and orchestrating containers across multiple nodes.

- **Scaling and Updating Services**: Techniques for dynamically scaling services and performing updates without downtime.

```
docker service create --replicas 5 --name my-web-app --publish published=8080,target
    =80 my-web-app:latest
docker service update --image my-web-app:v2 --update-parallelism 2 --update-delay 10s
    my-web-app
```

Managing Stateful Applications

The intermediate guide will also tackle the challenges of managing stateful applications that require persistent data storage in Docker.

- **Advanced Volume Management**: In-depth discussion on creating and managing Docker volumes to ensure data persistence across container lifecycles.

- **Database Management in Containers**: Configuring and optimizing databases such as MySQL and PostgreSQL within Docker containers for data persistence and performance.

CI/CD Integration with Docker

Integrating Docker into continuous integration and deployment pipelines is a crucial component of modern DevOps practices. The guide will explore how to build effective CI/CD workflows using Docker, with integration examples using popular tools like Jenkins, GitLab CI, and GitHub Actions.

- **Defining CI/CD Workflows**: Creating and managing CI/CD pipelines in Docker environments, including Docker-specific pipeline configurations.

- **Deployment Automation**: Practical advice on automating Docker deployments to streamline development cycles and improve deployment reliability.

Monitoring and Logging for Docker Environments

Comprehensive monitoring and effective logging are essential for maintaining the performance and health of Dockerized applications. The guide will introduce tools and strategies for robust monitoring and centralized logging.

- **Using Prometheus and Grafana**: Setting up Prometheus to collect Docker metrics and Grafana to visualize those metrics.

- **Implementing Centralized Logging**: Strategies for aggregating logs from Docker containers using tools like ELK Stack or Fluentd.

Conclusion

The intermediate-level guide to Docker is intended to transition users from basic understanding to a more comprehensive mastery, equipping them with the skills to manage advanced Docker functionalities. By exploring in-depth techniques and best practices, readers will be prepared to optimize their Docker environments, ensuring efficient, scalable, and secure containerized applications. This guide lays the groundwork for advanced Docker topics, setting the stage for professional growth towards Docker expertise.

Final thoughts and encouragement for continuous learning

As we conclude this exploration, it's essential to acknowledge that the journey through the realms of Docker and containerization is not ending here. The domains of technology are continuously evolving, with Docker being no exception. What we've discussed in this guide is merely an introduction to a broader, ever-expanding field of knowledge that requires ongoing engagement and learning to master fully.

The Necessity of Continuous Learning

In technology, staying stationary equates to falling behind. The swift advancement of technologies necessitates a constant commitment to education and skill enhancement. For professionals in this sector, continual learning is less an option and more a requisite to remain competent and competitive in a rapidly evolving industry.

Engaging with the Community and Resources

The collective wisdom of a community is a powerful asset in the learning process. Engaging with others in the field through various platforms offers unparalleled opportunities to gain insights, resolve challenges, and discover innovations. Actively participating in community discussions, attending relevant events, and networking can greatly accelerate your learning journey.

- **Community Forums and Online Platforms**: Engage with forums like Docker's community forums, GitHub, or Stack Overflow to dive into a wealth of knowledge and shared experiences that can help with practical problem-solving and staying updated with the latest trends.

- **Workshops and Tech Conferences**: Attending industry conferences, such as DockerCon, provides access to advanced workshops and presentations that showcase the forefront of Docker technology and application, offering a unique learning experience.

Setting Personal and Professional Goals

Adopting a structured approach to learning by setting specific goals can enhance the acquisition and application of knowledge. Personal learning objectives help maintain focus and drive throughout your educational endeavors, whether they involve mastering specific Docker functionalities or engaging with complex project deployments.

- **Project-Based Learning**: Tackling real-world projects or creating hypothetical scenarios to apply

Docker techniques can solidify your understanding and skills through practical application. For example, configuring a Docker network to handle intricate load-balancing tasks can provide hands-on experience that is both challenging and instructive.

Leveraging Documentation and Scholarly Resources

In-depth resources such as Docker's official documentation and relevant technical literature remain invaluable for anyone serious about mastering the platform. These resources provide comprehensive insights and are often the bedrock of technical understanding.

- **Regular Revision**: Periodically revisiting these materials to refresh your knowledge or to catch up on updates is crucial as Docker continues to evolve and introduce new features and best practices.

Practice and Continuous Experimentation

Consistent practice is the key to mastering any skill. Regularly engaging with Docker, experimenting with its various tools, and testing different configurations will deepen your understanding and enhance your operational efficiency.

- **Experimentation Labs**: Setting up a test environment where you can experiment with Docker without risk encourages innovation and deeper learning. This hands-on approach helps in better understanding the nuances of Docker and its applications.

Conclusion

This guide marks just the beginning of your learning curve with Docker. As new technologies and methodologies emerge, your journey with Docker should adapt and evolve. Continue to explore, practice, and connect with the community. Stay curious and motivated, and use this guide as a stepping stone to further your expertise in Docker and related technologies. Your path forward should be one of persistent learning and engagement, ensuring that you not only keep pace with technology trends but also contribute to shaping them.

Introduction

Introduction to optimizing Docker: Efficiency and workflows

As we delve into optimizing Docker, it's crucial to recognize that the growing complexity of Docker environments, with numerous containers spread across several hosts, calls for a meticulous approach to enhance performance and streamline operations. This introductory section lays the groundwork for understanding how to refine Docker workflows and maximize the efficiency of your containerized applications.

Key Performance Metrics in Docker

Grasping the fundamental performance metrics is the first step in Docker optimization. These metrics include CPU usage, memory consumption, I/O rates, and network bandwidth, which are vital indicators of how well containers are performing. Monitoring tools like Docker Stats, cAdvisor, and Prometheus offer detailed insights into these metrics, allowing for data-driven optimization strategies.

For example, using the **docker stats** command provides real-time data on container performance:

```
docker stats
```

This displays each container's CPU and memory utilization, helping identify potential bottlenecks or resource-heavy containers.

Enhancing Docker Images

The efficiency of Docker containers is significantly influenced by the images they are built from. Reducing the size of Docker images, which decreases download times and saves storage space, is a fundamental optimization tactic. Employing smaller base images, reducing the number of layers, and stripping unnecessary files or dependencies are effective strategies in achieving this.

Consider the implementation of multi-stage builds to minimize image size:

```
# Builder stage
FROM golang:1.15 as builder
WORKDIR /app
COPY . .
RUN go build -o myapp .

# Final lightweight image
FROM alpine:latest
COPY --from=builder /app/myapp .
CMD ["./myapp"]
```

This Dockerfile utilizes a multi-stage build where the final image is based on a smaller Alpine image, equipped only with the essential compiled application and its dependencies.

Advanced Container Management

Efficient container management is key to optimizing Docker workflows. Advanced techniques such as orchestrated container deployment, automated scaling, and strategic resource allocation play a pivotal role. Orchestration tools like Docker Swarm and Kubernetes offer functionalities that include load balancing, automatic scaling, and service recovery, facilitating comprehensive container management.

Example command to set resource limits on a Docker container:

```
docker run -d --name myservice --memory=500m --cpus="1.0" myservice:latest
```

This command restricts the **myservice** container to 500 MB of memory and one CPU, promoting fair resource distribution across all containers.

Optimizing Docker Networking

The networking capabilities within Docker enable efficient container communication. To tailor performance, especially in environments with high traffic, optimizing Docker's network settings is essential. This might involve creating user-defined bridge networks or opting for higher-performance network drivers like **overlay2**.

Here's a method to establish a user-defined bridge network:

```
docker network create -d bridge my-bridge-network
```

Using this network can improve performance over the default bridge by optimizing network traffic handling between containers.

Docker in CI/CD Pipelines

Incorporating Docker into CI/CD pipelines enhances the development lifecycle by automating the building, testing, and deployment of Docker containers. Automation tools such as Jenkins, GitLab CI, and GitHub Actions can be configured to handle these tasks efficiently.

Here's an example of a Jenkins pipeline script that automates Docker operations:

```
# Jenkins pipeline example
pipeline {
    agent any
    stages {
        stage('Build') {
            steps {
                script {
                    docker.build("myapp:${env.BUILD_ID}")
                }
            }
        }
        stage('Deploy') {
            steps {
                script {
                    docker.withRegistry('https://registry.hub.docker.com',
                        'docker-credentials-id') {
                        docker.image("myapp:${env.BUILD_ID}").push()
                    }
                }
            }
        }
    }
}
```

This script outlines a CI/CD workflow that builds a Docker image and pushes it to a Docker registry, automating the deployment process.

Conclusion

Optimizing Docker involves a holistic strategy that extends beyond simple tweaks to encompass comprehensive management of images, containers, resources, and workflows. As Docker utilization scales, these optimizations can significantly enhance system performance, reduce costs, and streamline operations. Continuous adaptation to the latest Docker practices and tools is essential to maintain an efficient and robust Docker environment. Engaging with these advanced strategies will ensure that your Docker setups are not just functional but are also optimized for peak performance.

Recap of core Docker concepts from the beginner's book

In our initial exploration of Docker within the beginner's guide, we covered an extensive range of foundational concepts essential for anyone new to this influential containerization platform. This recap is designed to reinforce the key principles we've discussed, ensuring a robust understanding as we progress to tackle more complex Docker functionalities.

Introduction to Docker

Docker is a platform-as-a-service product that utilizes OS-level virtualization to deliver software in packages called containers. These containers operate independently, contain all their own software, libraries, and configuration files, and can communicate with each other through predefined channels. All containers run on the host operating system's kernel, making them lighter and more efficient than traditional virtual machines.

Docker Containers and Docker Images

At the heart of Docker are Docker containers and Docker images.

Docker Images serve as the blueprints for Docker containers, providing a read-only template from which containers are instantiated. Images are constructed through commands in a Dockerfile or pulled from cloud-based registries like Docker Hub.

Example of building an image:

```
docker build -t my_image:latest .
```

Docker Containers are active runtime instances of Docker images. They can be managed via the Docker CLI where you can start, stop, and manage containers' settings and connectivity.

Example of launching a container:

```
docker run -d --name my_container my_image:latest
```

Dockerfile and Docker Hub

A **Dockerfile** is a script comprised of successive commands used to build a Docker image. It simplifies the process of automating the image creation, making it repeatable and easy to update.

Docker Hub functions as Docker's official repository for hosting and sharing container images. It is an invaluable resource for locating and distributing Docker images, facilitating collaboration and streamlining workflows in development pipelines.

Docker's Architecture

Docker operates on a client-server model:

- The **Docker Client** makes requests to the Docker Daemon which handles the heavy tasks of building, running, and distributing Docker containers.

- The interaction between client and daemon occurs through a RESTful API, which can be configured for communication over UNIX sockets or network interfaces.

Networking in Docker

Docker's sophisticated networking allows containers to interact both among themselves and with external networks. Docker configures three default networks automatically; however, users can create custom networks to suit more specific needs.

Data Persistence and Volumes

Despite containers being inherently ephemeral, Docker facilitates data persistence through volumes. Volumes are mounted file systems available to containers and are crucial for storing data that must persist beyond the life of a single container.

Example of managing data with a volume:

```
docker volume create my_volume
docker run -d --name my_app -v my_volume:/app/data my_image:latest
```

Conclusion

The foundational concepts from the beginner's guide are intended to provide a solid framework for understanding Docker's capabilities. From basic definitions and component descriptions to Docker's operational nuances like networking and volume management, these initial topics set the groundwork for more advanced learning. As we move forward into complex Docker use cases and configurations, revisiting these core principles will help solidify your understanding and enhance your ability to effectively deploy Docker in a variety of environments.

Preview of the advanced topics covered in this guide

As we advance from basic Docker education to more specialized knowledge, this guide aims to elevate your expertise with Docker, focusing on the application of its more complex features and operational techniques. Here is an outline of the sophisticated topics that this guide will cover, which are pivotal for those looking to master Docker at a professional level.

Docker Performance Optimization

A pivotal aspect of professional Docker use is the optimization of container performance. This section will address how to enhance the efficiency of Docker containers through fine-tuning Docker configurations, adjusting resource limits, and utilizing performance monitoring tools to ensure optimal operation.

```
docker stats --format "table {{.ID}}\t{{.CPUPerc}}\t{{.MemUsage}}"
```

This command helps customize the display of Docker statistics, focusing on CPU and memory utilization to assist in fine-tuning resource usage across containers.

Advanced Docker Networking

Deepening the understanding of Docker's networking capabilities, this section will explore advanced network configuration, including setting up and managing intricate network architectures such as overlay networks, and securing communication channels within Docker.

```
docker network create --driver overlay --subnet 10.0.9.0/24 secure-overlay
```

This example illustrates how to establish a secure overlay network, which is essential for facilitating effective communication across containers distributed over several hosts.

Strategic Data Management

Effective data management within Docker involves more than just basic volume usage. Here, we'll delve into advanced data storage strategies, including setting up reliable data backups, implementing data replication techniques, and ensuring robust data recovery processes.

```
docker run -d --name db -v dbdata:/data/db mongo
```

By using a named volume (**dbdata**), this command ensures data persistence for a MongoDB container, crucial for maintaining data integrity across container restarts.

Enhancing Docker Security

This guide will thoroughly explore how to bolster security within Docker environments, detailing methods to secure Docker daemons, effectively manage Docker secrets, and implement comprehensive audit logs to monitor container activities.

```
echo "ThisIsASecret" | docker secret create my_secret -
```

This command demonstrates creating a Docker secret, a secure method to manage sensitive information accessible to containers at runtime without exposing it in Dockerfiles or image data.

Docker and CI/CD Processes

Integrating Docker into continuous integration and deployment pipelines is critical for streamlining development operations. This section will provide insights into configuring automated CI/CD pipelines using Docker with tools like Jenkins, GitLab CI, and GitHub Actions.

```yaml
# Example .gitlab-ci.yml for Docker operations
image: docker:latest

services:
  - docker:dind

before_script:
  - docker login -u "$CI_REGISTRY_USER" -p "$CI_REGISTRY_PASSWORD" $CI_REGISTRY

build:
  stage: build
  script:
    - docker build -t $CI_REGISTRY_IMAGE:$CI_COMMIT_REF_SLUG .
    - docker push $CI_REGISTRY_IMAGE:$CI_COMMIT_REF_SLUG
```

This GitLab CI configuration demonstrates how to automate Docker image building and deployment within a CI/CD pipeline, facilitating consistent and efficient updates and releases.

Leveraging Kubernetes with Docker

For those managing large-scale Docker deployments, understanding Kubernetes' orchestration capabilities is indispensable. This part of the guide will cover how to deploy and manage Docker containers using Kubernetes, from setting up Kubernetes clusters to optimizing the distribution of workloads.

Conclusion

This advanced guide is crafted to deepen your Docker capabilities, addressing a broad spectrum of topics essential for sophisticated Docker use in professional environments. By engaging with detailed discussions on performance tuning, networking, security, and CI/CD integration, as well as effective Kubernetes deployment strategies, this guide prepares you to handle the complexities of extensive Docker implementations. Each section is designed to provide comprehensive insights and practical guidance to ensure you are fully prepared to optimize and secure your Docker operations.

Chapter One

Advanced Docker Configuration

Customizing Docker for enhanced performance

Enhancing the performance of Docker involves a series of strategic adjustments and optimizations to both Docker settings and the way containers are deployed and managed. In environments where performance and efficiency are critical, fine-tuning Docker configurations can lead to noticeable improvements in both application speed and resource utilization. This comprehensive discussion delves into various methods to customize Docker for better performance, focusing on actionable changes and practical implementations.

Tuning Docker Engine Settings

The Docker Engine's configuration offers multiple levers for performance optimization, including the choice of storage drivers and log levels.

- **Storage Drivers**: The choice of a storage driver affects the speed and efficiency of container data operations. For example, **overlay2** is often recommended for its performance and compatibility, but the optimal driver may vary based on specific workload requirements.

```
# Set overlay2 as the default storage driver
{
  "storage-driver": "overlay2"
}
```

This setting can be added to the Docker daemon configuration file, usually found at **/etc/docker/daemon.json**, to enhance file system performance.

- **Log Levels**: Reducing the verbosity of Docker's logging can conserve system resources that might otherwise be spent managing log output. This is especially valuable in production settings.

```
# Configure Docker to use a more conservative log level
{
  "log-level": "warn"
}
```

Setting the log level to **warn** helps reduce the overhead associated with logging less critical information.

Managing Container Resources

Setting explicit resource limits on containers helps prevent any single container from using an excessive share of the host machine's CPU and memory, which can improve overall system stability and performance.

- **CPU and Memory Limits**: These limits can be specified at container runtime using Docker's command-line options.

```
docker run -d --name resource-limited-container --memory=2g --cpus=2 my-image:latest
```

This command ensures that the **resource-limited-container** does not use more than 2 GB of RAM and 2 CPU cores, promoting fair resource usage across all containers.

Optimizing Network Configurations

Network performance is crucial for the responsiveness and speed of applications that communicate between containers or access the internet.

- **User-Defined Bridge Networks**: Compared to the default bridge network, user-defined bridges offer better performance and networking features.

```
docker network create --driver bridge enhanced-net
```

Creating a user-defined bridge network, **enhanced-net**, helps improve network efficiency and container-to-container communication.

Utilizing Performance Monitoring Tools

Effective monitoring is essential for identifying performance bottlenecks and optimizing container operations. Tools like Prometheus offer extensive capabilities to gather and analyze performance metrics.

- **Prometheus Integration**: Set up Prometheus to monitor Docker containers, providing insights into resource usage and system performance.

```
# Example of running Prometheus in a Docker container
docker run -d -p 9090:9090 -v /path/to/prometheus.yml:/etc/prometheus/prometheus.yml
    prom/prometheus
```

This command launches Prometheus inside a Docker container, configured to monitor metrics that help in fine-tuning performance.

Adhering to Performance Best Practices

Several best practices can aid in maintaining optimal performance in Docker environments:

- **Streamline Docker Images**: Keeping images small by using multi-stage builds and removing unnecessary files reduces build and deployment times.

- **Minimize Container Privileges**: Operating containers with only necessary privileges reduces security risks and can indirectly enhance performance.

- **Regular Software Updates**: Regularly updating Docker and container applications ensures access to the latest features and performance optimizations.

Conclusion

Customizing Docker to improve performance is a comprehensive process that involves tweaking engine settings, managing resources wisely, optimizing network setups, and employing effective monitoring tools. By implementing these strategies, you can significantly elevate the efficiency of your Docker containers. These optimizations ensure that your Dockerized applications are not only faster and more responsive but also more robust and secure in handling the demands of production environments.

Advanced Docker daemon configurations

Configuring the Docker daemon with advanced settings is crucial for tailoring and enhancing the Docker environment to better suit specific operational requirements. Advanced daemon configurations can significantly improve container performance, efficiently manage system resources, and provide enhanced control over Docker's operations and integration with the system's other components. Mastery of these configurations is vital for system administrators and engineers looking to optimize their Docker implementations.

Docker Daemon Configuration Overview

The Docker daemon can be configured with a variety of settings detailed in the daemon.json file, usually located at /etc/docker/daemon.json on Linux machines. Adjusting the Docker daemon through this configuration file ensures your custom settings are maintained after Docker restarts or system reboots.

Essential Advanced Configuration Options

1. **Storage Drivers**: The choice of a storage driver can greatly impact container performance, especially during high I/O operations. Docker supports several drivers, and selecting the appropriate one is key.

```
{
  "storage-driver": "overlay2"
}
```

Setting **overlay2** as the default storage driver is generally recommended due to its performance efficiency and compatibility with modern Linux kernels.

2. **Log Configuration**: Proper log management can enhance system performance and reduce disk space usage. Configuring log levels and specifying log options are important steps in this process.

```
{
  "log-level": "warn",
  "log-driver": "json-file",
  "log-opts": {
    "max-size": "10m",
    "max-file": "3"
  }
}
```

This configuration reduces log verbosity, switches to a JSON log format, and implements log rotation to maintain up to three log files, each with a maximum size of 10MB.

3. **Live Restore Feature**: Enabling the live restore feature allows Docker containers to continue running during a daemon restart, which is critical for minimizing downtime in production environments.

```
{
  "live-restore": true
}
```

With live restore active, the Docker daemon can be updated or restarted without stopping running containers, thus avoiding service disruption.

4. **Default Cgroup Driver**: Aligning Docker's cgroup driver with the system's default, particularly when using Kubernetes, can prevent conflicts and ensure consistent performance.

```
{
  "exec-opts": ["native.cgroupdriver=systemd"]
}
```

This setting configures Docker to use the **systemd** cgroup driver, ensuring it matches the configuration often recommended for systems managed with Kubernetes.

5. **Registry Mirrors**: Setting up registry mirrors can decrease the latency and increase the speed of image downloads by caching Docker images locally.

```
{
  "registry-mirrors": ["https://your-mirror.example.com"]
}
```

Configuring a registry mirror can enhance the efficiency of pulling images, which is particularly beneficial in distributed environments.

6. **Insecure Registries**: To facilitate interactions with private or internal registries that do not use HTTPS, they must be configured as insecure within Docker settings.

```json
{
  "insecure-registries" : ["myregistry.example.com:5000"]
}
```

This configuration allows Docker to communicate over HTTP or with registries that use an invalid SSL certificate.

Security Considerations

Enhancing Docker security through daemon configuration involves several critical practices, such as disabling outdated features, enforcing TLS authentication, and managing network traffic rules.

```json
{
  "disable-legacy-registry": true,
  "tlsverify": true,
  "tlscacert": "/path/to/ca.pem",
  "tlscert": "/path/to/server-cert.pem",
  "tlskey": "/path/to/server-key.pem",
  "iptables": false
}
```

These settings boost security by disabling support for legacy registries, enabling TLS verification for secure client-daemon communication, and opting out of automatic iptables configuration by Docker.

Conclusion

Advanced Docker daemon configurations provide a range of powerful options that can significantly enhance how Docker performs and interacts with host systems. By carefully tailoring these settings, system administrators and DevOps professionals can optimize Docker to meet specific performance benchmarks, manage resources more effectively, and ensure a secure operational environment. Keeping abreast of these advanced options is essential for anyone involved in the extensive use of Docker in enterprise settings.

Tips for optimizing Docker's runtime environment

Optimizing Docker's runtime environment is essential for maximizing system performance and ensuring efficient container management. By fine-tuning various Docker configurations, system administrators and developers can significantly improve how applications run and how resources are utilized. Here we outline several strategic approaches to enhance Docker's operational efficiency, focusing on system configuration, resource management, and network optimization.

Selecting the Optimal Storage Driver

Choosing the right storage driver is critical, as it impacts the performance of I/O operations within Docker containers. **Overlay2** is generally preferred for most scenarios due to its efficiency with layered file systems. However, depending on specific requirements such as compatibility with certain filesystems or performance criteria, other drivers like **aufs**, **btrfs**, or **zfs** might be more suitable.

```
{
  "storage-driver": "overlay2"
}
```

Applying this setting in the Docker daemon configuration file (**daemon.json**) can lead to improved disk performance and quicker container startup times.

Efficient Log Management

Proper management of log files is crucial to avoid unnecessary resource drain. Configuring Docker to manage logs properly, such as setting appropriate log levels and using Docker's native log rotation feature, can help maintain system efficiency.

```
{
  "log-driver": "json-file",
  "log-opts": {
    "max-size": "100m",
    "max-file": "3"
  }
}
```

This configuration limits each log file to 100 MB and stores only the last three files, effectively managing disk space usage.

Setting Resource Limits on Containers

Limiting the amount of CPU and memory that each container can use is vital to prevent any one container from degrading the performance of others or the entire system.

```
docker run -it --cpus="1.5" --memory="2g" my-container
```

This command configures a container to use no more than 1.5 CPU cores and 2 GB of memory, helping to balance resource allocation among multiple containers.

Enhancing Network Performance

Network configuration is another area where performance can be optimized. Using Docker's networking capabilities to their fullest can help reduce latency and increase throughput for communications between containers.

```
docker network create --driver overlay --attachable prod_network
```

Creating an overlay network facilitates better communication and data transfer across distributed containers, particularly in larger deployments.

Leveraging Multi-Stage Builds

Multi-stage builds in Dockerfiles allow for the creation of leaner images by separating the build environment from the runtime environment, reducing the final image size and speeding up deployment processes.

```
# Example of a multi-stage build
FROM golang:1.15 as builder
WORKDIR /app
COPY . .
RUN go build -o myapp .

FROM alpine:latest
COPY --from=builder /app/myapp .
CMD ["./myapp"]
```

This Dockerfile compiles an application in a Go environment and then copies the executable into a smaller, more secure Alpine image.

Implementing Regular Cleanup Routines

Maintaining a clutter-free Docker environment by regularly removing unused images, containers, and volumes is important for conserving disk space and optimizing performance.

```
docker system prune -a --volumes
```

This command cleans up unused Docker resources, helping to prevent resource leakage and maintain system cleanliness.

Continuous Performance Monitoring

Regular monitoring using tools like Prometheus, cAdvisor, or Docker's own **docker stats** is essential to understand the impact of your optimizations and to identify further improvement areas.

```
docker stats
```

This command gives a real-time view of container performance metrics, aiding in the proactive management of resource use.

Conclusion

By employing these optimization strategies, Docker users can ensure that their environments are not only more efficient but also more stable and capable of handling the demands of complex applications. These techniques provide a solid foundation for maintaining high performance in Docker deployments, enabling scalable and robust containerized solutions.

Chapter Two

Efficient Container Management

Techniques for managing container lifecycles efficiently

Efficiently managing the lifecycle of Docker containers is essential for ensuring robust, scalable, and efficient Docker environments. This involves understanding the various stages of a Docker container—from its creation, active management, and right through to its termination. Effective lifecycle management helps in optimal resource utilization and enhances operational flexibility. Below, we discuss several strategies to manage container lifecycles effectively, integrating best practices and automation techniques to streamline operations.

Effective Image Management

Managing Docker images efficiently is the cornerstone of container lifecycle management. This includes constructing streamlined images, keeping track of image versions, and regularly cleaning up unused images to conserve storage space.

- **Utilizing Multi-Stage Builds**: Multi-stage builds in Dockerfiles can minimize image sizes by segregating build dependencies from runtime necessities.

```
# Example of a multi-stage build
FROM golang:1.14 AS builder
WORKDIR /app
COPY . .
RUN go build -o application .

FROM alpine:latest
COPY --from=builder /app/application .
CMD ["./application"]
```

This Dockerfile example shows compiling an application in a Go environment and then transferring only the executable to a lighter Alpine image for deployment.

- **Pruning Images**: Regularly removing unused images can help maintain a lean system environment.

```
docker image prune -a --filter "until=24h"
```

This command deletes all images that were created more than 24 hours ago and are not currently used by any containers.

Automating Container Deployment

Automation plays a vital role in the efficient deployment of containers. Implementing CI/CD pipelines ensures smooth and consistent deployments and updates of applications.

- **Using Docker Compose**: For orchestrating multi-container applications, Docker Compose automates the configuration and management of multiple services through a **docker-compose.yml** file.

```
version: '3'
services:
  web:
    image: webapp:latest
    deploy:
      replicas: 4
      update_config:
        parallelism: 2
        delay: 10s
  database:
    image: redis:alpine
```

This setup specifies deployment behaviors, such as how many instances of each service should be run and how updates should be rolled out.

Effective Runtime Management

Proper management during the runtime phase is crucial for maintaining the stability and performance of Docker containers.

- **Resource Constraints**: Applying resource limits to containers can prevent any container from excessively using CPU or memory resources.

```
docker run -d --name effective_container --memory=500m --cpus=1 my_application:latest
```

This command restricts the container named **effective_container** to use only 500 MB of memory and 1 CPU.

- **Health Checks**: Configuring health checks helps in automatically assessing and managing the health of running containers.

```
HEALTHCHECK --interval=5m --timeout=3s \
  CMD curl -f http://localhost/ || exit 1
```

This Dockerfile instruction sets Docker to periodically check the health of the container, ensuring its operational integrity.

Handling Shutdown and Cleanup

Ensuring containers are gracefully shut down and cleaned up is critical for avoiding data loss and maintaining service continuity.

- **Monitoring Docker Events**: Docker's event system can be utilized to monitor and react to lifecycle changes such as container stops.

```
docker events --filter 'event=stop'
```

This command monitors for stop events, allowing for automated triggering of cleanup operations or other scripts upon container termination.

Conclusion

Efficient management of Docker container lifecycles involves meticulous planning, automated processes, and ongoing monitoring. By adopting these techniques, organizations can ensure that their containerized applications are managed more efficiently, remain robust, and can dynamically adapt to the needs of the business. Implementing these strategies leads to improved performance and stability across Docker deployments, enhancing the overall efficacy and responsiveness of IT operations.

Automating container creation, scaling, and teardown

In today's rapidly evolving software deployment landscape, the automation of container creation, scaling, and decommissioning is critical for optimizing efficiency and maintaining system reliability amid fluctuating workloads. Automation streamlines operations, reduces the likelihood of human error, and cuts operational costs. This discussion delves into using Docker and associated tools to automate key aspects of container lifecycle management, ensuring scalable and low-maintenance service delivery.

Streamlining Container Creation

Creating Docker containers efficiently involves using Dockerfiles and Docker Compose files to automate the setup and configuration processes.

- **Dockerfiles**: These are scripts used by Docker to automatically build images based on the instructions provided. They detail everything from selecting base images to installing applications and setting up environments.

```
# Example Dockerfile
FROM python:3.8-slim
WORKDIR /app
COPY . /app
RUN pip install -r requirements.txt
CMD ["python", "app.py"]
```

This Dockerfile demonstrates setting up a Python application, where dependencies are installed as defined in **requirements.txt** before the application is executed.

- **Docker Compose**: This tool allows for defining and running multi-container Docker applications with the help of a YAML file, which automates the deployment of linked services.

```
# Example docker-compose.yml
version: '3'
services:
  web:
    build: .
    ports:
      - "5000:5000"
  redis:
    image: "redis:alpine"
```

This configuration outlines how a web application is linked to a Redis service, showcasing the automation of service orchestration.

Facilitating Container Scaling

Effective container scaling ensures that applications can handle varying loads seamlessly. Docker Swarm and Kubernetes are prominent tools used for this purpose.

- **Docker Swarm** enables users to define the number of container replicas easily and maintains this state across the cluster.

```
docker service create --replicas 3 --name my_web -p 80:80 my_web_image
```

This command configures Docker Swarm to keep three replicas of a container running, distributing them across the available nodes.

- **Kubernetes** provides more complex scaling capabilities with configurations for automated scaling based on specific metrics.

```yaml
# Kubernetes deployment configuration
apiVersion: apps/v1
kind: Deployment
metadata:
  name: web-app
spec:
  replicas: 3
  selector:
    matchLabels:
      app: web
  template:
    metadata:
      labels:
        app: web
```

```yaml
    spec:
      containers:
      - name: web
        image: web-app:latest
        ports:
        - containerPort: 80
```

This deployment script instructs Kubernetes to manage three instances of the **web-app**, ensuring scalable application management.

Automating Container Teardown

Efficiently decommissioning containers is as important as scaling, especially in cloud environments where resource conservation impacts cost.

- **Docker Commands**: Specific Docker commands can be employed to remove containers and manage system resources after use.

```
docker container prune -f --filter "until=24h"
docker volume prune -f --filter "label!=keep"
```

These commands automate the removal of stopped containers and unused volumes, excluding those marked to be retained.

Integrating with CI/CD Pipelines

Incorporating container management into CI/CD pipelines facilitates automated testing, building, deployment, and scaling based on code updates, keeping production environments up-to-date and stable.

```
# CI/CD pipeline example in GitLab CI
stages:
  - build
  - deploy

build_app:
  stage: build
  script:
    - docker build -t my_web_image .
    - docker push my_web_image

deploy_app:
  stage: deploy
  script:
    - docker pull my_web_image
    - docker stack deploy --compose-file docker-compose.yml my_app
```

This pipeline configuration in GitLab CI demonstrates how changes in the repository trigger the automatic building and deployment of a Docker image, streamlining application updates.

Conclusion

Automating the creation, scaling, and teardown of Docker containers enhances not only operational efficiency but also application reliability and responsiveness. By leveraging Docker in conjunction with orchestration tools and integrating these processes into CI/CD workflows, organizations can maintain a robust, scalable, and self-sustaining deployment infrastructure. As business demands and technology landscapes evolve, the ability to manage container lifecycles efficiently becomes increasingly vital.

Advanced use of Docker CLI commands and utilities

Gaining expertise in Docker involves more than just understanding its basic operations; it requires mastery over the Docker Command Line Interface (CLI), which offers a robust suite of commands for deep interaction and management of Docker environments. This article explores the sophisticated capabilities of Docker CLI commands and utilities, aimed at enhancing operational efficiency and providing nuanced control over Docker processes.

Advanced Container and Image Management

Beyond the elementary commands like **docker run** and **docker build**, the Docker CLI facilitates intricate management of containers and images, encompassing monitoring, adjusting runtime settings, and optimizing the build process.

- **Detailed Container Operations**: Advanced management involves scrutinizing container logs, inspecting states, and dynamically adjusting configurations.

```
# Displaying detailed information about a specific container
docker inspect container_name

# Watching for real-time events from all containers
docker events --filter 'type=container'
```

These commands are vital for deep monitoring and troubleshooting within Docker environments.

- **Efficient Image Handling**: Optimizing how images are built, tagged, and stored is critical for maintaining a streamlined Docker setup.

```
# Using build cache and tags to minimize build times and manage versions
docker build -t my_image:latest -q .

# Removing unused images to conserve disk space
docker image prune -a
```

These techniques help in keeping the Docker environment clean and efficient by managing storage and build times effectively.

Networking Capabilities with Docker CLI

The Docker CLI also extends to managing complex networking setups, essential for connecting containers effectively and securely.

- **Creating Sophisticated Networks**: Advanced networking involves setting up networks that provide improved performance and security configurations.

```
# Setting up an overlay network suitable for distributed Docker environments
docker network create --driver overlay my_overlay
```

This command is crucial for applications where containers are distributed across multiple Docker hosts and need to communicate securely.

- **In-depth Network Analysis**: To effectively manage and troubleshoot network issues, Docker CLI offers comprehensive network inspection tools.

```
# Detailed inspection of Docker networks
docker network inspect my_overlay
```

This is essential for administrators looking to understand and optimize container networking.

Mastering Docker Volumes and Storage

For applications that require data persistence, Docker CLI provides commands to manage and secure data through volumes.

- **Volume Lifecycle Management**: Creating and maintaining volumes is fundamental for ensuring data persistence across container deployments.

```
# Commands for creating and inspecting volumes
docker volume create my_volume
docker volume inspect my_volume
```

These commands facilitate the management of data storage, crucial for stateful applications running in containers.

Automating Tasks Using Docker CLI

Automation using Docker CLI commands can significantly enhance productivity and consistency across deployments by scripting common operations.

- **Embedding Docker CLI in Scripts**: Automating container updates, deployments, and routine maintenance can be achieved through scripting Docker commands.

```
# Script for automated deployment or update of containers
#!/bin/bash
docker pull my_image:latest
docker stop my_container
docker rm my_container
docker run --name my_container -d my_image:latest
```

This script automates the update process for a Docker container, ensuring the application is always running the latest version without manual intervention.

Enhancing Security with Docker CLI

The Docker CLI also provides tools for conducting security audits and enhancements to ensure the Docker environment is secure against vulnerabilities.

- **Conducting Docker Security Audits**: Docker Bench for Security is a script that checks for dozens of common best practices around deploying Docker containers in production.

```
# Using Docker Bench for Security to perform security checks
git clone https://github.com/docker/docker-bench-security.git
cd docker-bench-security
sh docker-bench-security.sh
```

This tool is invaluable for administrators aiming to ensure their Docker configurations adhere to security best practices.

Conclusion

Mastering advanced Docker CLI commands and utilities equips users with the ability to optimize, automate, and secure their Docker environments effectively. Through detailed understanding and application of these commands, Docker users can achieve higher efficiency, robustness, and security in their containerized applications. As one grows more proficient with these advanced techniques, the potential to streamline Docker operations and maintenance significantly increases.

Chapter Three

Streamlining Docker Images

Techniques for minimizing Docker image sizes

Reducing the size of Docker images is critical for optimizing the deployment, performance, and scalability of containerized applications. Smaller Docker images result in faster pull times, reduced bandwidth consumption, and lower storage costs, especially in dynamic environments with frequent updates or numerous running instances. This article covers various strategies and best practices to effectively minimize Docker image sizes, ensuring efficient container management without compromising on the necessary features.

1. Selecting the Right Base Image

The foundation of a Docker image—its base image—substantially affects the final size. Opting for a minimal base image can drastically decrease the overall size.

- **Alpine Linux as a Base**: Known for its minimalism, Alpine Linux is an excellent choice for reducing image size due to its small footprint.

```
FROM alpine:latest
```

Using Alpine Linux as the base offers a streamlined starting point that includes only the most essential components.

216

2. Implementing Multi-Stage Builds

Multi-stage builds in Docker allow you to separate the build environment from the deployment environment in your Dockerfiles, using multiple FROM statements.

- **Multi-Stage Build Example**:

```
# Build environment
FROM golang:1.15 as builder
WORKDIR /app
COPY . .
RUN go build -o myapp .
```

```
# Deployment environment
FROM alpine:latest
COPY --from=builder /app/myapp .
CMD ["./myapp"]
```

This Dockerfile compiles a Go application in the first stage and then copies the executable into a leaner image based on Alpine Linux, minimizing the size of the final image.

3. Reducing Layers

Each command in a Dockerfile adds a new layer to the image. Consolidating commands can reduce the number of layers and thus the image size.

- **Combining RUN Commands**:

```
RUN apt-get update && apt-get install -y \
    package1 \
    package2 \
    && rm -rf /var/lib/apt/lists/*
```

217

By combining these commands, the image builds in fewer layers, each handling multiple tasks efficiently.

4. Cleaning Up Within Builds

Removing unnecessary files after installation processes within Dockerfiles can prevent them from inflating the image size. This includes clearing out caches and temporary files immediately after use.

- **Post-Installation Cleanup**:

```
RUN apt-get update && \
    apt-get install -y package1 && \
    apt-get clean && \
    rm -rf /var/lib/apt/lists/* /tmp/* /var/tmp/*
```

Executing these clean-up tasks in the same layer where installations occur ensures no unwanted files are left behind.

5. Utilizing .dockerignore

The **.dockerignore** file functions similarly to **.gitignore**, excluding unnecessary files and directories from being added to the Docker context, thus streamlining the build process.

- **.dockerignore File Example**:

```
node_modules
.git
.tmp
```

Creating such a file ensures that bulky or irrelevant directories do not clutter the build context, preserving efficiency.

6. Caching Optimization

Strategically ordering Dockerfile instructions to maximize the use of Docker's caching mechanism can reduce build times and minimize downloads.

- **Efficient Instruction Ordering**:

```
COPY requirements.txt /tmp/
RUN pip install --requirement /tmp/requirements.txt
COPY . /app
```

This sequence takes advantage of caching by handling dependency installation before copying application code, reducing rebuild time if **requirements.txt** has not changed.

Conclusion

Minimizing Docker image sizes plays a vital role in enhancing the efficiency of container deployments. Techniques such as selecting minimalist base images, utilizing multi-stage builds, optimizing layer construction, performing thorough clean-ups during builds, excluding unnecessary files, and leveraging caching are integral to producing smaller, more efficient images. These practices contribute to quicker deployments, lower operational costs, and improved scalability in production environments, ensuring that your Dockerized applications remain robust and agile.

Best practices for layering and caching in images

In the world of Docker, efficient management of image layers and caching mechanisms plays a critical role in optimizing the build process and runtime performance of containers. Docker images are built up from a series of layers—immutable files that represent instructions in the image's Dockerfile. Properly managing these layers and leveraging Docker's caching capabilities can significantly reduce build time, minimize bandwidth usage, and ensure rapid deployment. This article outlines best practices for layering and caching in Docker images, providing essential techniques to enhance your Docker workflows.

1. Understanding Docker Layers

When a Docker image is built, each instruction in the Dockerfile creates a new layer. These layers are stacked on top of each other, with each layer representing a change from the previous state. Since layers are cached and reused across builds, understanding how they work is essential to optimizing Docker builds.

- **Minimize Layer Count**: Combining multiple commands into a single RUN instruction reduces the number of layers created, which not only helps in keeping the build clean but also reduces the overall size of the image.

```
# Bad practice: Multiple RUN instructions
RUN apt-get update
RUN apt-get install -y package1
RUN apt-get install -y package2

# Good practice: Single RUN instruction
RUN apt-get update && \
    apt-get install -y package1 package2 && \
    rm -rf /var/lib/apt/lists/*
```

This example shows how to minimize layers by consolidating commands, which also helps in reducing the image size by removing unnecessary files within the same layer where they are added.

2. Leveraging Build Cache

Docker can reuse intermediate layers from previous builds that have not changed, known as caching. To effectively leverage the build cache, you should structure Dockerfiles so that instructions which are less likely to change are at the top.

- **Order Instructions Wisely**: Place instructions that change often (like copying source code) after those that change less often (like installing packages).

```
# Example of effective Dockerfile caching
FROM node:14
WORKDIR /app
COPY package.json package-lock.json ./
RUN npm install
COPY . .
```

In this Dockerfile, **npm install** is placed after copying **package.json** and **package-lock.json**, meaning any changes to the application's source code won't invalidate the cache created by **npm install**.

3. Avoid Cache Busting

Cache busting occurs when changes to one layer invalidate all subsequent layers in the cache. This can significantly increase build times and network traffic during builds.

- **Use Specific Copy Instructions**: Be specific about what you copy into the image to prevent unnecessary cache invalidation.

```
# Instead of copying everything
COPY . /app

# Copy only what's necessary
COPY ./static /app/static
COPY ./templates /app/templates
```

This approach ensures that changes to unrelated files don't invalidate the cache for layers that copy files into the image.

4. Multi-Stage Builds

Multi-stage builds allow you to use multiple FROM statements within a single Dockerfile. This practice enables you to use one stage for building the application with all necessary build tools and another, smaller stage for the runtime environment.

- **Implement Multi-Stage Builds**: This reduces the final image size by not including build dependencies in the runtime image.

```
# Multi-stage build to optimize size
FROM golang:1.15 as builder
WORKDIR /src
COPY . .
RUN go build -o /out/app .

FROM alpine:latest
COPY --from=builder /out/app /app
CMD ["/app"]
```

Here, the build dependencies are used in the first stage, but only the final compiled application is copied into the final image.

5. Cleaning Up

Ensuring that each layer in the build process is as lean as possible involves removing unnecessary files and artifacts the moment they are no longer needed.

- **Cleanup in the Same Layer**: Perform cleanup tasks in the same layer where changes are made to avoid bloating the image.

```
RUN apt-get update && \
    apt-get install -y mypackage && \
    apt-get clean && \
    rm -rf /var/lib/apt/lists/*
```

This command sequence prevents the update cache from becoming part of the image, thus avoiding unnecessary bloat.

Conclusion

Adhering to best practices for layering and caching can dramatically improve the efficiency and performance of

Docker images. By understanding and implementing these strategies, developers can optimize build processes, minimize image sizes, and accelerate deployment times in their Docker environments. This leads to better resource management, faster development cycles, and more efficient application delivery.

Advanced Dockerfile techniques and multi-stage builds

Advanced Dockerfile techniques, particularly multi-stage builds, play a crucial role in optimizing Docker image construction—making them more efficient, maintainable, and secure. Such practices help in significantly reducing image sizes by eliminating unnecessary dependencies and files, thereby enhancing the security and speed of deployments. This discussion will delve into various sophisticated Dockerfile strategies, focusing on multi-stage builds, efficient layer management, and dependency handling.

The Power of Multi-Stage Builds

Multi-stage builds in Docker allow the Dockerfile to separate the build into distinct stages, each potentially using different base images suitable for specific tasks. This method is especially effective for minimizing the final image size because it isolates build environments from production environments.

- **Multi-Stage Build Example**:

```
# Compilation stage using a larger base image equipped with necessary build tools
FROM golang:1.15 AS build-env
WORKDIR /src
COPY . .
RUN go build -o myapplication .

# Production stage using a smaller, cleaner base image
FROM alpine:latest
COPY --from=build-env /src/myapplication /app/
CMD ["/app/myapplication"]
```

In this Dockerfile, the application is compiled in the initial stage using a Go image, then the executable is transferred to a lighter Alpine-based image. This separation ensures that only essential artifacts persist in the final image.

Optimizing Docker Layers

Efficiently managing Docker layers is critical for reducing build time, image size, and enhancing caching efficacy.

- **Reduce Layer Count by Combining Commands**:

```
RUN apt-get update && apt-get install -y \
    package1 \
    package2 \
    && rm -rf /var/lib/apt/lists/*
```

By chaining commands together, the creation of unnecessary layers is minimized, and temporary files are removed within the same layer they're created, optimizing both the build process and the final image size.

Effective Caching Strategies

Docker's layer caching mechanism is a robust tool for speeding up image builds by reusing unchanged layers from previous builds.

- **Strategic Command Placement for Caching**:

```
COPY package.json /app/
RUN npm install
COPY . /app
```

This sequence takes advantage of caching by running **npm install** only if **package.json** changes, otherwise, it reuses the previously cached layer, speeding up subsequent builds.

Managing Dependencies and Enhancing Security

It's essential to manage software dependencies carefully to minimize the image size and reduce potential security vulnerabilities.

- **Install Only Necessary Dependencies**:

```
RUN apt-get update \
    && apt-get install -y --no-install-recommends build-essential \
    && make \
    && apt-get purge -y --auto-remove build-essential
```

This command installs necessary tools, uses them to build the application, and removes them all in one layer, which not only keeps the image clean but also reduces security risks by eliminating unnecessary software.

Utilizing .dockerignore

Using a **.dockerignore** file effectively excludes unnecessary files and directories from being sent to the Docker daemon, similar to **.gitignore** in version control contexts.

- **.dockerignore File Setup**:

```
.git
node_modules
Dockerfile*
*.md
```

Including items such as **node_modules** and version control directories ensures they do not bloat the build context, which optimizes the build speed.

Conclusion

Mastering advanced Dockerfile techniques and implementing multi-stage builds are key strategies for developers seeking to refine their Docker practices. By carefully managing layers, optimizing caching, and responsibly handling dependencies, you can create Docker images that are not only smaller and faster to deploy but also more secure. These advanced practices enable developers to maintain high efficiency and robust security standards in containerized application deployments.

Chapter Four

Docker Networking Deep Dive

In-depth networking models (bridge, host, overlay, macvlan)

Mastering Docker's networking options is crucial for effectively deploying and managing containerized applications across different environments. Docker offers several built-in network drivers, each tailored to specific network needs and operational requirements. This detailed examination explores Docker's primary networking models: bridge, host, overlay, and macvlan, explaining their functionalities, appropriate use cases, and configurations.

Bridge Networking

The bridge network is the default Docker network model. It enables communication between containers on the same host and uses Network Address Translation (NAT) to interact with external networks.

- **Appropriate Usage**: Bridge networks are ideal for isolating standalone containers that need to communicate with each other on the same Docker host.

- **Characteristics**:

  - Isolation: Containers on separate bridge networks are isolated by default.

o NAT: External interactions are managed through mapped ports.

- **Example Usage**:

```
# Creating a bridge network
docker network create --driver bridge my_bridge

# Running containers on this network
docker run -d --network=my_bridge --name container1 nginx
docker run -d --network=my_bridge --name container2 nginx
```

This setup establishes a bridge network named **my_bridge**, under which two containers can communicate internally.

Host Networking

Host networking configures a container to share the host's network namespace, using the host's IP address and port directly, which can improve network performance due to reduced overhead.

- **Appropriate Usage**: Use host networking for containers that manage high network traffic or require high-performance networking.

- **Characteristics**:

    o High Performance: Direct access to the host's network stack increases performance.

    o No Port Conflicts: Containers use the host's ports directly.

- **Example Usage**:

```
docker run -d --network host --name mycontainer nginx
```

This command runs an Nginx container using the host's network settings, directly accessible using the host's IP.

Overlay Networking

Overlay networks enable containers on different Docker hosts to communicate, encapsulating the traffic in a network overlay. This is particularly useful in clustered Docker environments like those managed by Docker Swarm.

- **Appropriate Usage**: Overlay networks are designed for environments where containers spread across multiple hosts need to connect.

- **Characteristics**:

  o Cross-Host Communication: Facilitates interaction across different Docker hosts.

  o Endpoint Discovery: Automatically discovers and manages service endpoints.

- **Example Usage**:

```
# Establishing an overlay network
docker network create --driver overlay --attachable my_overlay

# Connecting containers to the network
docker run -d --network=my_overlay --name service1 nginx
docker run -d --network=my_overlay --name service2 nginx
```

This configuration introduces an overlay network called **my_overlay** which supports inter-container communication across hosts.

Macvlan Networking

Macvlan networks make Docker containers appear as physical devices on your network by assigning them MAC addresses and full IP addresses from the network.

- **Appropriate Usage**: Macvlan is suited for scenarios where containers need to appear as physical devices or where legacy applications require traditional networking setups.

- **Characteristics**:

  - Network Integration: Containers behave like physical network devices.

  - Direct Access: Connects containers directly to the physical network without NAT.

- **Example Usage**:

```
# Creating a macvlan network
docker network create -d macvlan \
    --subnet=192.168.1.0/24 \
    --gateway=192.168.1.1 \
    -o parent=eth0 my_macvlan

# Running a container on the macvlan network
docker run -d --network=my_macvlan --name mycontainer nginx
```

Here, a Macvlan network is configured with a specific subnet and gateway, placing the container directly on the physical network.

Conclusion

The variety of Docker's networking models provides flexibility to accommodate different application needs and infrastructure setups. Whether the requirement is for simple inter-container communication, high-performance applications, complex multi-host environments, or integration with physical networks, Docker's networking options deliver robust solutions. Understanding when and how to utilize each networking model allows for the design of efficient, scalable, and secure network architectures for containerized applications.

Implementing custom network plugins

Custom network plugins in Docker allow for the extension of Docker's native networking capabilities to accommodate specific operational needs. These plugins are essential for situations where the default network drivers provided by Docker do not suffice. In this article, we explore how to develop, implement, and manage custom network plugins effectively, providing enhanced networking solutions tailored to unique requirements.

Overview of Docker Network Plugins

Docker network plugins are discrete components that integrate into Docker's ecosystem to provide additional or specialized network functionalities. They adhere to the

Container Network Model (CNM), which outlines a series of interfaces that plugins can implement to manage network configurations, resource allocation, and interactions with the network stack.

- **Types of Network Plugins**:

  - **Managed plugins**: These are hosted on Docker Hub, can be installed directly using Docker CLI, and are managed by Docker Engine.

  - **Legacy plugins**: These require manual installation and management on the host and are less integrated into Docker's management framework.

Developing a Custom Network Plugin

Creating a custom network plugin involves several key steps, from conceptualization to deployment, ensuring the plugin effectively meets the intended networking needs.

- **Steps for Development**:

  1. **Conceptualize the Plugin**: Define the functional scope of the plugin and which network lifecycle events it will handle (e.g., creation, modification, deletion of networks).

  2. **Implement the Plugin Logic**: Write the code that will handle the network operations. This often involves programming against Docker's API to manipulate network settings.

3. **Containerize the Plugin**: Package your plugin as a Docker image to simplify distribution and deployment.

4. **Testing and Deployment**: Deploy your plugin in a controlled environment to test its functionality and performance thoroughly.

- **Example Implementation**: Here's an example snippet of a plugin developed in Go, using Docker's network plugin helpers:

```go
package main

import (
    "github.com/docker/go-plugins-helpers/network"
)

type customNetworkDriver struct{}

func (d *customNetworkDriver) CreateNetwork(req network.CreateNetworkRequest) error {
    // Logic to handle network creation
    return nil
}

func (d *customNetworkDriver) DeleteNetwork(req network.DeleteNetworkRequest) error {
    // Logic to handle network deletion
    return nil
}
```

```go
func main() {
    driver := &customNetworkDriver{}
    handler := network.NewHandler(driver)
    handler.ServeUnix("root", "customnet")
}
```

This code sets up a basic network driver capable of creating and deleting networks.

Deploying Custom Network Plugins

Deployment involves integrating the plugin into Docker's runtime, making it available for containers to use.

- **Deployment Steps**:
    1. **Install the Plugin**: If it's a managed plugin, use Docker's CLI to install it.

```
docker plugin install --alias customnet your/pluginimage
```

    2. **Activate the Plugin**: Ensure the plugin is active and ready to use.

```
docker plugin enable customnet
```

    3. **Utilize the Plugin**: Specify your custom plugin when creating Docker networks.

```
docker network create --driver customnet --subnet=10.10.0.0/16 mynetwork
```

Key Considerations

When implementing custom network plugins, it's important to address several critical areas:

- **Security**: Verify that the plugin does not open up security vulnerabilities within the Docker ecosystem.

- **Performance**: Ensure that the plugin performs well under expected loads and does not degrade the performance of the host or containers.

- **Compatibility**: Check that the plugin is compatible with the specific versions of Docker Engine and respects all necessary networking protocols and standards.

Conclusion

Custom network plugins provide a mechanism to enhance and tailor Docker networking functionalities to specific requirements, offering solutions where default options are inadequate. By following thorough development practices and carefully managing these plugins, developers can significantly expand Docker's networking capabilities, achieving more adaptable, secure, and efficient network configurations for their containerized applications.

Network troubleshooting and optimization

Network troubleshooting and optimization are pivotal in ensuring that networks operate efficiently and support business processes effectively. As network environments become more sophisticated, mastering the ability to identify issues, enhance network performance, and safeguard data is paramount. This article outlines crucial strategies for network troubleshooting and optimization, providing insight into systematic approaches, advanced tools, and implementation practices.

Core Principles of Network Troubleshooting

Effective network troubleshooting is underpinned by a methodical approach to diagnosing and resolving issues that can affect performance, connectivity, and security. This structured method ensures precise problem identification and resolution.

- **Structured Troubleshooting Process**:
    1. **Identify the Issue**: Start by gathering accurate information about the problem from users and by analyzing network traffic.

    2. **Develop Hypotheses**: Formulate potential causes based on initial findings.

    3. **Conduct Tests**: Validate the hypotheses through diagnostic testing; revise as necessary.

    4. **Resolve and Implement**: Execute a solution to remedy the identified issue.

    5. **Confirm and Prevent**: Ensure the network is fully operational and take steps to prevent future issues.

    6. **Document**: Keep a detailed record of the problem and resolution process for future reference.

Network Optimization Practices

Optimizing a network involves configuring it to efficiently handle existing demands and to scale effectively as requirements grow.

- **Capacity Planning**: Regularly evaluate network traffic and performance to forecast bandwidth needs accurately.

- **Quality of Service (QoS) Implementation**: Apply QoS protocols to prioritize essential traffic, ensuring optimal bandwidth allocation.

- **Network Segmentation via VLANs**: Segmenting the network can enhance both performance and security by reducing broadcast traffic and isolating network segments.

Essential Tools for Diagnostics and Optimization

Employing the right tools is essential for both diagnosing network issues and for ongoing network optimization.

- **Basic Utilities**: Utilize **ping** for testing reachability and **traceroute** for tracking the path that packets take to a host.

```
ping 192.168.1.1
traceroute 192.168.1.1
```

- **Advanced Analysis Tools**: Use applications like Wireshark for in-depth traffic analysis and NetFlow or SFlow for traffic pattern analysis.

- **Network Performance Monitors**: Systems that continuously assess network performance, providing real-time alerts and insights.

Example of Network Optimization

Consider a network experiencing latency and slow data transfers, affecting operational efficiency. Addressing and optimizing such issues might involve:

- **Diagnostic Measures**: Implement **ping** and **traceroute** to locate delays or packet loss.

- **Analyzing Traffic and Bandwidth**: Deploy tools like NetFlow to identify traffic bottlenecks.

- **Implementation of Solutions**:

  - Modify QoS configurations to prioritize key applications.

  - Upgrade infrastructure based on detailed traffic analysis.

- **Ongoing Monitoring**: Utilize network performance monitoring tools to track the impact of changes and detect new issues promptly.

Advanced Network Management Strategies

- **Traffic Management**: Establish traffic shaping policies to control bandwidth utilization effectively.

- **Regular System Updates**: Consistently update network hardware and software to leverage enhancements and security updates.

- **Enhancing Network Security**: Continuously update and refine network security protocols to guard against emerging threats.

Conclusion

Effective network troubleshooting and optimization necessitate a thorough understanding of network operations, a strategic approach to problem-solving, and robust implementation skills. Utilizing cutting-edge diagnostic tools and adopting dynamic optimization strategies enable network professionals to ensure networks are not only performing optimally but are also secure and scalable. Regular evaluations and adjustments to network strategies, supported by proactive monitoring, are crucial in maintaining a high-performance network infrastructure that supports organizational needs effectively.

Chapter Five

Docker Storage Solutions

Detailed exploration of Docker storage drivers

Docker's storage drivers are integral components that dictate how data within Docker containers is stored and managed. A deep understanding of these drivers is essential for optimizing container performance and efficiency, particularly when dealing with persistent or shared data across containers. This article provides a thorough examination of Docker storage drivers, discussing their functions, common use cases, and considerations for selecting the most appropriate driver for specific needs.

Overview of Docker Storage Drivers

Storage drivers in Docker are tasked with managing the writable layer of containers and how image layers are handled and stored. Each driver employs a unique method to process container data, significantly influencing the container's performance. The primary role of a storage driver is to facilitate the layering of containers, a system that allows containers to share common files, which saves disk space and minimizes memory use.

Key Docker Storage Drivers

Docker supports a variety of storage drivers, each with specific strengths and operational characteristics. Among the most commonly used are **overlay2**, **aufs**, **devicemapper**, **btrfs**, and **zfs**.

- **Overlay2**: Recommended for most Docker users, **overlay2** leverages the OverlayFS filesystem for efficient layering and is known for its speed and disk usage optimization. It is widely supported across various Linux distributions.

```
# Configuring Docker to use Overlay2
{
    "storage-driver": "overlay2"
}
```

This setup specifies **overlay2** as the storage driver in Docker's configuration file **(/etc/docker/daemon.json)**.

- **AUFS**: Previously the default storage driver, AUFS is adept at managing extensive image layer sharing, making it a strong choice for environments with significant commonality between container images.

- **DeviceMapper**: Operating at the block device layer, **devicemapper** can be set up in loop-lvm for testing or direct-lvm for production use, the latter being preferred for its performance benefits.

- **Btrfs**: This modern filesystem supports the copy-on-write (COW) mechanism and offers functionalities like snapshots, although it requires careful management to maintain performance.

- **ZFS**: ZFS combines filesystem and volume management capabilities, offering comprehensive features like checksums and snapshots. It is robust for data-intensive applications but has specific licensing and compatibility requirements that may affect its use.

Selecting an Appropriate Storage Driver

The choice of storage driver should be guided by factors such as the host's OS, the specific needs for filesystem features, performance requirements, and the environment in which Docker is running. Here's what to consider:

- **Compatibility and Support**: Verify the compatibility of the storage driver with the host's Linux kernel and Docker's support policies.

- **Performance Requirements**: Assess the performance implications of each driver. Generally, **overlay2** is favored for its efficient performance and broad compatibility.

- **Advanced Filesystem Features**: Drivers like **btrfs** and **zfs** provide advanced features that may be beneficial for specific applications.

- **Ease of Management**: Consider the management overhead of each driver. Some, like **overlay2**, are simpler to configure and manage, whereas others like **devicemapper** require more complex setup and ongoing management.

Effective Configuration and Management

Proper setup and continual management of the chosen storage driver are crucial for maintaining optimal Docker performance. Ensuring adequate disk space, monitoring performance metrics, and understanding the drivers' operational characteristics can help avoid common pitfalls associated with storage in Docker environments.

Conclusion

Docker storage drivers are fundamental to the performance and operational efficiency of Docker containers. By comprehensively understanding the various drivers and their specific advantages, developers and system administrators can tailor their Docker setups to meet the precise demands of their applications, ensuring efficient and effective containerized solutions. Selecting the right storage driver, aligned with operational needs and environmental conditions, is key to achieving the best possible performance and reliability from Docker deployments.

Advanced volume management and strategies

Advanced management of Docker volumes is essential for ensuring robust data persistence, optimizing scalability, and maintaining high security within containerized environments. Docker volumes stand out as the method of choice for persistent storage, providing durability and stability beyond the ephemeral lifespan of container instances. This article delves into sophisticated strategies for effectively managing Docker volumes, highlighting approaches to enhance their functionality and performance in various operational scenarios.

Fundamentals of Docker Volumes

Docker volumes are designed to store data independently of container lifecycles, making them indispensable for applications requiring persistent data. These volumes are managed outside the containers by the Docker host's filesystem, allowing them to survive container restarts and removals, thereby facilitating better data integrity and I/O performance.

Role of Volume Drivers

Docker includes support for multiple volume drivers that facilitate the storage of volumes both locally and on remote resources like cloud storage or network-attached systems. These drivers enable Docker to integrate seamlessly with diverse storage solutions, enhancing flexibility in data management across distributed environments.

- **Local vs. Remote Storage**: Local drivers store data on the host machine, while remote drivers enable integration with external storage solutions, crucial for implementing high-availability systems.

Advanced Volume Management Techniques

Effective volume management requires aligning storage strategies with specific application needs and the broader system architecture. Here are several advanced techniques:

1. **Sharing Volumes Across Multiple Hosts**: Managing volumes across a cluster of machines is vital for applications deployed across several hosts. Technologies like Docker Swarm and Kubernetes natively manage such configurations, distributing volumes efficiently to maintain service continuity and data availability.

- ○ **Docker Swarm Example**:

```
# Create a multi-host compatible volume
docker volume create --driver rexray --name shared_volume

# Utilize the volume in a Docker service
docker service create --name myservice --mount type=volume,source=shared_volume
    ,target=/data myapp
```

2. **Automating Volume Backups**: Regular backups are critical for disaster recovery. Automating this process using scheduled tasks ensures data is regularly backed up without manual oversight.

- ○ **Automated Backup Example**:

```
#!/bin/bash
docker run --rm --volumes-from db_container -v $(pwd)/backup:/backup ubuntu tar
    cvf /backup/db_backup.tar /dbdata
```

3. **Dynamic Volume Provisioning**: For environments requiring rapid scaling, the ability to dynamically provision volumes is invaluable. Kubernetes, for instance, supports this through the StorageClass resource, allowing for on-the-fly volume creation as demands dictate.

- ○ **Kubernetes StorageClass Configuration**:

```
apiVersion: storage.k8s.io/v1
kind: StorageClass
metadata:
  name: dynamic
provisioner: kubernetes.io/aws-ebs
parameters:
  type: gp2
  fsType: ext4
```

246

4. **Optimizing Volume Performance**: Selecting the correct storage type and configuring specific performance metrics like IOPS is crucial, especially for I/O-intensive applications.

   o **Performance Configuration Tips**: When using cloud-based storage solutions such as AWS EBS, tailor the volume configuration to match the anticipated I/O workload to avoid performance bottlenecks.

5. **Enhancing Security Measures**: Security for Docker volumes includes using encrypted storage and implementing strict access controls to protect data both at rest and in transit.

   o **Encryption Practices**: Leverage encrypted volumes offered by cloud providers to enhance data security automatically.

Conclusion

In-depth volume management in Docker not only involves selecting the right storage configurations but also integrating them effectively to support containerized applications. By employing sophisticated management strategies, organizations can ensure their Docker volumes are not only high-performing but also secure and capable of meeting the demands of complex, distributed applications. Advanced volume management is key to leveraging the full potential of Docker technologies in today's dynamic IT environments.

Implementing and optimizing persistent storage solutions

Ensuring robust and efficient persistent storage solutions is pivotal for businesses aiming to maintain data integrity and availability throughout their application lifecycles. As organizations increasingly migrate to cloud-native frameworks, the strategic management of persistent storage becomes essential. This discussion provides insights into setting up persistent storage systems, highlights various techniques for optimizing these solutions, and offers best practices for maximizing operational efficiency and reliability.

Introduction to Persistent Storage

Persistent storage is crucial for applications that require data to be preserved across sessions or deployments, such as database management systems or any application where data permanence is necessary. Unlike transient storage, which is temporary and deleted when an application is shut down, persistent storage maintains data across various application instances.

Deploying Persistent Storage Solutions

The deployment of effective persistent storage must take into account several considerations to ensure that the storage solution aligns with application demands and performance expectations. Here are some critical deployment considerations:

1. **Choosing Suitable Storage Options**:

   o **Block Storage**: Highly effective for scenarios requiring fast data access, such as transactional databases. It attaches storage volumes directly to machines or containers for quick data retrieval.

   o **File Storage**: Ideal for applications that operate with shared access to files, commonly used by web servers and collaborative platforms.

   o **Object Storage**: Best suited for managing vast amounts of unstructured data, offering scalability and accessibility via simple APIs.

2. **Integrating Storage with Application Ecosystems**:

   o Seamless integration with application architectures is vital, particularly in scaling and managing data access patterns.

   o For container-based architectures like those managed with Kubernetes, leverage Persistent Volumes (PVs) and Persistent Volume Claims (PVCs) to decouple actual storage from its usage.

```
apiVersion: v1
kind: PersistentVolume
metadata:
  name: samplepv
spec:
  capacity:
    storage: 100Gi
  accessModes:
    - ReadWriteOnce
  awsElasticBlockStore:
    volumeID: "<aws-volume-id>"
    fsType: "ext4"
```

This Kubernetes PersistentVolume configuration demonstrates how to provision a volume with AWS Elastic Block Store, defining access modes and storage capacities.

Optimizing Persistent Storage

Optimization is key to enhancing the performance and cost-efficiency of persistent storage solutions. Strategies for effective optimization include:

1. **Performance Adjustments**:

   - Modify IOPS settings and utilize caching and solid-state drives (SSDs) to enhance data access speeds and throughput.

2. **Cost Management**:

   - Evaluate the financial impacts of different storage types and optimize usage to fit budget constraints.

   - Set up automated data lifecycle policies to move older, less frequently accessed data to more cost-effective storage solutions.

3. **Data Redundancy and Backup**:

   - Implement redundancy to prevent data loss, using techniques like RAID for hardware-level data protection.

   - Ensure comprehensive backup strategies are in place, with backups stored securely and in multiple locations.

4. **Security Protocols**:

   o Secure data with encryption both at rest and in transit to protect sensitive information.

   o Implement stringent access controls to manage who can interact with the storage systems.

Best Practices for Persistent Storage Management

To effectively manage persistent storage, organizations should adhere to several best practices:

- **Proactive Monitoring and Auditing**: Implement continuous monitoring solutions to keep track of storage performance and health. Regular audits help in optimizing storage use and maintaining compliance with regulatory standards.

- **Design for Scalability**: Architect storage solutions to be inherently scalable to handle growth seamlessly.

- **Leverage Automation**: Automate routine storage tasks such as provisioning, backups, and scaling to reduce the potential for human error and streamline operations.

Conclusion

Persistent storage is a cornerstone of effective IT infrastructure, supporting critical applications by ensuring data durability and accessibility. By carefully planning the deployment, optimization, and management of persistent storage solutions, organizations can achieve not only enhanced performance and cost efficiency but also greater operational resilience and compliance. Strategic management of persistent storage fosters an environment where business continuity is supported and data-driven decision-making thrives.

Chapter Six

Scaling Docker Containers

Strategies for scaling applications horizontally and vertically

Scaling applications to effectively handle increasing user demand and system load is a crucial aspect of modern application development and maintenance. Effective scaling strategies ensure applications can handle additional workload efficiently while maintaining performance and controlling costs. This discussion explores the methods of scaling applications both horizontally and vertically, detailing the advantages, challenges, and optimal scenarios for each.

Fundamentals of Application Scaling

Scaling strategies for applications are typically categorized into two primary methods: horizontal and vertical scaling.

- **Horizontal Scaling (Scaling Out/In)**: This method involves adding or removing nodes in a system, such as incorporating more servers into a pool to distribute workload more effectively. It enhances capacity by linking multiple hardware or software entities to function as a cohesive unit.

- **Vertical Scaling (Scaling Up/Down)**: This approach involves increasing the power (such as CPU and RAM) of an existing server, or enhancing its capabilities to support more load. Vertical scaling is often limited by the physical capabilities of the server.

Horizontal Scaling Strategies

Horizontal scaling is particularly beneficial for applications with a microservices architecture or those that are distributed by nature, where different components can be scaled independently to meet specific demands.

1. **Implementing Load Balancers**:

   o Utilizing load balancers can effectively distribute incoming network traffic or application requests across numerous servers, balancing the load.

   o Example: Employing load-balancing tools like NGINX or Apache to distribute requests evenly across a server pool.

```
http {
    upstream app {
        server srv1.example.com;
        server srv2.example.com;
        server srv3.example.com;
    }

    server {
        listen 80;
        location / {
            proxy_pass http://app;
        }
    }
}
```

2. **Designing Stateless Applications**:

   o Creating applications in a stateless manner allows each server to process requests independently of others, facilitating easier scaling.

3. **Utilizing Service Discovery Tools**:

   o Tools such as Consul, Etcd, or Kubernetes services can help in the discovery and management of services on a network as the number of hosts changes.

Vertical Scaling Strategies

Vertical scaling is often more straightforward to implement as it does not require the complex configuration needed for horizontal scaling, but it does have its limits in terms of server capacity.

1. **Upgrading Server Components**:

   o Periodically enhance server components such as CPUs and memory to increase processing power and capacity.

2. **Optimizing Resource Use**:

   o Fine-tune the settings of databases and application servers to maximize their efficiency using existing hardware.

   o Example: Configuring Java Virtual Machine (JVM) settings for optimized performance.

3. Applying Vertical Pod Autoscalers in Kubernetes:

- o For containerized environments managed with Kubernetes, utilize Vertical Pod Autoscalers (VPA) to automatically adjust resources allocated to pods based on their usage.

```yaml
apiVersion: "autoscaling.k8s.io/v1"
kind: VerticalPodAutoscaler
metadata:
  name: app-vpa
spec:
  targetRef:
    apiVersion: "apps/v1"
    kind: Deployment
    name: app
  resourcePolicy:
    containerPolicies:
      - containerName: '*'
        minAllowed:
          cpu: "500m"
          memory: "500Mi"
```

```yaml
        maxAllowed:
          cpu: "2000m"
          memory: "2Gi"
        controlledResources: ["cpu", "memory"]
```

Deciding Between Horizontal and Vertical Scaling

- **Cost Implications**: Horizontal scaling can often be more cost-effective, especially with the flexibility of cloud environments where adding resources does not necessarily require physical hardware investment.

256

- **Application Suitability**: Certain applications naturally align better with horizontal scaling (like those built with microservices), while others may only require vertical scaling (such as traditional databases).

- **Physical Limitations**: Vertical scaling is constrained by the server's maximum capacity, beyond which horizontal scaling is the only viable option.

Conclusion

The appropriate scaling strategy for an application depends on its unique requirements, architecture, and expected growth patterns. Both horizontal and vertical scaling have their roles in a comprehensive strategy for application deployment and management. Effective implementation of these strategies not only supports growth but also optimizes resource utilization and cost-efficiency, ensuring the application remains robust and responsive under varying loads. Understanding and implementing the right scaling strategies are crucial for maintaining resilient and adaptable applications in today's dynamic technology landscape.

Load balancing and traffic management with Docker

Load balancing and traffic management are pivotal for optimizing the performance and reliability of systems that deploy Docker for containerized applications. Effective load balancing ensures equitable distribution of network load and client requests across multiple servers, which optimizes resource utilization and enhances application availability and response time. This article delves into various strategies for integrating load balancing and traffic management in Docker setups, outlining effective techniques and practices for deployment.

Basics of Load Balancing in Docker

Load balancing within Docker environments can be implemented on different layers of the application stack, depending on the complexity and requirements of the applications:

- **Container-Level Load Balancing**: This method distributes the network load or client requests directly among the containers, often facilitated by Docker along with orchestration tools like Docker Swarm or Kubernetes.

- **Service-Level Load Balancing**: In Docker swarm mode, load balancing is inherently managed across all containers of a service, streamlining the process of handling incoming traffic.

Approaches to Load Balancing in Docker

Choosing the right load balancing method is critical and depends on the specific application and operational context. Several commonly utilized strategies include:

1. **Round Robin**: This basic approach cyclically distributes requests across all available servers. It is straightforward to implement and is often the default setting in many load balancers.

2. **Least Connections**: A more sophisticated strategy that routes new requests to the server currently handling the fewest connections, promoting a more even distribution of load.

3. **IP Hash**: This method assigns client requests based on their IP address, ensuring consistent routing to the same server which can be crucial for maintaining user session persistence.

Setting Up Load Balancers in Docker

Docker's capabilities can be augmented with internal features or through external tools for enhanced load balancing:

Native Load Balancing with Docker Swarm

Docker Swarm includes a built-in load balancer to distribute incoming traffic evenly across a service's active containers. Here is a simple example to deploy a service with inherent load balancing:

```
docker service create --name web-service --replicas 3 --publish 80:80 nginx
```

This command launches a service using the **nginx** image, with three replicas, and automatically configures load balancing across these replicas by publishing port 80.

Integrating External Load Balancers

For more complex traffic management needs, external load balancers such as HAProxy or NGINX can be used. These tools offer advanced configurations and capabilities beyond Docker's built-in options

- **NGINX Configuration Example**:

```
http {
    upstream docker_containers {
        server server1.example.com;
        server server2.example.com;
        server server3.example.com;
    }

    server {
        listen 80;
        server_name myapp.example.com;
        location / {
            proxy_pass http://docker_containers;
        }
    }
}
```

This setup creates a group of servers under the **docker_containers** upstream block and configures NGINX to proxy requests to these servers, effectively balancing the load among them.

Best Practices for Effective Traffic Management

Adopting best practices in traffic management ensures that Docker environments are not only effective but also robust and secure:

- **Health Checks**: Implement health checks to ensure traffic is not directed to non-functional containers, enhancing reliability.

- **Plan for Scalability**: Ensure that the load balancing architecture is scalable to accommodate increases in traffic without substantial changes.

- **Secure the Traffic**: Utilize TLS/SSL to encrypt data in transit, and configure security settings on load balancers to protect against unauthorized access.

Conclusion

Integrating load balancing and traffic management into Docker environments is essential for maintaining high availability, optimal performance, and scalability of applications. By employing Docker's built-in features or enhancing capabilities with external load balancing solutions, organizations can tailor their infrastructure to meet specific demands. Following strategic practices in deployment, health monitoring, and security will bolster the infrastructure's capacity to support dynamic application needs effectively.

Using Docker in high-availability environments

In the modern digital landscape, maintaining high availability for applications is crucial to ensure continuous service and minimize disruptions. Docker, a premier containerization technology, significantly aids in building environments that support high uptime through its robust features and integrations. This article discusses utilizing Docker to achieve high availability, emphasizing practical approaches, tools, and configurations conducive to building resilient systems.

Essentials of High Availability

High availability pertains to the design of systems that are dependable, available, and fault-tolerant, aiming to reduce downtime to the minimal possible extent. With Docker, high availability involves setting up Docker configurations such that services can recover swiftly from failures and continue operating without significant downtime.

Implementing High Availability with Docker

Docker facilitates high availability through containerization—encapsulating applications in containers with all necessary dependencies, which promotes easy replication and distribution across multiple hosts. Key strategies include clustering, load balancing, and continuous health monitoring.

1. **Docker Clustering Options**

    o   **Docker Swarm**: Docker's native clustering tool, Docker Swarm, transforms a group of Docker engines into a single, virtual Docker engine. This orchestration capability is crucial as it ensures the cluster maintains the desired state, like keeping multiple container instances running for the same service.

```
docker swarm init
docker service create --replicas 3 --name my-service --publish published=8080,target
    =80 my-image
```

These commands start a Docker Swarm and deploy a service with three replicas, enhancing the service's fault tolerance.

    o   **Kubernetes**: Frequently used alongside Docker, Kubernetes offers sophisticated orchestration features that manage Docker containers, ensuring that services are not disrupted despite individual container failures.

262

2. Load Balancing Techniques

- Integral for distributing network traffic or requests across several servers, load balancing helps maintain service efficiency and accessibility. While Docker Swarm includes basic load balancing features, integrating advanced external load balancers can optimize traffic distribution.

```
http {
    upstream app {
        least_conn;
        server server1.example.com;
        server server2.example.com;
    }

    server {
        listen 80;
        location / {
            proxy_pass http://app;
        }
    }
}
```

This sample NGINX setup demonstrates a load balancing configuration that distributes incoming traffic based on the least connections strategy.

3. Ensuring Redundancy and Replication

- Running multiple container replicas across different hosts or regions is vital for redundancy. Docker's ability to configure services with multiple replicas and to replicate Docker

263

volumes ensures data is not lost even if one instance fails.

4. Proactive Health Checks and Monitoring

- o Docker's native health checks can restart unresponsive containers, while Docker Swarm keeps track of all containers and nodes. For comprehensive monitoring, integrating with tools like Prometheus or Grafana offers detailed insights into system performance and health.

```
HEALTHCHECK --interval=30s --timeout=30s --start-period=5s --retries=3 \
  CMD curl -f http://localhost/ || exit 1
```

Adding a health check command in the Dockerfile helps monitor application health within the container.

5. Planning for Disaster Recovery

- o High availability is complemented by effective disaster recovery planning. Regularly backing up container data and Docker configurations ensures that services can be rapidly restored after any failure.

Conclusion

Employing Docker in high-availability configurations necessitates a strategic approach incorporating clustering, effective load balancing, and robust monitoring. Docker's architecture supports these strategies, making it possible to create resilient, scalable, and highly available systems. By meticulously planning and implementing these practices, organizations can safeguard their applications against failures, ensuring operational continuity and reliability.

Chapter Seven

Orchestrating Containers with Docker Swarm

Introduction to Docker Swarm

Docker Swarm is Docker's official clustering and orchestration solution, designed to control, coordinate, and manage multiple Docker engines into a unified service deployment. This powerful feature turns clusters of Docker nodes into a single virtual Docker engine, streamlining the deployment and scalability of applications across various Docker hosts. This discussion provides a foundational overview of Docker Swarm, including its architecture, essential functionalities, and guidance on initializing and managing a Swarm environment.

Overview of Docker Swarm

Docker Swarm serves as an orchestration tool that manages the lifecycle of containers deployed across a number of machines. Integral to Docker, it operates seamlessly with Docker containers, requiring no additional software installations to orchestrate a cluster of Docker engines.

Core Features of Docker Swarm

Docker Swarm comes equipped with several robust features that facilitate efficient deployment and management of containerized applications on a large scale:

- **High Availability**: Docker Swarm enhances application uptime by distributing containers evenly across the cluster and automatically replacing any containers that fail, ensuring persistent service availability.

- **Load Balancing**: Swarm mode includes a load-balancing feature that distributes incoming external requests evenly across all containers associated with a service.

- **Declarative Deployment Model**: Users specify their desired service state, and Docker Swarm automatically maintains this state, ensuring the service runs the specified number of container instances.

- **Scalability**: Users can easily scale their applications by increasing or decreasing the number of container replicas through simple commands.

- **Networking Features**: Docker Swarm also provides robust networking capabilities, enabling secure and efficient inter-container communication.

Docker Swarm Architecture

The architecture of Docker Swarm is structured around several key components:

- **Manager Nodes**: These nodes manage and orchestrate the cluster, handling tasks like maintaining the cluster state, scheduling service deployments, and managing worker node tasks. The manager nodes use the Raft Consensus Algorithm to provide a consistent operating environment and enhance fault tolerance.

- **Worker Nodes**: These nodes are responsible for executing the containers and reporting back to the manager nodes. They perform the tasks assigned by the managers.

- **Services and Tasks**: In Docker Swarm, a 'service' defines the application's configuration, such as the container image to use and the number of replicas. A 'task' acts as a single instance of a service, which runs one container.

Initializing Docker Swarm

Setting up a Docker Swarm involves initializing a Swarm, adding nodes, and configuring services. Below is a simple guide on how to start:

1. **Initialize the Swarm**: On your desired manager machine, start the Swarm:

```
docker swarm init
```

This command transforms your Docker engine into a Swarm manager and outputs a command to add workers to this Swarm.

2. **Join Worker Nodes**: On each potential worker node, run the join command provided by the manager's **swarm init**:

```
docker swarm join --token <TOKEN> <MANAGER_IP:PORT>
```

This token secures the process, preventing unauthorized nodes from joining the Swarm.

3. **Deploy a Service**: You can then deploy applications as services within the Swarm. For instance, to launch an Nginx service, you could use:

```
docker service create --name my-nginx --replicas 3 --publish 80:80 nginx
```

This command establishes a service named **my-nginx**, starts three instances of Nginx containers, and maps port 80 on the host to port 80 on the containers.

Conclusion

Docker Swarm is an invaluable orchestration tool within the Docker ecosystem, enabling streamlined and efficient management of containerized applications across multiple hosts. It facilitates not only high availability and scalability but also ensures that applications remain resilient and easy to manage. By leveraging Docker Swarm, system administrators and developers can maintain applications that are both robust and flexible, effectively managing their deployments with simplicity and precision.

Setting up and managing a Swarm cluster

Deploying and managing a Docker Swarm cluster is essential for developers and administrators who aim to streamline application deployments across multiple Docker hosts. Docker Swarm is a robust orchestration tool that clusters several Docker engines into a single virtual engine, enhancing high availability, and improving overall system resource management. This article outlines the process of establishing a

Docker Swarm cluster, managing services within the cluster, and maintaining optimal performance.

Introduction to Setting Up Docker Swarm

Docker Swarm enables a group of Docker hosts to function collectively, coordinating as managers or workers within the cluster. Managers handle cluster management tasks and orchestration, while workers execute containerized applications.

Steps to Initialize a Docker Swarm Cluster

Creating a Docker Swarm cluster involves several key steps, from initiating the cluster to integrating worker nodes and setting up necessary networking. Here's a structured approach:

1. **Initializing the Swarm**: Select one Docker host as the manager and initiate the Swarm:

```
docker swarm init --advertise-addr <MANAGER_IP>
```

Replace **<MANAGER_IP>** with your manager node's IP address. This action designates this node as the manager and generates a join token for adding worker nodes.

2. **Joining Worker Nodes**: Utilize the join token on other Docker hosts that you wish to add as workers:

```
docker swarm join --token <JOIN_TOKEN> <MANAGER_IP:2377>
```

Execute this on each Docker host intended to be a worker to connect them to the manager node.

3. **Creating Overlay Networks**: Establish an overlay network to allow inter-container communication across different hosts:

```
docker network create --driver overlay --attachable my_overlay
```

This command sets up a network that supports container communication across the cluster, vital for distributed applications.

Managing Docker Swarm Services

With the Swarm operational, the next step involves deploying and scaling services across the cluster.

1. **Deploying Services**: Launch services using the Docker CLI:

```
docker service create --name nginx_service --replicas 3 --network my_overlay --publish
    80:80 nginx
```

This creates a service named **nginx_service** with three Nginx container replicas, connected to the overlay network and exposing port 80.

2. **Scaling Services**: Adjust the number of service replicas based on demand:

```
docker service scale nginx_service=5
```

This command upscales the **nginx_service** to five replicas.

3. **Updating Services**: Apply updates to the service configuration seamlessly:

271

```
docker service update --image nginx:latest nginx_service
```

This updates the Nginx service to the latest image version without downtime.

Monitoring and Routine Maintenance of the Swarm

Effective monitoring and maintenance are vital for ensuring the stability of a Docker Swarm cluster.

1. **Cluster Monitoring**: Use Docker commands to monitor the health and configuration of the Swarm:

```
docker service ls
docker service ps nginx_service
docker node ls
```

These commands provide insights into service statuses, node health, and overall cluster configuration.

2. **Accessing Logs for Troubleshooting**: Retrieve logs to diagnose issues within services:

```
docker service logs nginx_service
```

This command pulls the logs for **nginx_service**, aiding in troubleshooting.

3. **Managing Nodes**: Adjust node availability for maintenance or updates:

```
docker node update --availability drain <NODE_ID>
```

Setting a node's availability to **drain** prevents new tasks from starting on it and gracefully stops existing tasks.

Conclusion

Setting up and maintaining a Docker Swarm cluster requires a thoughtful setup of managers and workers, deployment of services, and ongoing monitoring and maintenance. Following the outlined steps ensures that administrators can effectively leverage Docker Swarm for deploying scalable, fault-tolerant applications across multiple Docker hosts, thus optimizing application availability and resource usage. By mastering these techniques, developers and system administrators can ensure their applications are robust and capable of adapting to varying loads and operational demands.

Deploying applications across Swarm nodes

Deploying applications across Docker Swarm nodes is essential for optimizing container workload distribution across multiple Docker hosts, enhancing application robustness, scalability, and performance. Docker Swarm, Docker's native clustering and orchestration tool, simplifies this by managing a group of Docker engines as a cohesive unit. This article covers the essentials of setting up a Docker Swarm environment, effectively deploying applications, and maintaining optimal application performance.

Overview of Docker Swarm Deployment

Docker Swarm facilitates the configuration of a network of Docker nodes that operate as a single, seamless entity, streamlining the deployment and management of containerized applications. Below is a guide on configuring and utilizing Docker Swarm for deploying applications.

Preparing the Swarm Environment

Proper setup and configuration are prerequisites before deploying applications in a Docker Swarm:

1. **Swarm Initialization**: Begin by establishing the manager node, which orchestrates and manages the swarm:

```
docker swarm init --advertise-addr <MANAGER_IP>
```

This command designates your Docker engine as the swarm manager, generating necessary credentials to connect worker nodes.

2. **Adding Worker Nodes**: Integrate additional Docker hosts as worker nodes using the manager's join token:

```
docker swarm join --token <JOIN_TOKEN> <MANAGER_IP:2377>
```

Run this command on each host you intend to include as a worker.

3. **Overlay Network Creation**: Construct an overlay network to enable inter-container communication across different Docker hosts:

```
docker network create --driver overlay --attachable my_network
```

This network ensures that containers on different hosts can communicate effectively, which is crucial for distributed applications.

Deploying and Managing Swarm Services

Deploying applications involves creating scalable groups of containers, known as services, within the swarm:

1. **Service Deployment**: Initiate your application as a Docker service, defining parameters such as number of replicas, network settings, and port mappings:

```
docker service create --name my_app --replicas 3 --network my_network --publish 80:80
    my_image
```

This sets up a service called **my_app** with three replicas of **my_image**, linked to **my_network**, and maps port 80 externally to port 80 on the containers.

2. **Service Scaling**: Modify the number of service replicas based on application demand:

```
docker service scale my_app=5
```

This increases the replicas for **my_app** to five.

3. **Service Updates**: Periodically update the service to change configurations or update to newer image versions:

```
docker service update --image my_image:new_version my_app
```

This command updates **my_app** to use a newer image version, facilitating seamless upgrades.

Best Practices for Successful Deployments

Implementing best practices ensures robust and efficient application deployments across Docker Swarm:

- **Load Balancing and Service Discovery**: Leverage Docker Swarm's built-in load balancing and service discovery to efficiently route traffic across all containers.

- **Health Checks Implementation**: Configure health checks to automatically manage the lifecycle of containers based on their health status:

```
docker service create --name my_app --replicas 3 --network my_network --publish 80:80
  --health-cmd "curl -f localhost:80 || exit 1" my_image
```

- **Resource Management**: Specify resource limits and reservations to ensure balanced resource allocation among services:

```
docker service create --name my_app --limit-cpu 0.5 --limit-memory 256M --reserve-cpu
  0.25 --reserve-memory 128M my_image
```

- **Ongoing Monitoring**: Employ monitoring solutions to continuously monitor service performance and health. Tools such as Prometheus, Grafana, or Docker's **docker stats** are effective for keeping tabs on your deployments.

Conclusion

Deploying applications across Docker Swarm nodes necessitates careful orchestration to ensure that the applications are not only well-distributed across multiple hosts but also maintained in an optimal operational state. By systematically setting up the swarm, deploying services correctly, and adhering to established best practices, administrators and developers can harness the full potential of Docker Swarm for managing scalable, highly available, and efficient application environments.

Chapter Eight

Continuous Integration and Deployment with Docker

Setting up CI/CD pipelines using Docker

Integrating Docker into CI/CD pipelines enhances the software development lifecycle by ensuring consistency across environments from development through to production. Docker's containerization technology encapsulates software in standardized environments, which streamlines the release process and minimizes integration issues. This guide outlines the procedure for implementing Docker within CI/CD frameworks, providing a roadmap for setting up an efficient pipeline.

Advantages of Docker in CI/CD Workflows

Using Docker in CI/CD pipelines offers significant benefits:

1. **Uniformity**: Docker ensures that applications operate under consistent conditions at every stage, which simplifies debugging and development.

2. **Modularity**: Docker's ability to isolate environments and scale applications across multiple containers and hosts makes it ideal for handling complex applications.

3. **Control**: By running each task in a separate container, Docker minimizes conflicts and facilitates straightforward updates and rollbacks.

Implementing Docker in CI/CD Pipelines

The process to deploy a CI/CD pipeline utilizing Docker involves several stages, from integrating with source control systems to deploying the application in production environments.

1. **Source Control Setup**:

   o CI/CD pipelines typically start with a source control system trigger, like a push to a Git repository.

   o Configuration example: Setting up GitHub webhooks to initiate CI processes when new commits are pushed.

2. **Building with Docker**:

   o Configure the CI system to execute builds inside Docker containers based on specifications in a Dockerfile.

   o Example Dockerfile for a Python application:

```
FROM python:3.8-slim
WORKDIR /app
COPY requirements.txt .
RUN pip install -r requirements.txt
COPY . .
CMD ["python", "app.py"]
```

- This Dockerfile configures a Python environment, installs dependencies, and prepares the app for execution.

3. **Automated Testing**:

   - Define steps within the CI pipeline to execute tests in Docker containers to validate the application's behavior.

   - Example Jenkins pipeline configuration:

```
pipeline {
  agent any
  stages {
    stage('Build') {
      steps {
        script {
          docker.build("my-app:${env.BUILD_ID}")
        }
      }
    }
    stage('Test') {
      steps {
        script {
          docker.run("my-app:${env.BUILD_ID}", "pytest")
        }
      }
    }
  }
}
```

   - This Jenkins setup builds and tests the application using Docker, ensuring all tests pass in the containerized environment.

4. **Deployment**:

   - Automatically deploy the Dockerized application upon successful testing.

280

o   Example Docker Compose deployment:

```yaml
version: '3'
services:
  web:
    image: "my-app:${env.BUILD_ID}"
    deploy:
      replicas: 3
      resources:
        limits:
          cpus: "0.1"
          memory: 50M
      restart_policy:
        condition: on-failure
    ports:
      - "80:80"
    networks:
      - webnet
networks:
  webnet:
```

o   This configuration outlines deployment settings, including replication, resource constraints, and networking.

Optimizing Docker-based CI/CD Pipelines

- **Minimize Image Size**: Utilize multi-stage builds and smaller base images to reduce build time and resource consumption.

- **Enhance Caching**: Arrange Dockerfile instructions to maximize layer caching, speeding up repeated builds.

- **Incorporate Security**: Regularly scan Docker images for vulnerabilities and enforce security best practices in image creation and container runtime.

- **Monitor Systematically**: Employ monitoring tools to continually assess the pipeline's performance and make necessary adjustments.

Conclusion

Embedding Docker into CI/CD pipelines significantly refines the process of software development, testing, and deployment. By adhering to the described methodologies and best practices, development teams can build dynamic, reliable, and scalable application deployments. This ensures that applications are developed, tested, and deployed more efficiently, enhancing productivity and reducing deployment risks.

Best practices for building and deploying with Docker in pipelines

Incorporating Docker into CI/CD pipelines offers a streamlined approach to software development, enabling consistent, efficient, and scalable application deployments. Docker simplifies the process of container management, making it ideal for automation in build, test, and deployment stages. This article discusses effective practices for integrating Docker into CI/CD workflows, highlighting strategies for Dockerfile configuration, security enhancements, and deployment techniques.

Docker Build Best Practices

1. **Efficient Dockerfile Design**

   o **Start with Official Images**: Base your Dockerfiles on official images from Docker Hub to ensure a secure and stable foundation. For instance, start with **FROM node:14-alpine** for a Node.js application.

   o **Consolidate Instructions**: Reduce the number of layers by combining RUN, COPY, and ADD instructions, which helps minimize the image size and build time.

```
RUN set -ex \
    && apt-get update \
    && apt-get install -y \
       package1 \
       package2 \
    && apt-get clean \
    && rm -rf /var/lib/apt/lists/*
```

   o **Optimize for Caching**: Arrange Dockerfile commands to maximize the use of Docker's build cache, placing instructions that change less frequently towards the top.

   o **Use Multi-Stage Builds**: Minimize your final image size by compiling or building in an initial stage and then copying the necessary artifacts to a lighter base image.

```
# Build stage
FROM maven:3.6.3-jdk-8 as builder
WORKDIR /app
COPY . .
RUN mvn clean install

# Final stage
FROM openjdk:8-jre-slim
COPY --from=builder /app/target/myapp.jar /app/myapp.jar
CMD ["java", "-jar", "/app/myapp.jar"]
```

2. Security Practices

- **Run as Non-Root**: Configure your container to run as a non-root user to enhance security.

```
RUN useradd -m myappuser
USER myappuser
```

- **Secure Secrets**: Avoid embedding secrets into your Docker images. Instead, utilize external secret management tools or environment variables at runtime.

- **Automate Security Scans**: Include steps in your CI pipeline to perform security scans on your images using tools like Docker Bench or Trivy.

3. Configuration Best Practices

- **Configuration via Environment Variables**: Keep your Docker containers adaptable by configuring them with environment variables, which can be set when starting your container.

```
docker run -e "DATABASE_HOST=db.production.example" myapp
```

- o **Implement .dockerignore**: Speed up the build process by creating a **.dockerignore** file to exclude files and directories that are not necessary for building the Docker image.

Docker Deployment Best Practices

1. **Immutable Containers**

   - o Deploy containers without modifications once they are built; instead, replace containers with new ones to update or change configurations, facilitating consistent rollbacks and deployments.

2. **Utilize Orchestrators**

   - o Employ Docker Swarm or Kubernetes to manage container deployments. These tools help scale, monitor, and maintain container health effectively.

3. **Container Health Checks**

   - o Integrate health checks in your container definitions to enable the orchestrator to assess container health and replace unhealthy instances automatically.

```
HEALTHCHECK --interval=5m --timeout=3s \
  CMD curl -f http://localhost/ || exit 1
```

4. **Monitor and Log**

   o Set up comprehensive monitoring and logging to track the performance and status of your containers. Use solutions like Prometheus for monitoring and ELK Stack for logging to gather insights and ensure operational transparency.

5. **Deployment Strategies**

   o Implement advanced deployment techniques such as blue-green or rolling updates to minimize downtime and reduce deployment risks during updates.

Conclusion

Employing Docker within CI/CD pipelines necessitates a disciplined and strategic approach to Dockerfile creation, security practices, and deployment methodologies. By following these recommended practices, development teams can leverage Docker to enhance their CI/CD pipelines, resulting in more reliable, secure, and efficient software delivery processes. This not only accelerates time to market but also ensures high-quality releases, supporting dynamic business needs effectively.

Tools and services for CI/CD with Docker

Incorporating Docker into Continuous Integration (CI) and Continuous Deployment (CD) pipelines facilitates streamlined and robust software development processes. Docker's containerization ensures consistent environments, which are crucial for the reliable deployment of applications. This article discusses various tools and services optimized for integrating Docker within CI/CD workflows, detailing their functionalities and typical applications.

Utilizing Jenkins for Docker-based CI/CD

Overview: Jenkins is a widely-used open-source automation server that supports Docker through various plugins, enhancing its capabilities to manage CI/CD pipelines efficiently.

Key Features:

- **Robust Plugin Ecosystem**: Jenkins supports a multitude of plugins, including those specifically designed for Docker integration.

- **Pipeline as Code**: Jenkins enables defining build pipelines as code, stored with the source code for versioning and easy edits.

Use Case:

- Full lifecycle automation from code commit to deployment, leveraging Docker to ensure environment consistency.

- Example configuration in Jenkins:

```
pipeline {
    agent any
    stages {
        stage('Build') {
            steps {
                script {
                    def dockerImage = docker.build 'myapp'
                }
            }
        }
```

```
        stage('Test') {
            steps {
                script {
                    dockerImage.inside {
                        sh 'make test'
                    }
                }
            }
        }
        stage('Deploy') {
            steps {
                script {
                    dockerImage.push('myapp:latest')
                }
            }
        }
    }
}
```

GitLab CI/CD with Docker

Overview: GitLab provides a comprehensive CI/CD solution embedded within its platform, which is particularly effective for projects hosted on GitLab, using Docker to streamline pipelines.

288

Key Features:

- **Integrated CI/CD**: Seamless integration within the GitLab platform, including a private Docker Container Registry.

- **Auto DevOps**: Automatically configures CI/CD pipelines for applications based on best practices.

Use Case:

- Automated pipeline configuration for Docker-based projects, managing everything from build to deployment.

- Example **.gitlab-ci.yml**:

```
build:
  image: docker:19.03.12
  services:
    - docker:19.03.12-dind
  script:
    - docker build -t my-image:$CI_COMMIT_REF_SLUG .
    - docker push my-image:$CI_COMMIT_REF_SLUG

deploy:
  image: my-image:$CI_COMMIT_REF_SLUG
  script:
    - deploy_to_production.sh
```

CircleCI Integration

Overview: CircleCI offers a cloud-native CI/CD service that excels in fast-paced development environments requiring Docker support.

Key Features:

- **Performance Optimization**: Supports parallelism and caching to speed up builds.

- **Docker Layer Caching**: Enables faster builds by reusing Docker layers.

Use Case:

- Ideal for projects requiring frequent integration and fast feedback loops.

- Configuration example in **.circleci/config.yml**:

```
version: 2
jobs:
  build:
    docker:
      - image: circleci/ruby:2.4.1
    steps:
      - checkout
      - setup_remote_docker

      - run:
          name: Build and Push Docker Image
          command: |
            docker login -u $DOCKER_USER -p $DOCKER_PASS
            docker build -t myorg/myapp .
            docker push myorg/myapp
```

Leveraging Docker Hub for CI/CD

Overview: Docker Hub provides a central repository for Docker images, offering automated build features and integration with GitHub and Bitbucket.

Key Features:

- **Automated Builds**: Automatically builds Docker images from GitHub or Bitbucket repositories upon code changes.

- **Webhooks Support**: Triggers further actions after successful builds or pushes.

Use Case:

- Streamline the process of building and sharing Docker images within teams and the public.

- Example of setting up automated builds connected to a GitHub repository.

Conclusion

Integrating Docker into CI/CD pipelines using tools like Jenkins, GitLab CI/CD, CircleCI, and Docker Hub provides development teams with powerful, scalable, and efficient methods for software delivery. These tools ensure that applications are not only built and tested within consistent environments but also deployed with reliability, adhering to modern development practices. By selecting the appropriate tools and configuring them to harness Docker's capabilities, teams can enhance their development workflows, leading to more predictable and successful software releases.

Chapter Nine

Monitoring and Logging Docker Environments

Tools and strategies for monitoring Docker containers and hosts

Monitoring Docker containers and hosts is essential for ensuring the efficient, secure, and reliable operation of containerized applications. As Docker environments grow in scale and complexity, adopting effective monitoring tools and strategies becomes crucial. This guide outlines various tools and methodologies for adeptly monitoring Docker setups, detailing how these can be implemented to maintain robust container ecosystems.

Essential Metrics for Docker Monitoring

Effective Docker monitoring focuses on various critical metrics and logs that provide insights into the operations and health of both containers and their host environments. Key metrics include:

- **Container Performance Metrics**: Including CPU usage, memory usage, network I/O, and disk I/O.

- **System-Level Metrics**: Such as CPU utilization, memory consumption, load averages, and the overall health of the Docker daemon.

- **Application Logs**: Capturing standard output and errors from containers.

- **Events and Errors**: Monitoring Docker-specific events and runtime errors that could impact application performance and stability.

Top Tools for Docker Monitoring

A variety of specialized tools are available to facilitate comprehensive monitoring of Docker environments:

1. Prometheus and Grafana

Overview: Prometheus is an open-source system monitoring and alerting toolkit, while Grafana is a metric analytics and visualization suite.

Features:

- **Prometheus** effectively scrapes and stores metrics as time-series data, with powerful queries and real-time alerting.

- **Grafana** provides extensive visualization options using data from Prometheus, enhancing the ability to interpret and act on the collected information.

Implementation:

- Set up Prometheus to collect metrics from Docker environments, using it in conjunction with Grafana for advanced data visualization.

```
# Example docker-compose.yml setup for Prometheus and Grafana
version: '3'
services:
  prometheus:
    image: prom/prometheus
    ports:
      - "9090:9090"
    volumes:
      - ./prometheus.yml:/etc/prometheus/prometheus.yml

  grafana:
    image: grafana/grafana
    ports:
      - "3000:3000"
```

2. cAdvisor

Overview: Developed by Google, cAdvisor (Container Advisor) provides analytics regarding resource usage and performance characteristics of running containers.

Features:

- It monitors and gathers information about containers, helping users understand the resource and performance characteristics of their operations.

Implementation:

- Deploy cAdvisor to monitor container metrics, which can be integrated with broader monitoring setups like Prometheus.

3. Elastic Stack (ELK)

Overview: Comprising Elasticsearch, Logstash, and Kibana, the Elastic Stack is used to search, analyze, and visualize large volumes of data in real time.

Features:

- **Elasticsearch** stores and retrieves data efficiently, **Logstash** processes incoming data feeds, and **Kibana** visualizes the data with various charts and graphs.

Implementation:

- Configure Docker logs to feed into Logstash, processed and stored in Elasticsearch, and visualized through Kibana for a comprehensive logging solution.

4. Datadog

Overview: Datadog is a cloud-based service that provides monitoring of servers, databases, tools, and services through a SaaS-based data analytics platform.

Features:

- Offers integrated solutions for monitoring Docker containers, providing dashboards, alerts, and machine learning-based insights for complex environments.

Implementation:

- Utilize Datadog's Docker integration to track and analyze metrics and logs across all containers and hosts seamlessly.

Monitoring Best Practices for Docker

- **Centralize Log Management**: Aggregate all logs and metrics to a central platform for easier correlation and analysis.

- **Set Proactive Alerts**: Configure alerts for critical metrics to proactively manage potential issues before they escalate.

- **Define Resource Quotas**: Implement resource quotas in Docker configurations to prevent any single container from monopolizing system resources.

- **Monitor Security Posture**: Regularly monitor for vulnerabilities and anomalies within containers and hosts using specialized security tools.

Conclusion

Implementing robust monitoring for Docker containers and hosts is pivotal for the health and performance of containerized applications. By integrating tools like Prometheus, Grafana, cAdvisor, the Elastic Stack, and Datadog into Docker CI/CD pipelines, teams can achieve deeper insights, proactive management, and enhanced operational visibility. Adhering to recommended practices for monitoring ensures Docker environments are both performant and secure, supporting ongoing operational excellence.

Implementing effective logging practices

Effective logging practices are crucial for maintaining robust, efficient, and secure software systems. Logs provide invaluable insights into application behavior, user actions, system failures, and performance metrics, facilitating prompt troubleshooting and aiding in compliance and security monitoring. This article discusses key strategies for establishing and maintaining a practical logging framework, focusing on the collection, management, and analysis of log data.

The Role of Logging in Software Systems

Logging involves recording events and data during the runtime operation of a system to a persistent storage medium. It is essential for:

- **Troubleshooting and Error Resolution**: Logs provide detailed diagnostics that help identify and rectify errors.

- **Performance Optimization**: Logs help detect performance issues by tracking slow operations and system bottlenecks.

- **Regulatory Compliance and Auditing**: Logs support compliance by recording access and changes, essential for audits.

- **Development Support**: Detailed logs can assist developers in understanding application flow and system state during debugging.

Best Practices for Effective Logging

1. Choose Relevant Log Content

Determining the right amount and type of information to log is vital to avoid overwhelming log files with noise or missing critical events.

- **Content to Log**: Focus on significant events like user transactions, system errors, and status changes. Include pertinent details like timestamps, user identifiers, and transaction identifiers.

- **Structured Logging**: Adopt structured logging formats, such as JSON, to facilitate easier parsing and analysis.

```
{
  "time": "2023-11-01T12:00:00Z",
  "severity": "ERROR",
  "message": "Failed to process payment",
  "userId": "98765",
  "transactionId": "12345",
  "errorDetails": "Insufficient funds"
}
```

2. Implement Log Levels Strategically

Use log levels to differentiate the importance of log entries, enabling focused analysis and storage efficiency.

- **DEBUG**: For detailed debugging information.

- **INFO**: General operational entries confirming proper operation.

- **WARNING**: Indications of potential issues.

- **ERROR**: For serious issues affecting operation but not causing shutdown.

- **CRITICAL**: For severe situations where the system's stability is compromised.

3. Centralize Logs

In complex systems, especially distributed architectures, centralizing logs from all sources into a unified platform is essential for correlated analysis and management.

- **Tools**: Implement centralized logging solutions like the ELK Stack, Graylog, or Splunk. These tools aggregate logs in a central repository and provide advanced search and analytics capabilities.

4. Ensure Log Security and Compliance

Protecting log information is critical, especially logs containing sensitive data.

- **Security Measures**: Encrypt logs during transmission and at rest. Control access to logs based on user roles.

- **Retention Policies**: Define and enforce policies for log retention based on legal and operational requirements, ensuring efficient storage management.

5. Set Up Alerts and Monitoring

Active monitoring of logs with real-time alerts can accelerate incident response times and enhance system reliability.

- **Alerting Setup**: Configure monitoring tools like Prometheus to trigger alerts based on predefined criteria such as error rates exceeding thresholds.

```
alerting:
  rules:
    - alert: HighErrorRate
      expr: rate(errors[10m]) > 0.05
      for: 10m
      labels:
        severity: critical
      annotations:
        summary: High error rate detected
```

Conclusion

Implementing robust logging practices is foundational to effective software system management. By strategically collecting and managing logs, organizations can enhance operational intelligence, streamline troubleshooting, bolster security, and ensure compliance. Effective logging involves capturing relevant data, using structured formats, employing appropriate log levels, centralizing log management, securing log data, and utilizing proactive monitoring strategies. These practices not only support day-to-day operations but also significantly improve the resilience and security of applications, thereby enhancing overall business performance.

Visualizing Docker performance data

Effective visualization of Docker performance metrics is essential for optimizing the operation of containerized environments. It enables developers and system administrators to monitor application health, manage resources judiciously, and troubleshoot issues promptly. This article outlines various tools and methods for tracking and visualizing Docker performance, providing guidance on their implementation.

Importance of Docker Performance Visualization

Visualizing Docker performance metrics allows for:

- **Efficient Resource Usage**: Monitoring the consumption of CPU, memory, network, and storage helps in managing resources effectively.

- **Troubleshooting**: Visualization tools can help pinpoint problems within Docker containers and their host environments quickly.

- **Cost Management**: Optimizing resource usage can lead to significant cost savings in operational expenses.

- **Performance Enhancements**: Insights from data visualization guide adjustments to improve stability and responsiveness.

Leading Tools for Docker Performance Visualization

The following tools are highly regarded for their ability to gather and display Docker performance data effectively:

1. cAdvisor (Container Advisor)

Overview: Google's cAdvisor is a specialized container monitoring tool that provides detailed information about resource usage and performance characteristics of running containers.

Key Features:

- Delivers real-time, per-container resource usage statistics.

- Features an accessible web-based user interface for easy data access.

How to Deploy:

- **Running cAdvisor within Docker**:

```
docker run \
  --volume=/:/rootfs:ro \
  --volume=/var/run:/var/run:rw \
  --volume=/sys:/sys:ro \
  --volume=/var/lib/docker/:/var/lib/docker:ro \
  --publish=8080:8080 \
  --detach=true \
  --name=cadvisor \
  google/cadvisor:latest
```

- Access the web interface via **http://<Docker_Host_IP>:8080** to view real-time metrics.

2. Grafana

Overview: Grafana is a sophisticated, open-source platform for monitoring and data visualization that supports a wide array of databases.

Key Features:

- Offers extensive visualization tools like graphs and dashboards that are highly customizable.

- Can integrate with numerous data sources, including Prometheus, to create comprehensive monitoring solutions.

Setting It Up:

- **Deploy Grafana to view Docker metrics:**

```
docker run \
  --name grafana \
  -p 3000:3000 \
  grafana/grafana
```

- Configure Grafana to pull data from Prometheus, which collects Docker metrics, to visualize various performance indicators.

3. Prometheus

Overview: Known for its powerful monitoring capabilities, Prometheus is particularly adept at collecting and storing time-series data from Docker environments.

Key Features:

- Stores data in a time-series format with strong querying capabilities, making it ideal for the dynamic nature of container monitoring.

- Offers alerting functionalities that can notify administrators about critical issues.

Example Setup:

- **Configuring Prometheus for Docker monitoring**:

```
global:
  scrape_interval: 15s

scrape_configs:
  - job_name: 'docker'
    static_configs:
      - targets: ['localhost:9323']
```

- Prometheus can be set to scrape Docker Daemon metrics available on specified ports, providing a detailed view of performance across all containers.

Best Practices for Visualizing Docker Performance

- **Continuous Monitoring**: Maintain ongoing surveillance of all Docker containers to manage performance proactively.

- **Alert Configuration**: Establish alerts for predefined performance thresholds to address potential issues swiftly.

- **Holistic Approach**: Monitor both specific container metrics and overall system health to gain a comprehensive understanding of the infrastructure.

- **Security Measures**: Ensure all monitoring interfaces and data transmissions are secured to protect sensitive information.

Conclusion

By employing tools such as cAdvisor, Grafana, and Prometheus, organizations can effectively visualize performance data from Docker environments. These tools not only help in tracking vital metrics but also assist in proactive management, troubleshooting, and optimization of containerized applications. Implementing these tools enhances visibility into operations, leading to more informed decision-making and ultimately, improved performance and resource efficiency.

Chapter Ten

Docker Security Enhancement

Advanced security techniques and best practices

In today's digital landscape, where cyber threats continually evolve, it's crucial for organizations to embrace sophisticated security measures and best practices to protect their technological infrastructure. This article outlines effective advanced security techniques and practices essential for safeguarding digital assets against modern cyber threats.

Crucial Advanced Security Techniques

Adopting state-of-the-art security methods is vital for defense against cyber threats and ensuring compliance with regulatory requirements. Below are essential strategies for enhancing an organization's security framework:

1. Data Encryption

Securing sensitive information through encryption is fundamental for protection both in storage and during transmission. Advanced encryption protocols, like AES-256, are critical for maintaining data integrity and confidentiality.

- **Best Practice**: Deploy TLS protocols to secure all network transmissions. Employ cryptographic libraries, such as OpenSSL, to facilitate encryption within your applications.

```
openssl enc -aes-256-cbc -salt -in filename.txt -out filename.enc
```

2. Identity and Access Management (IAM)

Effective IAM ensures that only authorized users can access specific resources within an organization, enforcing policies like multi-factor authentication (MFA), role-based access control (RBAC), and the principle of least privilege (PoLP).

- **Best Practice**: Integrate MFA for all critical system interactions to strengthen security measures, especially for administrative and external accesses.

3. Advanced Threat Detection

Implementing systems like SIEM, SOAR, and IDS/IPS is crucial for timely detection and mitigation of threats.

- **Best Practice**: Equip IDS/IPS systems with capabilities to detect and actively mitigate threats based on set rules.

```
# Example Snort IDS rule to detect and block a specified threat
alert tcp $EXTERNAL_NET any -> $HOME_NET 443 (msg:"Suspected Malware Activity";
    sid:1000001; rev:1;)
```

4. Zero Trust Architecture

Adopting a Zero Trust framework means not trusting any entity by default, whether inside or outside the network, necessitating strict verification for every access attempt.

- **Best Practice**: Use micro-segmentation and continuous verification to control network access and reduce the risk of insider threats.

5. Continuous Security Assessments

Regular security evaluations such as audits and penetration testing are essential to identify and address vulnerabilities effectively.

- **Best Practice**: Engage in third-party audits and frequent penetration testing to ensure security weaknesses are identified and remediated. Use automated scanning tools for regular assessments.

```
# Command for starting a vulnerability scan using OWASP ZAP
zap-cli start
zap-cli open-url http://example.com
zap-cli active-scan -r http://example.com
zap-cli alerts
```

Foundational Security Best Practices

To support advanced techniques, organizations must also adhere to foundational best practices:

- **Ongoing Monitoring and Logging**: Implement sophisticated monitoring solutions to oversee all network and system activities, ensuring prompt detection of unusual behavior.

- **Timely Patch Management**: Automate the process of updating software to patch known vulnerabilities, maintaining the security integrity of all systems.

- **Security Awareness Training**: Regularly conduct training sessions to enhance employee awareness about current security threats and preventive measures.

- **Prepared Incident Response**: Maintain an up-to-date incident response plan outlining procedural responses to potential security incidents.

- **Integrate Security in SDLC**: Embed security measures early in the software development lifecycle, ensuring all new software is secure by design.

Conclusion

By implementing these advanced security techniques and adhering to established best practices, organizations can effectively shield themselves against sophisticated cyber threats. Techniques such as robust encryption, stringent access controls, proactive threat detection, and the Zero Trust model are integral to a comprehensive security strategy. Together with regular security assessments, continuous monitoring, and a proactive approach to software maintenance, these strategies ensure organizations maintain a strong defense against potential cyber attacks, thereby safeguarding their critical data and systems.

Securing Docker images, networks, and storage

Ensuring robust security measures for Docker environments involves securing Docker images, networks, and storage systems effectively. Given the scalable nature of containers, it is imperative to establish stringent security protocols to guard against vulnerabilities and ensure that containerized applications operate securely and efficiently. This article outlines essential strategies and best practices for fortifying Docker images, networks, and storage, with practical implementation examples.

Securing Docker Images

Docker images serve as the templates for Docker containers; thus, their security is crucial. The integrity of an image affects all containers derived from it, making image security a fundamental aspect of container security.

Best Practices for Docker Image Security:

1. **Utilize Trusted Base Images**: Always opt for official or verified images from reputable registries such as Docker Hub. Regularly perform vulnerability scans on these images.

```
docker pull ubuntu:latest
```

2. **Reduce the Attack Surface**: Limit the number of packages and layers in your Docker images. Opt for minimal base images like Alpine or distroless images from Google.

```
FROM alpine:latest
RUN apk --no-cache add nginx
```

3. **Keep Images Updated**: Continually update images to incorporate the latest security patches. Automate updates using CI/CD pipelines.

```
FROM ubuntu:latest
RUN apt-get update && apt-get upgrade -y
```

4. **Implement Multi-Stage Builds**: Use multi-stage builds to include only the necessary components in the final image, avoiding the inclusion of unnecessary build tools.

```
# Build stage
FROM golang:1.15 as builder
WORKDIR /app
COPY . .
RUN go build -o myapp .

# Final stage
FROM alpine:latest
COPY --from=builder /app/myapp /myapp
ENTRYPOINT ["./myapp"]
```

5. **Regular Vulnerability Scanning**: Employ tools like Clair, Trivy, or Docker's built-in scanning features to detect vulnerabilities within the images.

```
trivy image ubuntu:latest
```

Securing Docker Networks

Docker networks connect containers to each other and to the external world, making network security critical to prevent unauthorized access and safeguard data.

Best Practices for Docker Network Security:

1. **Implement Network Segmentation**: Use user-defined bridge networks to isolate groups of containers, reducing the risk of cross-container breaches.

311

```
docker network create --driver bridge isolated_network
```

2. **Disable Inter-container Communication**: Prevent containers on the same network from communicating unless explicitly required.

```
docker network create --internal --driver bridge no_comm_network
```

3. **Enable Network Encryption**: For sensitive communications, enable encryption on Docker networks using protocols like IPSec to secure data in transit.

```
docker network create --opt encrypted --driver overlay secure_network
```

4. **Use Firewalls and Security Groups**: Control both inbound and outbound network traffic to and from Docker containers using firewall rules and security groups.

Securing Docker Storage

Docker storage mechanisms like volumes and bind mounts should be secured to protect the data used by containers.

Best Practices for Docker Storage Security:

1. **Encrypt Persistent Volumes**: Protect Docker volumes using encryption solutions to secure data at rest.

```
# Creating an encrypted volume using dm-crypt
cryptsetup luksFormat /dev/sda
cryptsetup luksOpen /dev/sda enc_vol
mkfs.ext4 /dev/mapper/enc_vol
mount /dev/mapper/enc_vol /mnt
```

2. **Restrict Access to Bind Mounts**: Limit the access permissions for bind mounts to prevent unauthorized data access from containers.

```
docker run -v /secured/data:/data:ro myapp
```

3. **Develop Backup and Recovery Procedures**: Establish reliable backup and recovery processes for Docker volumes to ensure data integrity and availability.

```
docker run --volume /data --volume-driver backup-driver mybackup-container
```

Conclusion

Securing Docker images, networks, and storage is vital for the integrity and security of containerized applications. By implementing practices such as using trusted base images, minimizing image attack surfaces, enforcing network segmentation, enabling data encryption, and securing storage solutions, organizations can effectively mitigate risks associated with their Docker environments. Regular updates, continuous monitoring, and vulnerability scanning further enhance the security measures, ensuring ongoing protection against potential threats.

Compliance and vulnerability management in Docker environments

Maintaining compliance and effectively managing vulnerabilities are pivotal components of securing Docker environments. As containerization becomes a staple in modern IT infrastructures, it is imperative for organizations to align their Docker deployments with prevailing industry regulations while safeguarding them against potential security vulnerabilities. This article outlines essential methodologies and best practices to ensure robust compliance and vulnerability management within Docker ecosystems.

Ensuring Compliance in Docker Environments

Compliance in the context of Docker involves adhering to statutory and regulatory requirements designed to secure data and operations within containerized applications. These regulations, which may include GDPR, HIPAA, PCI-DSS, and others, mandate rigorous security controls, precise data management, and systematic audits.

Strategic Approaches to Compliance:

1. **Data Security and Encryption**: Encrypt data stored within Docker containers and secure data in transit using network security protocols like TLS to prevent unauthorized access.

```
# Example of creating a secure Docker network with encryption
docker network create --opt encrypted --driver overlay secure_network
```

2. **Implementing Access Controls**: Leverage Docker's capabilities to manage sensitive data securely using

Docker secrets and enforce role-based access control (RBAC) to limit resource access based on user roles.

```
# Example of using Docker secrets in a Docker Compose file
version: '3.1'
services:
  mysql:
    image: mysql
    environment:
      MYSQL_ROOT_PASSWORD_FILE: /run/secrets/db_password
    secrets:
      - db_password

secrets:
  db_password:
    file: ./password.txt
```

3. **Auditable Logging and Monitoring**: Establish comprehensive logging for all Docker container activities and implement monitoring solutions to ensure continuous oversight and reporting. Logs should be immutable and securely stored to support audit requirements.

```
# Example of configuring logging for a Docker service
services:
  web:
    image: nginx
    logging:
      driver: syslog
      options:
        syslog-address: "tcp://192.168.0.42:123"
```

4. **Routine Compliance Audits**: Regularly perform audits to evaluate adherence to compliance standards, utilizing automated tools to benchmark against

established standards such as the CIS Docker Benchmark.

Managing Vulnerabilities in Docker Environments

Vulnerability management is the proactive approach to identifying, evaluating, and remediating security weaknesses in Docker containers and images.

Effective Vulnerability Management Practices:

1. **Regular Vulnerability Scanning**: Conduct thorough scans of Docker images and containers to identify vulnerabilities using tools like Clair, Trivy, or Docker Bench.

```
# Example command for scanning a Docker image with Trivy
trivy image my-org/my-app:latest
```

2. **Dependency Management**: Monitor and manage software dependencies within Docker containers to ensure they are up-to-date and secure. Tools like Snyk or Dependabot can help automate dependency updates.

3. **Securing Image Supply Chain**: Use only trusted, verified Docker images for your deployments. Implement measures like Docker Content Trust to sign and verify images, reinforcing security policies regarding image provenance.

```
# Enabling Docker Content Trust to ensure image integrity
export DOCKER_CONTENT_TRUST=1
docker pull my-org/my-app:latest
```

4. **Efficient Patch Management**: Swiftly apply patches to Docker images and redeploy containers to mitigate vulnerabilities. Automate these processes via CI/CD pipelines to reduce exposure to risks.

```
# Example CI/CD pipeline script to automatically rebuild and deploy Docker images
jobs:
  build_and_deploy:
    runs-on: ubuntu-latest
    steps:
    - uses: actions/checkout@v2
    - name: Build and push updated Docker image
      uses: docker/build-push-action@v2
      with:
        context: .
        push: true
        tags: my-org/my-app:latest
```

Conclusion

Effective compliance and vulnerability management are essential to safeguarding Docker environments. By encrypting data, implementing stringent access controls, maintaining detailed logs, and conducting regular security audits, organizations can ensure they meet compliance standards. Additionally, robust vulnerability management through regular scanning, diligent patching, and careful management of dependencies and image integrity helps fortify Docker environments against threats. These strategies collectively enhance the security, resilience, and compliance of Docker deployments, supporting an organization's overall cybersecurity framework.

317

Chapter Eleven

Docker APIs and SDKs

Utilizing Docker APIs for custom integration

Leveraging Docker APIs offers developers a robust mechanism for programmatically managing containers, images, and networks, significantly enhancing automation capabilities within Docker environments. This capability is particularly useful in complex setups where manual management of Docker resources would be cumbersome and inefficient. This article delves into how Docker APIs can be utilized for custom integrations, providing examples of API usage and their practical applications in diverse scenarios.

Overview of Docker APIs

The Docker API, a RESTful interface, allows developers to interact with the Docker daemon remotely via HTTP requests. This interface supports a variety of operations such as initiating or halting containers, manipulating images, configuring networks, and more. Docker ensures backward compatibility through versioned API releases.

Configuring the Docker API

To interact with the Docker API, you must configure the Docker daemon to listen on a specific port or socket. This configuration is usually specified in the Docker daemon's settings file, typically located at **/etc/docker/daemon.json**.

Below is an example configuration that enables API access over HTTP:

```
{
    "hosts": ["unix:///var/run/docker.sock", "tcp://0.0.0.0:2375"]
}
```

Security Note: Exposing the Docker API over the network without stringent security measures can pose significant risks, as it would allow anyone with network access to manage Docker. It is critical to secure the API using firewalls and, preferably, HTTPS with TLS.

Using the Docker API

With the Docker API accessible, interactions can be performed using any HTTP client. Below are examples using **curl** to demonstrate basic Docker operations:

1. Listing Docker Containers

To list all Docker containers, a GET request is made to the **/containers/json** endpoint:

```
curl -s --unix-socket /var/run/docker.sock http://localhost/containers/json
```

This command returns a JSON array containing details such as container IDs, names, and statuses.

2. Starting and Stopping Containers

Containers can be started or stopped by issuing POST requests to specific endpoints:

```
# To start a container
curl -X POST --unix-socket /var/run/docker.sock http://localhost/containers
    /{container_id}/start

# To stop a container
curl -X POST --unix-socket /var/run/docker.sock http://localhost/containers
    /{container_id}/stop
```

Replace **{container_id}** with the actual container ID.

3. Managing Images

To download a new image from Docker Hub, the **/images/create** endpoint is utilized:

```
curl -X POST --unix-socket /var/run/docker.sock "http://localhost/images/create
    ?fromImage=ubuntu&tag=latest"
```

This pulls the latest Ubuntu image from Docker Hub.

Practical Applications of Docker APIs

Incorporating Docker APIs can streamline operations and enable automation in several practical ways:

1. **CI/CD Automation**: Docker APIs can be integrated into CI/CD pipelines to automate tasks such as pulling new images, updating containers, and managing deployment workflows.

2. **Provisioning Environments**: APIs enable dynamic provisioning and teardown of development, test, or staging environments, adapting to varying workload demands.

3. **Custom Monitoring Solutions**: Develop tailored monitoring tools using Docker APIs to track container performance, resource usage, and overall system health.

4. **Building Custom User Interfaces**: Create intuitive user interfaces for Docker management that allow users to interact with containers without direct CLI operations.

Conclusion

Utilizing Docker APIs for custom integration empowers developers and system administrators with the ability to manage Docker resources programmatically. By setting up secure API access, professionals can harness Docker's capabilities to facilitate custom integrations that boost productivity, enhance system reliability, and ensure robust security. Docker APIs serve as versatile tools in the DevOps arsenal, enabling a wide range of automated solutions from deployment pipelines to custom management interfaces.

Building applications and tools with Docker SDKs

Docker SDKs (Software Development Kits) offer a powerful suite of tools that enable developers to programmatically manage Docker environments, thereby enhancing automation capabilities across various Docker operations. These SDKs support a range of functionalities, including container management, image handling, network configurations, and volume management, all from within an application. This article delves into how developers can utilize Docker SDKs to develop robust applications and tools, complete with practical code examples to demonstrate their application.

Introduction to Docker SDKs

Docker provides several SDKs tailored to different programming languages such as Python, Go, and JavaScript (Node.js). Each SDK provides a simplified, high-level interface to the Docker Engine API, abstracting some of the complexities of direct API communication and facilitating easier and more efficient Docker operations.

Setting Up Docker SDKs

To begin developing applications with Docker SDKs, you need to prepare your development environment:

1. **Install Docker**: Ensure Docker is installed and operational on your development system. Docker can be downloaded from its official website.

2. **Select and Install an SDK**: Depending on your programming language preference, install the corresponding Docker SDK. For instance, if you are using Python, you would install the Docker Python SDK as follows:

```
pip install docker
```

3. **Configure Docker Engine Access**: Your application will need to interact with the Docker Engine API, typically accessible through the Docker daemon. By default, this connection is made through the Unix socket **/var/run/docker.sock** on Linux or named

pipes on Windows. Verify that your application has the necessary permissions to access these interfaces.

Examples of Utilizing Docker SDKs in Application Development

1. Container Management with Python

Below is an example using the Docker Python SDK to perform basic container management tasks such as listing containers, starting or stopping a container, and pulling an image:

```python
import docker

client = docker.from_env()

# List all containers
for container in client.containers.list(all=True):
    print(container.id)

# Start a container
client.containers.get('container_id').start()

# Stop a container
client.containers.get('container_id').stop()

# Pull a new image
client.images.pull('nginx:latest')
```

This script provides a straightforward demonstration of how the Docker Python SDK can simplify interactions with Docker containers.

2. Building and Running Containers with Go

The Docker Go SDK, also known as **go-docker**, enables developers to automate building images and running containers as shown in the following Go application:

```go
package main

import (
    "context"
    "fmt"
    "io/ioutil"
    "os"

    "github.com/docker/docker/api/types"
    "github.com/docker/docker/client"
    "github.com/docker/docker/pkg/archive"
)

func main() {
    ctx := context.Background()
    cli, err := client.NewClientWithOpts(client.FromEnv, client
        .WithAPIVersionNegotiation())
    if err != nil {
        panic(err)
    }
```

```go
    // Create a tar of the current directory
    tar, err := archive.TarWithOptions(".", &archive.TarOptions{})
    if err != nil {
        panic(err)
    }

    // Build an image using the Dockerfile in the current directory
    buildResponse, err := cli.ImageBuild(ctx, tar, types.ImageBuildOptions{
        Tags: []string{"my-custom-app:latest"},
    })
    if err != nil {
        panic(err)
    }
    defer buildResponse.Body.Close()
    response, err := ioutil.ReadAll(buildResponse.Body)
    if err != nil {
        panic(err)
    }
    fmt.Println(string(response))
```

```go
// Run a container from the built image
resp, err := cli.ContainerCreate(ctx, &container.Config{
    Image: "my-custom-app:latest",
}, nil, nil, nil, "")
if err != nil {
    panic(err)
}

if err := cli.ContainerStart(ctx, resp.ID, types.ContainerStartOptions{}); err !=
    nil {
    panic(err)
}

fmt.Printf("Container %s is started\n", resp.ID)
```

This Go code illustrates how to build a Docker image from a Dockerfile and initiate a container using the resulting image, showcasing the automation capabilities of the Docker Go SDK.

Conclusion

Docker SDKs equip developers with the tools necessary to integrate Docker functionality into their applications or to create specialized tools that meet their specific needs. Whether through automating deployment processes, managing container lifecycles, or developing custom solutions for monitoring and management, Docker SDKs offer extensive possibilities to streamline operations and enhance productivity. The examples presented in Python and Go highlight just a snippet of what can be achieved with these powerful tools.

Examples of API and SDK utilization in real-world scenarios

APIs (Application Programming Interfaces) and SDKs (Software Development Kits) play a pivotal role in bridging disparate software systems, enhancing functionality, and automating operations across various industries. This article explores how APIs and SDKs are effectively utilized in real-world scenarios to facilitate seamless interactions and drive innovation, complete with practical code examples for a clearer understanding of their applications.

Financial Industry: Facilitating Seamless Transactions

In the realm of finance, APIs are integral to integrating seamless payment solutions into e-commerce platforms. Payment service providers such as Stripe and PayPal offer APIs that enable online stores to embed payment processing directly into their websites, providing a fluid user experience during checkout.

Example Usage:

```
import stripe
stripe.api_key = "your_private_key"

stripe.Charge.create(
    amount=2000,
    currency="usd",
    source="tok_mastercard",  # Obtained via Stripe.js
    description="Invoice payment #001"
)
```

This Python code snippet shows how to process a payment using Stripe's API, demonstrating the ease with which financial transactions can be integrated into applications.

Healthcare: Streamlining Patient Care

APIs in healthcare allow for the efficient exchange of patient information across various systems, enhancing the delivery of medical care. They enable healthcare providers to access up-to-date patient records securely and quickly, essential for effective medical decision-making.

Example Usage:

```javascript
fetch('https://api.medicalprovider.com/patient/98765/details', {
  method: 'GET',
  headers: {
    'Authorization': 'Bearer securetoken456'
  }
})
.then(response => response.json())
.then(data => console.log(data));
```

This JavaScript fetch example illustrates how a medical application can access a patient's records securely, facilitating improved healthcare services and patient outcomes.

Telecommunications: Enriching User Connectivity

Telecommunications entities leverage SDKs to incorporate sophisticated communication functionalities into their applications, such as in-app messaging and VoIP services. Twilio's SDKs, for instance, allow the integration of these features to foster richer user interaction.

Example Usage:

```java
import com.twilio.sdk.Twilio;
import com.twilio.sdk.resource.api.v2010.account.Message;

public class MessageApp {
  public static final String ACCOUNT_SID = "ACxxxxxxxxxxxxxxxxxxxxxxxx";
  public static final String AUTH_TOKEN = "your_auth_token_here";

  public static void main(String[] args) {
    Twilio.init(ACCOUNT_SID, AUTH_TOKEN);
```

```java
    Message message = Message.creator(
      new com.twilio.type.PhoneNumber("+15558675309"),
      new com.twilio.type.PhoneNumber("+15551234567"),
      "Message sent via Twilio SDK"
    ).create();

    System.out.println(message.getSid());
  }
}
```

This Java code demonstrates how to send an SMS using Twilio's SDK, showing how telecommunication applications can enhance communication options within their services.

E-commerce: Enhancing Customer Experience

E-commerce platforms use APIs to deliver personalized shopping experiences by recommending products based on user preferences and past behaviors. These APIs connect to advanced analytics services that analyze user data to provide customized product suggestions.

Example Usage:

```javascript
fetch('https://api.ecommerce.com/user/4321/recommendations', {
  method: 'POST',
  headers: {
    'Content-Type': 'application/json'
  },
  body: JSON.stringify({sessionId: 'session123', viewedItems: ['123', '456']})
})
.then(response => response.json())
.then(data => console.log(data));
```

This API usage example in an e-commerce context shows how platforms can tailor product recommendations to enhance user engagement and increase sales by catering to individual tastes.

Smart Home Applications: Integrating Device Functionality

Smart home technology providers utilize APIs and SDKs to link various home automation devices, allowing them to be managed via central applications or voice-activated systems. This integration facilitates a more interconnected and automated home environment.

Example Usage:

```python
import home_automation_sdk

# Setup home environment
home = home_automation_sdk.setup()

# Command to turn off all lights
home.lights.off()
```

This Python script provides an example of how smart home applications might use an SDK to control lighting systems, showcasing the convenience and automation capabilities available in modern smart home setups.

Conclusion

The strategic use of APIs and SDKs across different sectors emphasizes their fundamental role in enhancing software functionality and user experience. From processing secure payments and accessing critical health data to facilitating advanced communications and personalizing retail experiences, these tools enable a wide array of automated and sophisticated features. By embedding APIs and SDKs into their platforms, developers can streamline operations, foster innovation, and deliver richer, more responsive services.

Chapter Twelve

Performance Tuning in Docker

Techniques for performance analysis and bottleneck identification

Performance analysis and bottleneck identification are crucial techniques in software optimization, aimed at improving system response times and operational efficiency. By employing these methods, developers can uncover areas within an application or system that limit overall performance and address them effectively. This article explores several strategies for conducting performance analysis and pinpointing performance bottlenecks, complete with practical examples to demonstrate their application.

Overview of Performance Analysis

Performance analysis involves evaluating the effectiveness and speed of a system under various workloads. Its primary goal is to determine a system's throughput, identify performance limits, and detect sections of the application that may be optimized for better efficiency.

Identifying Bottlenecks

Bottlenecks occur when a particular component slows down the data flow, resulting in reduced performance across the system. Identifying these bottlenecks is vital as it directs focus to the most impactful areas for performance improvement.

Techniques for Analyzing Performance and Identifying Bottlenecks

1. Profiling

Profiling is a method used to understand the resource usage of different parts of a program, including CPU time and memory usage. There are primarily two types of profilers:

- **CPU Profilers**: Analyze the amount of time each function takes, helping pinpoint where optimizations can make the most impact.

- **Memory Profilers**: Track how much memory is being used by the program, which is crucial for identifying memory leaks or inefficiencies.

Example Usage: Profiling a Python function using **cProfile**:

```python
import cProfile
import re

def sample_function():
    return re.compile('foo|bar').search('foobar')

cProfile.run('sample_function()')
```

This will output the number of function calls and the time spent in each, aiding in the identification of slow functions.

2. Tracing

Tracing provides a detailed record of a program's execution, offering insights into the sequence of operations and where delays occur.

Example Usage: Implementing tracing in Java with the Logger API:

```java
import java.util.logging.*;

public class TraceExample {
    private static final Logger logger = Logger.getLogger(TraceExample.class.getName());

    public static void main(String[] args) {
        logger.setLevel(Level.ALL);
        logger.entering("TraceExample", "main");

        // Simulated application logic

        logger.exiting("TraceExample", "main");
    }
}
```

This sets up basic tracing, logging entry and exit points in the application's flow, which can help track down where delays or issues occur.

3. Benchmarking

Benchmarking measures the performance of a system's components under specific conditions, typically to compare against an industry standard or to measure improvements.

Example Usage: Using **timeit** in Python to benchmark a small snippet of code:

```python
import timeit

result = timeit.timeit('"-".join([str(n) for n in range(100)])', number=1000)
print(result)
```

This code benchmarks how long it takes to execute the specified Python code snippet a thousand times, which can be useful for comparing performance before and after optimizations.

4. Monitoring and Logging

Continuous monitoring and logging are vital for observing a system's operation in real-time. They help in identifying unusual patterns or spikes in resource usage that may indicate bottlenecks.

Example Usage: Configuring monitoring with tools like Prometheus and Grafana to visualize performance metrics:

Set up Prometheus to collect data and Grafana to display this data through intuitive dashboards. This can help in tracking performance trends and quickly identifying anomalies.

5. Load Testing

Load testing simulates high demand on a system to understand how it behaves under stress and to identify its maximum capacity.

Example Usage: Conducting load testing with Apache JMeter on a web application to measure its performance under simulated traffic conditions.

Conclusion

Employing performance analysis and bottleneck identification techniques is essential for maximizing software efficiency. Techniques such as profiling, tracing, benchmarking, continuous monitoring, and load testing are invaluable in diagnosing performance issues and facilitating targeted optimizations. By implementing these strategies, developers can ensure their applications are not only robust but also optimized to deliver the best possible performance.

Performance tuning for Docker applications

Performance tuning for Docker applications is crucial for ensuring that these containerized systems run efficiently and effectively utilize available system resources. This article explores several strategies for enhancing the performance of Docker applications, detailing practical adjustments and configurations that can significantly improve system responsiveness and resource management.

Overview of Performance Considerations in Docker

Docker containers operate on a shared Linux kernel, which means they run more lightweight than traditional virtual machines but also share system resources. To optimize Docker performance, it's important to manage how these resources are allocated and used among containers.

Essential Techniques for Enhancing Docker Performance

1. Effective Container Management

Proper container management is essential for maintaining optimal performance across Docker applications. This involves careful control of container lifecycle events such as creation, deployment, scaling, and termination.

- **Setting Resource Limits**: Limiting the resources each container can use prevents any single application from monopolizing system resources.

Example Command:

```
docker run -d --name optimized_container --memory=512m --cpus=2 nginx
```

This command restricts the container to 512 MB of memory and 2 CPU cores, ensuring it does not consume excessive system resources.

2. Optimizing Networking Configurations

The default network settings for Docker might not suit all applications, especially those requiring high throughput and low latency.

- **Selecting Network Drivers**: Using the appropriate Docker network driver, like the host network, can decrease network overhead for performance-critical applications.

Example Command:

```
docker run -d --name network_optimized_app --network host my_app
```

This command uses the host network for the Docker container, reducing network-related performance overhead.

3. Enhancing Persistent Storage Performance

I/O operations are critical in applications that require persistent storage. Performance can be greatly improved by properly configuring Docker volumes.

- **Utilizing Data Volumes**: Data volumes facilitate direct data storage access by the host system, which can enhance I/O performance compared to storing data within container layers.

Example Command:

```
docker run -d --name data_intensive_app -v /opt/data:/var/data my_app
```

This command maps a host directory as a data volume in the container, improving the speed and efficiency of data access.

4. Image Optimization

The efficiency of Docker containers is also influenced by the size and structure of the images they run from. Smaller, well-organized images often lead to better performance.

- **Implementing Multi-Stage Builds**: Multi-stage builds help minimize Docker image sizes by separating build environments from production environments.

Example Dockerfile:

```
# Build stage for compiling resources
FROM node:14 AS builder
WORKDIR /app
COPY . .
RUN npm install && npm run build

# Production stage with runtime environment
FROM alpine
COPY --from=builder /app/build /app
CMD ["node", "/app/server.js"]
```

This Dockerfile example showcases how to use multi-stage builds to keep production images clean and lightweight, enhancing container startup times and reducing resource load.

5. Systematic Logging and Monitoring

Effective monitoring and logging strategies are vital for continuously assessing and tuning the performance of Docker applications.

- **Configuring Log Drivers**: Using centralized logging drivers can help manage log data efficiently, reducing the impact of logging on container performance.

Example Configuration:

```
docker run -d --name log_managed_app --log-driver=gelf --log-opt gelf-address=udp://logserver
    :12201 my_app
```

This setup directs container logs to a Graylog server using the GELF driver, minimizing local storage and I/O usage on the container host.

Best Practices for Docker Performance Tuning

- **Consistent Benchmarking**: Regular benchmarking can help track the impacts of changes and identify further areas for improvement.

- **Security Optimizations**: Enhancing security settings can also improve performance by eliminating unnecessary processing.

- **Contextual Tuning**: Always tailor performance tuning efforts to the specific needs and operational contexts of your applications.

Conclusion

Performance tuning for Docker applications involves a comprehensive approach to configuring and managing containers, networks, and storage options effectively. By applying these strategies—such as setting resource limits, optimizing network configurations, managing persistent storage intelligently, refining Docker images, and implementing robust logging—developers can ensure that their Docker applications are not only efficient but also scalable and reliable under various operational loads.

Case studies on performance optimization

Performance optimization is pivotal in improving software application functionality and enhancing user interaction across various industries. This article delves into several real-world case studies where strategic performance optimizations have significantly bolstered system responsiveness and operational efficacy, detailing the challenges encountered, the solutions implemented, and the results achieved.

Case Study 1: Optimization of an E-Commerce Portal

Background: A leading e-commerce retailer experienced slow website response times during high-traffic periods, negatively impacting user experience and sales.

Challenge: The main issues were rooted in inefficient database operations and inadequate content delivery mechanisms, leading to increased load times.

Solution: The retailer implemented a multi-pronged approach to address these issues:

- **Database Enhancements**: Modifications were made to optimize SQL queries and introduce indexes, which facilitated quicker data access.

- **Implementation of a CDN**: A Content Delivery Network (CDN) was deployed to manage the distribution of static content more efficiently, reducing latency.

- **Scalability Enhancements**: They conducted extensive scalability testing to better understand and enhance the infrastructure's handling of peak loads.

Results: The optimizations led to a 50% improvement in page load times, a 30% drop in bounce rates, and an overall increase in user conversions.

Case Study 2: Financial Transaction System Enhancement

Background: A financial institution needed to optimize its transaction processing software to accommodate growing transaction volumes without delays.

Challenge: The software struggled with long processing times, particularly during peak periods like financial year-ends.

Solution:

- **Algorithm Enhancement**: The institution optimized critical processing algorithms to speed up operations, leveraging more efficient computational methods.

- **Server Upgrades**: The system was moved to higher-capacity servers, and specific operations were optimized to leverage this new hardware effectively.

- **Performance Profiling**: Detailed profiling was conducted to identify and rectify performance bottlenecks.

Results: These changes resulted in a 40% reduction in processing times, ensuring the system could handle increased loads efficiently.

Case Study 3: Mobile Game Performance Enhancement

Background: A popular mobile game was facing issues with lag and frequent crashes on lower-specification devices.

Challenge: The game was graphics-intensive and not optimized for varying hardware capabilities, affecting its performance and user ratings.

Solution:

- **Code Optimization**: The game's source code was refined to reduce memory usage and optimize graphics rendering.

- **Dynamic Asset Management**: The game was updated to load assets dynamically based on current usage, reducing unnecessary memory consumption.

- **User Feedback Utilization**: Feedback from users was analyzed to pinpoint specific performance issues, which were then specifically addressed through targeted optimizations.

Results: Post-optimization, the game saw a 60% decrease in crash reports and significant improvements in user ratings across all devices.

Case Study 4: Healthcare Patient Management System Optimization

Background: A healthcare provider aimed to reduce the time taken to access patient records in order to improve response times in patient care.

Challenge: Delays in data retrieval from their patient management system were leading to inefficiencies in medical care.

Solution:

- **Database Optimization**: The patient database was optimized with new indexing strategies and more efficient query configurations to quicken data retrieval.

- **User Interface Improvements**: The system interface was upgraded to load data asynchronously, enhancing the perceived responsiveness.

- **Advanced Caching Techniques**: Caching mechanisms were introduced for frequently accessed data, reducing direct queries to the database and speeding up data access.

Results: These improvements reduced the time to access patient records by 70%, significantly enhancing operational efficiency and patient care quality.

Conclusion

These case studies highlight the transformative potential of performance optimization in various sectors. By carefully diagnosing performance issues and implementing targeted solutions, businesses can enhance their operational capabilities and improve user experiences. From leveraging advanced database optimizations and scaling solutions in e-commerce to dynamic resource management in mobile gaming, these initiatives underscore the importance of tailored performance strategies in achieving substantial improvements in efficiency and customer satisfaction.

Chapter Thirteen

Advanced Troubleshooting Techniques

Advanced debugging of Docker containers

Advanced debugging of Docker containers is essential for ensuring the robustness and efficiency of applications operating within Docker environments. This article outlines sophisticated methods and tools that facilitate deep troubleshooting and problem-solving in complex containerized setups.

Context for Docker Debugging

Docker containers operate as isolated environments running on the host's kernel, making debugging sometimes challenging due to the layers of abstraction involved. Effective debugging thus demands a comprehensive grasp of Docker's architecture alongside specialized tools tailored for these environments.

Advanced Docker Debugging Techniques and Tools

1. Leveraging Docker Logs

Accessing logs is often the initial step in debugging Docker containers. Docker's built-in logging capabilities can be accessed using the **docker logs** command, which provides immediate insights into container operations.

Example Command:

```
docker logs [container_id]
```

This retrieves a container's logs, which can be continuously monitored in real-time using the **-f** option, similar to using the tail command on traditional log files:

```
docker logs -f [container_id]
```

2. Inspecting Container Configurations

The **docker inspect** tool offers a deep dive into a container's configuration and state, providing vital information for debugging configuration-related issues.

Example Command:

```
docker inspect [container_id]
```

This command outputs comprehensive details in JSON format about the container's settings, including network setups and mounted volumes.

3. Interactive Container Debugging

For direct debugging, Docker allows command execution inside a running container using **docker exec**, which is especially useful for examining the internal state and environment.

Example Command:

```
docker exec -it [container_id] /bin/bash
```

This opens a bash shell inside the container, allowing real-time investigation and interaction.

4. Diagnosing Network Issues

Docker containers can sometimes experience network-related issues, which require specific tools to diagnose.

Example Command:

```
docker network inspect [network_name]
```

This reveals detailed network configuration and how containers are linked, assisting in troubleshooting network issues.

5. Monitoring Container Performance

For performance-related debugging, Docker provides a built-in command to monitor resource usage.

Example Command:

```
docker stats
```

This displays ongoing resource usage statistics for containers, aiding in identifying resource-intensive processes.

External tools like Prometheus and Grafana can also be implemented for more detailed performance tracking and anomaly detection.

6. Using Debuggers Inside Containers

For in-depth application debugging, traditional debuggers can be used within Docker containers to attach to specific processes.

Example Setup for Debugging with GDB:

1. Install GDB in the container.

2. Identify the process ID of the target application.

3. Attach GDB to the process.

```
docker exec -it [container_id] gdb -p [process_id]
```

This setup facilitates step-through debugging and detailed inspection of running processes.

Recommendations for Effective Docker Container Debugging

- **Maintain minimal Docker images**: Simplify debugging by reducing the number of components within your Docker images.

- **Use version-specific tags**: This ensures that environments are consistent and that specific versions can be targeted for debugging.

- **Implement health checks**: These can help monitor container health and automatically recover unresponsive applications.

- **Employ multi-stage builds**: Reduce complexity in production containers by separating build and deployment environments, minimizing potential bug sources.

Conclusion

Mastering advanced debugging techniques for Docker containers is key to managing and maintaining stable and efficient Dockerized applications. By combining Docker-specific commands with general debugging tools, developers and system administrators can effectively resolve issues, ensuring smooth operation and optimal performance of their containerized applications.

Troubleshooting complex Docker networking and storage issues

Troubleshooting complex Docker networking and storage issues is crucial for ensuring the optimal performance and reliability of applications running in Docker environments. This article outlines methods to identify and resolve such issues, with a focus on the specialized techniques and tools that facilitate effective troubleshooting.

Understanding Docker Networking and Storage Complexities

Docker networking enables communication among containers and between containers and external networks. It supports various network drivers like **bridge**, **host**, **overlay**, and **macvlan**, each suited to different operational needs. Problems typically arise from network misconfigurations, overlapping settings among containers, or driver-specific limitations.

For Docker storage, challenges mainly revolve around data persistence, volume management, and storage driver efficiency. These issues are pivotal as they directly affect data integrity and application performance.

Effective Strategies for Troubleshooting Docker Networking

1. Diagnosing Connectivity Problems

Network connectivity issues can prevent containers from communicating internally or externally. Understanding the network setup is the first step in troubleshooting.

- **Inspecting Network Configurations**: Using **docker network inspect** helps provide a comprehensive view of an individual network's configuration and health.

Example Command:

```
docker network inspect bridge
```

- **Verifying Container Connections**: Ensure each container is correctly connected to the intended network and assigned the appropriate IP addresses.

Example Command:

```
docker inspect --format '{{ .NetworkSettings.Networks }}' container_name_or_id
```

2. Resolving Port Conflicts

When containers are set up to use the same host ports, conflicts can occur, often preventing containers from launching.

- **Identifying Port Usage**: Checking the port mappings of all active containers can highlight any existing conflicts.

Example Command:

```
docker ps
```

- **Adjusting Port Settings**: Modify container port settings to resolve overlaps, ensuring each container has unique port assignments.

3. Leveraging Advanced Network Drivers

For complex networking requirements, such as across multiple Docker hosts, switching to an advanced network driver like **overlay** might be necessary.

- **Creating and Managing Overlay Networks**: This is particularly useful in environments utilizing Docker Swarm.

Example Command:

```
docker network create -d overlay my_overlay
```

Strategies for Addressing Docker Storage Challenges

1. Ensuring Data Persistence

Loss of data upon container restart is typically due to misconfigured or non-persistent storage settings.

- **Proper Volume Configuration**: Setting up persistent volumes ensures data remains intact across container restarts.

Example Command:

```
docker run -v /my/data:/data my_image
```

2. Optimizing Volume Performance

Performance issues with volumes often stem from suboptimal storage driver configurations or the nature of the underlying storage hardware.

- **Inspecting and Tuning Volumes**: Reviewing volume configurations and adjusting them can enhance performance.

Example Command:

```
docker volume inspect my_volume
```

3. Addressing File Permission Issues

Incorrect file permissions or ownership can prevent containers from accessing mounted volumes.

- **Configuring Permissions and Ownership**: Ensuring the right permissions and ownership are set on host directories and files used by Docker.

Example Commands:

```
chmod -R 775 /path/to/data
chown -R user:group /path/to/data
```

Recommended Tools and Practices

- **Network Monitoring Tools**: Implementing tools like Wireshark or tcpdump can help capture and analyze packet transfers, useful in diagnosing network issues.

- **I/O Performance Monitoring**: Tools such as **iostat** or **iotop** can be instrumental in monitoring and diagnosing storage performance issues.

- **Routine Data Backups**: Maintaining regular backups of data volumes can safeguard against data loss and facilitate quick recovery from storage-related issues.

Conclusion

Navigating the complexities of Docker networking and storage requires a blend of careful configuration management, the use of sophisticated diagnostic tools, and adherence to best practices. By systematically applying these troubleshooting strategies, developers and system administrators can effectively resolve issues and maintain the high performance and reliability of their Dockerized applications.

Case studies of real-world problem solving

Case studies offer profound insights into practical problem-solving across various industries, providing a clear perspective on the challenges faced, solutions implemented, and the outcomes achieved. This article presents a collection of real-world case studies that illustrate how different sectors have successfully addressed complex issues through innovative strategies.

Case Study 1: Enhancing Efficiency in Retail Logistics

Background: A prominent global retailer was experiencing inefficiencies in its logistics operations, leading to inventory discrepancies and delays in product deliveries.

Challenge: The retailer's existing logistics system was inadequate for predicting accurate inventory needs, resulting in frequent overstocking and shortages.

Solution:

- **Advanced Predictive Analytics**: The company integrated artificial intelligence and machine learning to refine its demand forecasting methods. These technologies utilized past sales data, alongside external factors like weather conditions and economic trends, to enhance prediction accuracy.

- **Automated Inventory Management**: Inventory replenishment processes were automated to allow real-time updates and automatic ordering, minimizing human error and delays.

Results: The retailer saw a 25% reduction in inventory costs and an increase in customer satisfaction due to more reliable stock levels and quicker fulfillment times.

Case Study 2: Streamlining Data Processes in Healthcare

Background: A healthcare provider was struggling with the management of vast amounts of unstructured patient data scattered across multiple systems.

Challenge: The fragmented nature of the data storage made it difficult to efficiently access and leverage patient information for medical care.

Solution:

- **Unified Data Management System**: A centralized data management platform was developed to standardize and consolidate patient data into a single system.

- **Cloud-Based Solutions**: By adopting cloud technologies, the provider enhanced the accessibility and scalability of the data storage solutions.

- **Enhanced Security Protocols**: Strong encryption and robust access controls were implemented to secure sensitive patient data.

Results: The new system simplified the management of patient data, ensured greater data security, and provided medical staff with quicker access to necessary information, thereby improving patient care services.

Case Study 3: Advanced Risk Management in Finance

Background: A financial institution faced challenges in managing risks associated with market volatility and regulatory demands.

Challenge: The existing risk models were insufficient, lacking the agility to incorporate real-time data and adapt to new regulatory requirements.

Solution:

- **Real-time Market Data Analysis**: The institution developed a system capable of processing live market data for immediate analysis.

- **Sophisticated Risk Modeling**: New statistical and machine learning models were introduced to predict and mitigate potential risks more effectively.

- **Automated Compliance Systems**: Systems were automated to ensure adherence to international finance regulations, reducing human error and oversight.

Results: These innovations enabled the firm to react quickly to market changes, reduce risk exposure, and maintain compliance more efficiently.

Case Study 4: Scaling IT Infrastructure in a Tech Startup

Background: A fast-growing tech startup was encountering significant challenges in scaling its IT infrastructure to meet increasing user demand.

Challenge: The initial IT setup could not sustain the rapid growth in user base, causing service interruptions and poor user experiences.

Solution:

- **Adopting Scalable Cloud Infrastructure**: The startup migrated to a cloud infrastructure designed to scale automatically with increased traffic.

- **Streamlined Deployment Processes**: A continuous deployment framework was implemented to facilitate frequent updates with minimal downtime.

- **Ongoing Performance Monitoring**: Continuous monitoring solutions were put in place to track system performance and identify operational bottlenecks promptly.

Results: This strategic overhaul reduced service disruptions, accommodated growth efficiently, and enhanced the overall quality of service.

Conclusion

The case studies discussed highlight the effectiveness of applying targeted, innovative solutions to resolve industry-specific challenges. Whether through enhancing logistic operations with AI, centralizing healthcare data on cloud platforms, employing advanced risk management strategies in finance, or scaling IT operations in technology startups, these examples show that thoughtful strategy implementation can lead to substantial improvements in operational efficiency and customer satisfaction. Each case study serves as a testament to the transformative power of adopting new technologies and processes in response to evolving business needs and market conditions.

Chapter Fourteen

The Docker Community and Future Trends

Engaging with the Docker community for support and collaboration

Engaging with the Docker community offers substantial benefits, providing a platform for support, learning, and sharing within a network of professionals. Docker's ecosystem includes a diverse array of users, from developers to system admins, all contributing to and leveraging the collective knowledge base. This article explores how involvement in this community can enhance one's Docker expertise, resolve challenges, and offer opportunities for collaboration.

Advantages of Docker Community Involvement

1. **Technical Support**: Docker's forums and real-time chat channels are prime resources for troubleshooting assistance, where experienced users often provide insights and solutions to complex issues.

2. **Educational Growth**: Regular interactions with experienced Docker users accelerate the learning process, keeping participants at the forefront of Docker technology and practices.

3. **Networking Opportunities**: Active participation in the community can lead to connections with industry peers and thought leaders, opening doors to potential collaborations and career advancements.

4. **Influencing Docker Evolution**: Community feedback and contributions play a crucial role in shaping the future directions and improvements of Docker technologies.

Strategies for Engaging with the Docker Community

Active Participation in Online Forums and Chats

- **Docker Forums**: These forums are a hub for Docker users to pose questions, exchange knowledge, and provide solutions specific to varied Docker challenges.

Example Interaction:

```
User Query: "What are the best practices for managing Docker volumes?"
Experienced User Response: "Always prefer named volumes for data persistence and ease of
    management, and regularly back up your volumes."
```

- **Docker Community Slack**: This platform facilitates dynamic exchanges with other Docker users, providing a space for real-time problem solving and networking.

Contributing to Docker's Open Source Projects

- **GitHub Contributions**: Engaging with Docker's GitHub repositories allows users to contribute code, suggest features, or enhance documentation, directly influencing the development of Docker.

Example GitHub Contribution:

```
git clone https://github.com/docker/docker.git
cd docker
# Implement changes or improvements
git commit -am "Refine volume management functionality"
git push
```

- **Documentation Enhancement**: Contributing to Docker's documentation can help clarify functionalities and extend its usability to a broader audience.

Engaging in Docker-Focused Events

- **DockerCon**: Attending DockerCon exposes participants to the latest Docker innovations and best practices through sessions conducted by experts.

- **Local Community Meetups**: These gatherings are opportunities to share experiences and learn from local Docker practitioners in a more informal setting.

Leveraging Blogs and Social Media

- **Blogging About Docker**: Sharing personal experiences, tips, or comprehensive guides through blogs helps disseminate knowledge and establish oneself as a thought leader in the Docker community.

- **Engaging on Social Media**: Regular interaction with Docker's social media feeds keeps one informed about the latest updates and community news.

Community Engagement Best Practices

1. **Professional Conduct**: Respectful and constructive engagement is essential for a healthy community dynamic.

2. **Continuous Learning**: Keeping up-to-date with Docker's latest features and community insights ensures relevant and effective community interactions.

3. **Sharing Expertise**: Contributing solutions and advice not only aids others but also enhances one's profile within the community.

Conclusion

Participating in the Docker community is highly beneficial, fostering not just individual growth but also contributing to the broader Docker ecosystem. By engaging through problem-solving forums, contributing to open-source projects, participating in events, and sharing insights online, community members can gain significant technical expertise, network with peers, and influence the development of Docker. This active engagement helps cultivate a rich environment of collaboration and innovation.

Current trends and future developments in Docker technology

Docker technology has significantly transformed the deployment and management landscape, solidifying its role as a cornerstone in the containerization domain. As this technology continues to evolve, it aligns with emerging trends and future projections that suggest a trajectory towards more advanced, secure, and scalable container solutions. This article explores these ongoing developments and future directions in Docker technology.

Current Trends in Docker Technology

1. Enhanced Security Measures

Security remains paramount as Docker containers often host critical applications. Recent advancements show a trend towards strengthening security protocols:

- **Non-root User Containers**: Efforts are being made to enable containers to operate without requiring root privileges, reducing potential security vulnerabilities.

- **Advanced Image Scanning**: Docker Scan, integrated with Docker Desktop and Docker Hub, offers automated scanning of images for vulnerabilities at both development and deployment stages.

2. Deeper Integration with DevOps and CI Tools

Docker's compatibility with continuous integration and continuous deployment (CI/CD) pipelines is enhancing, thereby smoothing the development cycles for quicker, more reliable delivery. Tools such as Jenkins, GitLab, and GitHub Actions are embedding Docker to ensure uniformity across environments from development through to production.

3. Widespread Adoption of Kubernetes for Orchestration

While Docker Swarm is still supported, Kubernetes has become the preferred orchestration solution within the Docker ecosystem, attributed to its scalability and robust community support. Docker Desktop includes Kubernetes support, allowing seamless local development and testing.

4. Expanding Presence in Cloud Platforms

As cloud-native development ascends, Docker's role continues to grow, with major cloud platforms like AWS, Azure, and Google Cloud offering extensive Docker integrations. These integrations simplify container management, allowing developers to focus more on their core development work without the operational overhead.

5. Emergence in Edge Computing and IoT

Docker is proving crucial in edge computing where lightweight, reliable containers are vital. It ensures consistent deployments across diverse environments, crucial for IoT applications that need to operate under varied conditions. Docker facilitates remote updates and management, minimizing downtime for countless devices.

Future Developments in Docker Technology

1. Integration with Serverless Computing

Looking ahead, Docker is likely to blend more with serverless computing frameworks, offering even lighter container solutions that are optimized for ephemeral, event-driven architectures. This could further reduce operational complexity and enhance scalability.

2. Support for AI and Machine Learning

With AI and ML becoming ubiquitous, Docker is expected to play a bigger role in ensuring reproducible environments for developing and deploying machine learning models. Future enhancements may include Docker images and configurations specially designed to optimize AI and ML workflows.

3. Focus on Sustainability and Efficient Resource Use

As the focus on sustainability intensifies, Docker's role in optimizing resource usage to minimize energy consumption will become more critical. Future Docker updates may incorporate smarter resource management tools that help reduce the carbon footprint of digital operations.

4. Advancements in Platform Independence

Docker's core promise of "build once, run anywhere" might expand to ensure seamless operation across an even broader array of platforms. This could entail more sophisticated solutions for managing cross-platform dependencies and configurations, simplifying deployments across diverse ecosystems.

Conclusion

The path of Docker technology is marked by a consistent drive towards innovation influenced by the need for more robust security, operational efficiency, and adaptability. The integration of Docker with cutting-edge trends like serverless architectures, AI, and IoT, alongside its strengthening foothold in cloud and edge computing, underscores its enduring relevance and potential for future growth. As Docker technology continues to evolve, it promises to enhance how businesses deploy and manage applications, making it an essential tool for modern software strategies.

Preparing for enterprise-grade Docker deployments

Deploying Docker in an enterprise setting requires meticulous planning and strategic implementation to ensure that container deployments are secure, scalable, and integrate seamlessly with existing systems. This article provides a comprehensive guide on how to prepare for enterprise-grade Docker deployments, emphasizing essential considerations and practices for a successful rollout.

Initial Planning and Infrastructure Evaluation

Needs Assessment: Begin with a detailed evaluation of your organization's specific requirements including scalability, security, compliance, and performance. Understanding how Docker will fit into and enhance your existing infrastructure is key.

Infrastructure Preparation: Check your current IT infrastructure's capability to support Docker containers. This may involve upgrading servers, enhancing storage capabilities, or improving network configurations to handle the anticipated demands of Docker deployment.

Architectural Design for Docker Implementation

Designing the Docker Architecture: Develop an architecture that meets your organization's needs, selecting an appropriate orchestration tool like Kubernetes, Docker Swarm, or Apache Mesos based on the complexity and scale required.

Ensuring System Resilience: Design your Docker architecture with high availability in mind. Implement strategies across multiple data centers or clouds to provide failover and disaster recovery solutions. Plan for regular backups of Docker images and configuration settings to mitigate data loss.

Security Measures and Regulatory Compliance

Securing Containers: Adopt stringent security practices from the start. Utilize secure base images, conduct regular vulnerability assessments, manage container access, and keep containers updated with the latest security patches.

Network Security Protocols: Establish robust network security policies to control traffic to and from containers. Utilize Docker's network drivers to create isolated networks that segment container traffic and enhance security.

Compliance with Regulations: Align your Docker operations with applicable regulations by setting up compliant logging and monitoring systems and ensuring data protection measures are in place.

Resource Management Strategies

Resource Allocation Policies: Set limits on container resources to prevent any container from monopolizing system resources, which can be specified when starting containers using Docker.

Example Command:

```
docker run -d --name app_container --memory=4g --cpus=2 my_app_image
```

Monitoring and Optimization: Leverage tools like Prometheus for system monitoring and either the ELK Stack or Fluentd for logging to gain insights into container performance and health.

Integrating Docker with CI/CD Pipelines

CI/CD Integration: Embed Docker into your continuous integration and deployment pipelines to automate the build, test, and deployment processes of containerized applications, ensuring consistent and error-free deployments.

Infrastructure as Code: Use tools such as Docker Compose, Ansible, or Terraform to manage Docker configurations and deployments systematically. This practice supports scalability and manageability.

Example Docker Compose Usage:

```yaml
version: '3.8'
services:
  api:
    image: my_api:latest
    deploy:
      replicas: 4
      resources:
        limits:
          cpus: '1.0'
          memory: 100M
      restart_policy:
        condition: on-failure
    ports:
      - "1234:1234"
    networks:
      - apinet
networks:
  apinet:
```

Staff Training and External Support

Team Training: Regularly train and update your IT team on Docker technologies and best practices. Ensure they understand the specifics of your Docker setup and how it integrates with the broader IT environment.

Engaging External Support: For larger deployments, consider engaging with Docker Enterprise or other specialized vendors for expert support and services.

Conclusion

Successfully deploying Docker at an enterprise level involves strategic preparation and execution across multiple domains from infrastructure readiness and security to integration with development pipelines and staff training. By following these guidelines, organizations can harness the full potential of

Docker to streamline and enhance their operations while ensuring that the deployments are secure, efficient, and compliant with industry standards.

Conclusion

Recap of the skills and knowledge gained

Reflecting on educational or professional development is crucial for solidifying acquired skills and knowledge. This recapitulation aims to provide an exhaustive review of the critical competencies developed, how they have been applied effectively, and their impact on professional growth.

Core Competencies Developed

1. Technical Mastery

A significant level of expertise has been developed in key technical areas, particularly in programming languages like Python, JavaScript, and SQL. These skills are vital for addressing complex tasks in software development and IT operations.

Illustrative Python Example:

```python
def find_max(numbers):
    max_number = numbers[0]
    for number in numbers:
        if number > max_number:
            max_number = number
    return max_number
```

This algorithm demonstrates the capability to implement solutions for common programming problems, such as identifying the maximum number in a list.

2. Analytical Proficiency

The ability to analyze problems, process data effectively, and make informed decisions has been greatly enhanced. Skills in utilizing tools such as Excel, R, and various data visualization software have been honed to conduct thorough data analyses and presentations.

3. Project Management Acumen

Competencies in managing project timelines, resource allocation, risk assessment, and quality assurance have been strengthened. Familiarity with Agile and Scrum methodologies has been acquired, facilitating the management of projects with agility and effectiveness.

4. Interpersonal and Communication Skills

Through teamwork and collaborative projects, skills in communication, negotiation, and conflict resolution have been refined, ensuring effective interactions and task execution within teams.

Application of Skills

The acquired skills have been leveraged in several real-world scenarios:

- **Software Creation**: Applying programming skills to develop functional software that aligns with user needs.

- **Strategic Data Analysis**: Using analytical abilities to extract actionable insights from data, significantly impacting strategic decisions.

- **Project Oversight**: Employing project management skills to lead diverse teams and ensure the successful execution of projects.

Impact on Professional Growth

The integration of these skills has markedly enhanced professional capabilities:

- **Expanded Career Paths**: The advanced technical and managerial skills have facilitated access to new opportunities in data analysis, software development, and project management.

- **Improved Job Performance**: A deeper understanding of technical and project tasks has led to enhanced job performance and output quality.

- **Leadership Opportunities**: Enhanced management and communication skills have enabled leadership roles, managing teams, and steering projects to fruition.

Areas for Further Enhancement

While substantial progress has been made, there are areas where additional development is necessary:

- **Ongoing Technical Education**: Continuous learning in emerging technologies and advanced programming is essential.

- **Advanced Data Science Techniques**: Further knowledge in data analysis, statistics, and machine learning will enhance competitiveness.

- **Understanding of Global Project Management**: Learning international project management standards is critical for handling global projects effectively.

Conclusion

The skills and knowledge accrued thus far lay a solid foundation for continued professional development, enhancing current capabilities and opening avenues for future growth. The next steps involve deepening existing skills and exploring new areas to stay relevant and effective in a dynamically changing professional landscape. This ongoing commitment to learning and development is crucial for sustained success and professional satisfaction.

How to apply these optimizations in various environments

Optimizing across different environments is essential to maximize performance, minimize costs, and ensure scalability. This process involves tailoring general improvements to fit specific contexts such as development, testing, production, and cloud-based environments. This article discusses a systematic approach for implementing these optimizations, with techniques and examples illustrating how to adapt these strategies effectively across various settings.

Understanding Optimization Categories

Before applying specific optimizations, it's critical to identify the types of improvements needed:

- **Performance Enhancements**: This includes refining code, optimizing database interactions, and reducing response times.

- **Resource Efficiency**: Managing CPU, memory, and storage to utilize them effectively without excess.

- **Security Measures**: Strengthening security to safeguard operations, particularly in environments exposed to external threats like public and hybrid clouds.

- **Cost Efficiency**: Identifying inefficiencies in resource usage to cut operational expenses.

Development Environment Optimizations

Development environments focus on rapid iteration and creativity. Optimizations here aim to accelerate development cycles and enhance testing effectiveness.

- **Code Refinement**: Using tools to identify and refactor inefficient code segments enhances both performance and maintainability.

Example: Utilizing Python's **cProfile** to pinpoint performance issues.

```python
import cProfile
import re

def sample_function():
    return re.match('foo.*', 'foobar').group()

cProfile.run('sample_function()')
```

- **Automated Testing Locally**: Setting up automated tests to detect issues early, minimizing bugs in more critical stages.

Example: Creating an automated test using pytest for a Python application.

Testing Environment Tactics

Testing environments require stability and should mirror production settings closely. Applying optimizations here ensures applications perform under load as expected.

- **Load Testing**: Using tools to simulate user traffic helps understand application behavior under stress.

- **Appropriate Resource Allocation**: Aligning resources in testing to reflect production settings aids in accurate performance evaluation.

Production Environment Enhancements

Optimizations in production are vital for boosting performance and minimizing downtime.

- **Database Tuning**: Regularly optimizing queries and maintaining databases ensure swift data access.

Example SQL: Reviewing and optimizing slow queries.

```
EXPLAIN SELECT * FROM orders WHERE date >= '2021-01-01';
```

- **Implementing Caching**: Using solutions like Redis or Memcached reduces database load and speeds up response times.

- **Utilizing CDNs**: Deploying CDNs enhances content accessibility and decreases latency.

Cloud-Based Optimizations

Cloud environments offer unique optimization opportunities, especially regarding scalability and cost management.

- **Dynamic Scaling**: Leveraging auto-scaling features of cloud platforms ensures resources are efficiently adjusted according to demand.

- **Effective Cost Management**: Utilizing cloud vendor tools to monitor and manage expenditures helps avoid unnecessary spending.

Example: Configuring AWS EC2 auto-scaling to efficiently manage workloads.

```
aws autoscaling create-auto-scaling-group --auto-scaling-group-name my-group \
    --launch-configuration-name my-config --min-size 1 --max-size 10 --desired-capacity 5 \
    --vpc-zone-identifier subnet-12345678
```

Cross-Environment Optimization Best Practices

- **Regular Monitoring**: Consistent monitoring across all settings ensures optimizations are effective and identifies areas needing attention.

- **Feedback Integration**: Creating channels for feedback from production back to development informs ongoing development and testing phases.

- **Thorough Documentation and Regular Review**: Keeping detailed records of implemented changes and periodically reviewing their impacts helps refine strategies and adjust as necessary.

Conclusion

Successfully applying optimizations in various environments demands an in-depth understanding of each setting's specific requirements and challenges. By customizing strategies to suit development, testing, production, and cloud scenarios, organizations can achieve enhanced performance, efficiency, and cost-effectiveness, while maintaining robust security and compliance. Continuous monitoring, feedback, and adaptation are crucial to navigating the evolving landscape of technological capabilities and business needs.

Preview of advanced topics in the upcoming book

The forthcoming book delves into a range of sophisticated subjects designed to expand the reader's understanding and capabilities within contemporary technological realms. This preview highlights the intricate topics to be covered, tailored for an audience already versed in foundational concepts, and showcases how these advanced discussions can be applied in practice.

In-Depth Exploration of Advanced Algorithms

The book begins with a comprehensive examination of complex algorithms essential to modern computing. It discusses graph theory algorithms, advanced machine learning models, and techniques for processing data in real time, complete with code examples that bring these concepts to life.

Example Topic: Graph Theory Algorithms

- **Usage**: Solving problems related to network flows, shortest paths, and connectivity.

- **Code Example**:

```python
import networkx as nx

G = nx.DiGraph()
G.add_edge('A', 'B', capacity=10.0)
flow_value, flow_dict = nx.maximum_flow(G, 'A', 'B')
print("Flow Value:", flow_value)
```

This segment aims to demonstrate how critical these algorithms are for developing complex network systems and efficient data structures.

Frontiers of Artificial Intelligence

The book will cover the cutting edge of artificial intelligence, including sections on deep learning, reinforcement learning, and generative adversarial networks (GANs), with an emphasis on their practical uses and the ethical considerations they raise.

Example Topic: Generative Adversarial Networks (GANs)

- **Applications**: Enhancing images, augmenting data, and refining model training methods.

- **Sample Code**:

```
from keras.models import Sequential
from keras.layers import Dense, LeakyReLU, BatchNormalization, Reshape
from keras.optimizers import Adam
```

```
# Example code for initializing a GAN
def build_generator():
    model = Sequential()
    model.add(Dense(256, input_shape=(100,)))
    model.add(LeakyReLU(alpha=0.2))
    model.add(BatchNormalization(momentum=0.8))
    model.add(Dense(512))
    model.add(LeakyReLU(alpha=0.2))
    model.add(BatchNormalization(momentum=0.8))
    model.add(Dense(1024))
    model.add(LeakyReLU(alpha=0.2))
    model.add(BatchNormalization(momentum=0.8))
    model.add(Dense(784, activation='tanh'))
    model.add(Reshape((28, 28)))
    return model
```

The insights from this section will enable readers to apply AI technologies across diverse industries effectively.

Advanced Cybersecurity Methods

Addressing the ever-evolving digital threats requires increasingly sophisticated cybersecurity measures. This section discusses the latest in cryptography, blockchain applications for security, and advanced network security protocols.

Example Topic: Quantum Cryptography

- **Usage**: Implementing secure communication based on quantum mechanics.

379

- **Insight**: Exploring the foundations of quantum key distribution (QKD) and its future impact on secure communications.

High-Performance and Parallel Computing

High-performance computing (HPC) and strategies for parallel processing are also critical themes, focusing on utilizing modern computing resources to enhance performance and efficiency.

Example Topic: GPU Acceleration

- **Usage**: Utilizing GPU hardware to accelerate complex computations and data-intensive tasks.

- **Code Example**:

```python
import tensorflow as tf
print(tf.config.list_physical_devices('GPU'))
```

Innovations in Cloud Computing

The final discussions address advanced cloud computing concepts, including serverless architectures, enhanced cloud security measures, and the integration of hybrid cloud solutions.

Example Topic: Serverless Computing

- **Usage**: Developing applications that automatically scale without managing servers.

- **Considerations**: Evaluating the cost-effectiveness and scalability challenges of serverless architectures.

Conclusion

The book promises to equip readers with a deep and actionable understanding of these advanced topics, preparing them for the challenges of applying such knowledge in real-world settings. Through a blend of theoretical insights and practical applications, it aims to provide a holistic view of the current and future landscape of technology. Readers will emerge with not only a broader understanding but also practical techniques that can be directly applied to their professional and research endeavors.

Introduction

Recap of essential Docker concepts from previous books

As we progress into the detailed exploration of Docker in "Docker: A Pro-Level Guide to Cutting-Edge Techniques in Docker Performance Tuning," it is essential to revisit the fundamental Docker concepts previously discussed in earlier volumes. This summary ensures readers are equipped with the necessary foundational knowledge to engage with more complex subject matter. The content will recap Docker's key functionalities, architecture, and common practices, offering a thorough review of critical elements foundational to Docker proficiency.

Overview of Docker

Docker simplifies the process of developing, deploying, and running applications using containers. These containers package an application with all its dependencies, ensuring it runs seamlessly across any Linux system, irrespective of varying configurations or setups.

Docker Containers and Images

Understanding containers and images is crucial as they represent core components of Docker's functionality:

- **Docker Images**: These are immutable files that contain all necessary components such as source code, libraries, and dependencies needed for an application to run. Think of an image as a blueprint (image) from which a house (container) is built.

Example Command: Building an image from a Dockerfile:

```
docker build -t myapp:1.0 .
```

- **Docker Containers**: These are executable instances of images. Containers run in isolation but share the OS kernel, launching quickly and consuming minimal resources.

Example Command: Starting a Docker container:

```
docker run -d --name my-running-app myapp:1.0
```

Docker Architecture

Grasping Docker's architecture is essential for mastering its use. Docker operates on a client-server model:

- **Docker Daemon**: This server-side component manages Docker containers, handling tasks and communications between containers and the Docker client through a REST API.

- **Docker Client**: The user interface for Docker, where commands are entered and transmitted to the Docker daemon for execution.

Docker Networking and Storage

Networking and storage management are vital for Docker functionality:

- **Docker Networks**: Docker's networking features enable containers to communicate within and outside the Docker environment. Docker supports several network types, like bridge, host, and overlay, which simplify the setup of communication pathways between containers.

Example Command: Exploring a Docker network:

```
docker network inspect bridge
```

- **Docker Volumes**: For data persistence, Docker utilizes volumes which are directories on the host system managed by Docker and are isolated from the core filesystem.

Example Command: Managing Docker volumes:

```
docker volume create my-volume
docker run -d --name devtest -v my-volume:/app nginx:latest
```

Dockerfile and Docker Compose

- **Dockerfile**: A script comprised of successive commands used to assemble an image automatically.

- **Docker Compose**: This tool manages multi-container setups using a YAML file to define services, networks, and volumes, streamlining the configuration and instantiation of all components with one command.

Example Docker Compose Configuration:

```yaml
version: '3'
services:
  web:
    build: .
    ports:
      - "5000:5000"
  redis:
    image: "redis:alpine"
```

Conclusion

This overview reiterates the indispensable Docker concepts that form the groundwork for the advanced techniques discussed in the upcoming chapters. With a robust understanding of these basics, readers will be well-prepared to navigate the complexities of optimizing Docker deployments, enhancing both their theoretical knowledge and practical skills in Docker applications. This foundation is crucial for both newcomers and seasoned Docker users who aim to elevate their capabilities in Docker's performance tuning.

Introduction to high-performance Docker environments

Setting up high-performance Docker environments is crucial for organizations that depend on quick, dependable, and scalable application delivery. This guide provides an introductory framework for developers and IT specialists to enhance Docker's capabilities to support demanding operational needs effectively. Below, we explore the necessary components, configurations, and techniques to maximize Docker performance.

Fundamentals of High-Performance Docker Environments

High-performance Docker environments are engineered to manage resources efficiently, ensuring optimal speed and reliability for containerized applications under various usage scenarios. These environments are vital for applications that require immediate data processing, consistent uptime, and low response times.

Essential Components for High-Performance Docker

Creating a robust Docker setup involves several critical components:

- **Robust Hardware**: The foundation of high performance is strong hardware capable of handling intensive tasks. This includes multi-core CPUs, ample RAM, and fast SSDs to reduce input/output latency.

- **Optimized Docker Images**: Tailoring Docker images to be as lightweight as possible—by using minimal base images and removing unnecessary packages—helps reduce container startup times and conserve resources.

- **Enhanced Networking Solutions**: Optimizing Docker's networking capabilities is essential for reducing latency and maximizing data throughput.

Custom bridge networks or high-performance networking plugins can be beneficial.

Example Command:

```
docker network create --driver bridge --subnet 192.168.1.0/24 high-perf-net
```

- **Scalable Storage Configurations**: Employing fast, scalable storage solutions, like direct-attached SSD storage or distributed filesystems that excel in high I/O operations, is crucial.

Performance-Enhancing Configurations

To ensure Docker operates at peak efficiency, specific configurations and tuning are necessary:

- **Resource Constraints**: Setting CPU and memory limits on containers can prevent any single application from consuming disproportionate resources, ensuring stable performance across all services.

Example Command:

```
docker run -it --cpus="1.5" --memory="1000m" ubuntu /bin/bash
```

- **Lifecycle Management Optimizations**: Implementing Docker features such as restart **policies** and **health checks** helps manage containers effectively, promoting uptime and reliability.

Example Health Check in Docker Compose:

```
healthcheck:
  test: ["CMD-SHELL", "curl -f http://localhost || exit 1"]
  interval: 30s
  timeout: 10s
  retries: 5
```

- **Performance Monitoring Tools**: Tools like Prometheus and Grafana are instrumental in monitoring Docker performance, providing insights that help fine-tune operations in real time.

High-Performance Best Practices

Maintaining high performance involves consistent best practices:

- **Routine Maintenance**: Regular updates to Docker and all containerized applications ensure access to the latest features and security enhancements.

- **Efficient Security Measures**: Implementing security protocols that do not degrade performance, such as streamlined encryption processes, is essential.

- **Effective Load Distribution**: Utilizing load balancers to evenly distribute requests can prevent overloading individual containers, aiding performance consistency across services.

Advanced Performance Strategies

For those looking to advance Docker's capabilities:

- **Cross-Host Networking**: Employing orchestration tools like Docker Swarm or Kubernetes facilitates container management across multiple hosts, enhancing load management and redundancy.

- **Leveraging GPU Resources**: For computation-heavy tasks, configuring Docker containers to access GPU resources can significantly boost processing power.

Example Command:

```
docker run -it --gpus all nvidia/cuda:11.0-base nvidia-smi
```

Conclusion

Developing a high-performance Docker environment entails a comprehensive understanding of Docker's capabilities, along with strategic configuration and management to ensure resource efficiency. By optimizing both the hardware and Docker configurations, implementing robust resource management practices, and utilizing advanced monitoring tools, organizations can construct durable, scalable, and highly efficient environments that meet the demands of high-performance applications. This foundational knowledge empowers IT professionals to transform their Docker setups to accommodate advanced operational requirements effectively.

Overview of advanced performance tuning concepts covered in this book

This book delves deeply into advanced performance tuning techniques for Docker, aimed at professionals seeking to push their Docker environments to new heights of efficiency and responsiveness. It elaborates on a variety of sophisticated strategies for refining Docker containers, networking, and storage, alongside comprehensive methods for effective monitoring and systematic troubleshooting. Below is an outline of the pivotal themes and methodologies that will be meticulously explored throughout this guide, providing a framework for readers to customize Docker performance enhancements according to their specific operational demands.

Enhanced Container Performance Techniques

Optimizing the performance of Docker containers involves detailed adjustments related to how resources are allocated and managed. This book will introduce complex techniques to ensure container performance is maximized, covering:

- **CPU and Memory Allocation**: Detailed strategies for assigning CPU cores and memory to containers to ensure critical applications perform at their best. Docker allows for precise resource allocation to balance loads effectively.

Example Command:

```
docker run -it --cpus="2" --memory="4g" my-application
```

- **Kernel Adjustments**: Techniques for tweaking kernel parameters that impact the performance of containers, such as modifying I/O scheduler settings or enhancing the network stack to support higher data throughput.

Network Performance Tuning

As networking is crucial, especially in distributed systems, this book explores advanced network configurations and tuning strategies to improve data transfer efficiency and secure container communications. Topics include:

- **Choosing Network Drivers**: Analysis of Docker network drivers and configurations like overlay or custom bridge networks that optimize communication between containers.

Example Configuration:

```
networks:
  custom_network:
    driver: bridge
```

- **Network Enhancements**: Implementing traffic shaping, adjusting port forwarding rules, and employing updated TCP/IP stacks to streamline network performance.

Optimizing Storage Solutions

For applications requiring frequent disk access, optimizing storage performance is crucial. This section will discuss:

- **Volume Configuration**: Strategies for Docker volume management to boost I/O performance, including choices between bind mounts and volumes for data persistence.

Example Command:

```
docker volume create --driver local --opt type=tmpfs --opt device=tmpfs optimized_volume
```

- **Utilizing Efficient File Systems**: Advantages of using sophisticated file systems such as ZFS or Btrfs in Docker setups to enhance data operation speeds.

Advanced Monitoring and Logging

Maintaining optimal performance requires robust monitoring and systematic logging. This book presents:

- **Monitoring Tools**: Using powerful tools like Prometheus or Docker's native monitoring capabilities to track real-time performance metrics of Docker containers.

Example Setup:

```
docker run -d -p 9090:9090 prom/prometheus
```

- **Centralized Logging Approaches**: Setting up centralized logging with systems like the ELK Stack or Fluentd to consolidate logs for easier performance analysis and troubleshooting.

Profiling and Debugging

Identifying and addressing performance issues is key to maintaining efficiency. This book will guide readers through:

- **Profiling Containers**: Employing advanced profiling tools to gather detailed performance data.

- **Identifying Bottlenecks**: Techniques for pinpointing issues related to CPU, memory, or I/O using Docker-specific commands and external tools.

Conclusion

The book equips readers with a thorough set of advanced techniques and tools for tuning and maintaining high-performance Docker environments. By integrating the discussed concepts, professionals will not only elevate their Docker operations but will also acquire the skills necessary to proactively tackle complex performance challenges. Each chapter offers actionable advice and practical examples, enabling readers to apply their newfound knowledge to enhance their Docker setups effectively.

Chapter One

Advanced Container Architecture

Designing containers for high performance and efficiency

Designing Docker containers for high performance and efficiency is essential in today's technology landscape where speed and resource management are paramount. This guide outlines key practices for optimizing Docker container architecture, ensuring they operate efficiently under various loads. We will explore container design, configuration, and management strategies to maximize their performance.

Core Principles of High-Performance Container Design

1. Optimal Base Image Selection:

Choosing the right base image is crucial for container performance. Lightweight images such as Alpine Linux can dramatically reduce the overhead, enhancing startup times and operational efficiency compared to bulkier images like Ubuntu.

Example: Adopting Alpine Linux

```
FROM alpine:3.12
RUN apk add --no-cache python3 py3-pip
COPY . /app
WORKDIR /app
RUN pip install -r requirements.txt
CMD ["python3", "app.py"]
```

This Dockerfile demonstrates using Alpine Linux to minimize image size while maintaining necessary functionalities.

2. Layer Management in Dockerfiles:

Effective management of Docker image layers can streamline builds and minimize image sizes. Merging frequently changed layers can reduce build times and resource consumption.

Example: Streamlining layers

```
RUN apt-get update && apt-get install -y \
    package1 \
    package2 \
    && rm -rf /var/lib/apt/lists/*
```

This method consolidates several layer updates into a single instruction, optimizing the build process.

Configuration Enhancements

3. Resource Allocation Controls:

Setting resource limits is fundamental to preventing resource hogging by any single container, ensuring a balanced distribution of system resources.

Example: Configuring resource limits

```
docker run -d --name constrained-container --memory=500m --cpus=1.5 nginx
```

This command restricts the container to specific CPU and memory limits, promoting equitable resource use.

4. Network Configuration for Performance:

Improving Docker's networking setup can significantly enhance container communication efficiency. Switching to host networking or user-defined bridges can increase throughput and reduce latency.

Example: Utilizing host networking

```
docker run -d --name network-optimized-container --network host nginx
```

This setup allows the container to use the host's networking stack, improving performance but reducing isolation.

Advanced Resource Handling

5. Effective Volume Management:

Proper handling of Docker volumes is vital for data-intensive applications. Volumes generally provide better performance than bind mounts and are easier to manage.

Example: Setting up a Docker volume

```
docker volume create log_data
docker run -d --name log-volume-container -v log_data:/data nginx
```

This approach uses Docker-managed volumes to optimize data access and management.

6. Caching Mechanisms:

Caching is a powerful method to boost application response times and reduce load on back-end systems. Implementing caching at the application level or through dedicated caching services like Redis can dramatically improve performance.

Continuous Performance Evaluation

Regularly monitoring container performance is essential for maintaining and adjusting configurations to meet changing demands. Utilizing tools such as Prometheus and Grafana can help track and visualize performance metrics effectively.

Example: Setting up Prometheus for monitoring

```
docker run -p 9090:9090 -v /path/to/prometheus.yml:/etc/prometheus/prometheus.yml prom
    /prometheus
```

Deploying Prometheus in this manner allows for detailed tracking of Docker performance, facilitating proactive management and tuning.

Conclusion

To achieve and maintain high-performance Docker containers, it is critical to employ strategic design principles, meticulous configuration, and ongoing management. By incorporating minimalist design approaches, precise resource allocation, and continuous monitoring, developers can optimize Docker containers for speed, efficiency, and reliability. These strategies ensure that containers are well-prepared to handle the demands of modern application deployments, leading to more scalable and robust solutions.

Best practices for container lifecycle management

Effective management of the container lifecycle is critical to ensure the stability, scalability, and efficiency of applications deployed using Docker. This guide delineates the best practices for managing the lifecycle of Docker containers, from creation through to decommissioning, providing a streamlined framework for developers and operations teams.

Stages of the Container Lifecycle

1. Creation of Containers: The creation phase is foundational in container lifecycle management. It involves crafting precise, reproducible Docker images through Dockerfiles to ensure uniformity across development, testing, and production environments.

Example Dockerfile:

```
FROM python:3.8-slim
WORKDIR /app
COPY requirements.txt .
RUN pip install -r requirements.txt
COPY . .
CMD ["python", "app.py"]
```

This Dockerfile outlines the setup for a lightweight Python application, focusing on consistency and minimal overhead.

2. Deployment of Containers: Deployment is about orchestrating and running containers in the designated environments. Utilizing tools like Kubernetes or Docker Swarm for orchestrating deployments ensures containers are managed efficiently, adhering to health checks and configuration specifications.

Example Kubernetes Deployment Configuration:

```yaml
apiVersion: apps/v1
kind: Deployment
metadata:
  name: python-app
```

```yaml
spec:
  replicas: 3
  selector:
    matchLabels:
      app: python
  template:
    metadata:
      labels:
        app: python
    spec:
      containers:
      - name: python
        image: python-app:latest
        ports:
        - containerPort: 80
```

This configuration automatically manages multiple instances of a container, providing robustness and load distribution.

3. Operational Management of Containers: Operational management includes monitoring, logging, and resource allocation. Tools like Prometheus for monitoring and the ELK Stack or Fluentd for logging are instrumental in maintaining the health and performance of containers.

Example Prometheus Monitoring Configuration:

```
global:
  scrape_interval: 15s
scrape_configs:
  - job_name: 'docker'
    static_configs:
      - targets: ['172.17.0.1:9100']
```

This setup enables continuous monitoring, facilitating early detection of issues and performance optimization.

4. Updating and Scaling Containers: Containers may need updates or adjustments in scale based on performance demands or updates. Employing orchestration tool features for rolling updates and automatic scaling ensures services remain available without interruption.

Example of Kubernetes Rolling Update Strategy:

```
strategy:
  type: RollingUpdate
  rollingUpdate:
    maxSurge: 1
    maxUnavailable: 0
```

This approach allows for seamless updates by incrementally replacing containers.

5. Decommissioning of Containers: The end of a container's lifecycle involves decommissioning, which should be handled carefully to ensure that all related resources, like volumes and networks, are also appropriately managed and cleaned.

Example Docker Removal Command:

```
docker stop container_id && docker rm container_id
```

Comprehensive Best Practices

- **Automation**: Automating the container lifecycle where possible minimizes human error and optimizes efficiency.

- **Immutability**: Adhering to the principle of immutability, where changes prompt a new container deployment rather than modifying existing containers.

- **Security Practices**: Ensuring each lifecycle stage incorporates robust security measures to protect against vulnerabilities.

- **Documentation**: Keeping detailed records of configurations and operations procedures helps maintain consistency and facilitates knowledge sharing among team members.

Conclusion

Managing Docker containers across their lifecycle involves a blend of detailed planning, disciplined execution, and utilization of advanced tools. By following these best practices, teams can ensure their containerized applications are not only high-performing but also secure and scalable. This level of management supports a robust infrastructure that is adaptable and capable of meeting modern application demands.

Analyzing and refining container design

Optimizing the design of Docker containers is crucial for enhancing application performance, scalability, and security. This process involves a systematic review of container configurations, aiming to streamline them to better align with specific operational goals. Here, we outline several strategies and tools that facilitate the refinement of container designs for improved efficiency and effectiveness.

Assessing Container Architecture

The refinement process begins with a comprehensive assessment of the current container setup. This evaluation encompasses understanding application architecture, pinpointing dependencies, and assessing how current container configurations impact performance. Key focus areas include:

- **Base Images and Container Size**: Analyzing the use of base images and the overall container size is critical. Opting for smaller, more secure base images like Alpine Linux can enhance startup times and reduce security risks.

Example: Using a minimal base image in Dockerfile:

```
FROM alpine:latest
RUN apk add --no-cache python3 py3-pip
```

- **Layer Optimization**: Reviewing and optimizing the layers within Docker images for more efficient builds and fewer vulnerabilities is also vital.

- **Resource Usage**: Ensuring containers are configured with appropriate resource limits to prevent performance bottlenecks is essential.

Example: Configuring resource limits:

```
docker run -d --name optimized-instance --memory=500m --cpus="1.0" my-application:latest
```

Reducing Resource Consumption

Minimizing resource usage without compromising functionality is key to container optimization:

- **Multi-Stage Builds**: Implementing multi-stage builds helps keep production containers streamlined by separating build environments from runtime environments.

Example: A multi-stage build process:

```
# Build stage
FROM golang:1.14 AS builder
WORKDIR /app
COPY . .
RUN go build -o main .

# Final stage
FROM alpine:latest
COPY --from=builder /app/main .
CMD ["./main"]
```

- **Build Caching**: Properly utilizing Docker's build cache by structuring Dockerfile instructions can enhance build speeds and decrease resource use.

Security Enhancements

Container security is paramount, and enhancing protective measures includes:

- **Trusted Base Images**: Employing base images from trusted sources and regularly scanning them for vulnerabilities is recommended.

- **Security Practices**: Implementing stringent security practices such as running containers with non-root users and minimizing the use of sensitive data in environment variables.

Example: Configuring a container to run as a non-root user:

```
FROM node:14
RUN useradd -m appuser
USER appuser
COPY . /app
WORKDIR /app
RUN npm install
CMD ["node", "app.js"]
```

Integrating into CI/CD Pipelines

Incorporating container design refinements into continuous integration and deployment pipelines ensures that changes are consistently and automatically tested and deployed. Tools like Jenkins, GitLab CI, and GitHub Actions can automate the processes of building, testing, and deploying container changes.

Example: A GitLab CI pipeline for Docker builds:

```
build:
  image: docker:19.03.12
  services:
    - docker:dind
  script:
    - docker build -t my-application:$CI_COMMIT_REF_SLUG .
    - docker push my-application:$CI_COMMIT_REF_SLUG
```

Continuous Monitoring and Adaptation

Regular monitoring and proactive adjustments based on performance data are crucial for maintaining optimal container operation. Utilizing monitoring tools like

Prometheus, Grafana, or the Elastic Stack provides insights into performance and helps identify areas needing attention.

Example: Configuring Prometheus to monitor Docker containers:

```
docker run \
  -p 9090:9090 \
  -v /etc/prometheus/prometheus.yml:/etc/prometheus/prometheus.yml \
  prom/prometheus
```

Conclusion

Refining container design is an ongoing process that demands a detailed examination of the current configurations, effective resource management, stringent security measures, and seamless integration into CI/CD processes. By adhering to these best practices, organizations can ensure their containerized applications are not only optimized for performance but are also secure and robust, capable of adapting to changing demands while minimizing operational disruptions.

Chapter Two

Deep Dive into Docker Engine

Exploring Docker engine internals

Delving into the Docker Engine internals provides crucial insights for those looking to optimize, troubleshoot, and extend Docker capabilities more effectively. As the core component that enables building, shipping, and running containerized applications, understanding the Docker Engine's architecture and functional mechanisms is essential. This exploration focuses on the Docker Engine's key elements, operational processes, and how various internal modules interact.

Overview of Docker Engine

The Docker Engine operates on a client-server model and includes:

- **The Server (dockerd)**: This is the Docker daemon that handles all requests for Docker API and manages Docker objects such as images, containers, networks, and volumes. It can also communicate with other Docker daemons.

- **The REST API**: This API allows external programs to communicate with the Docker daemon, executing commands and managing Docker tasks.

- **The Client (docker)**: The Docker CLI is used to interact with Docker. Through the CLI, commands are sent to the Docker daemon which executes them.

Architectural Components of Docker Engine

The Docker Engine's architecture is built around several key components:

- **Docker Daemon (dockerd)**: The backbone of Docker that processes all API requests and manages Docker's services.

- **Docker Client (docker)**: This is the primary interface for users to interact with Docker, sending commands to the daemon.

- **REST API**: The API used by the Docker client to communicate with the daemon, it supports direct REST calls and scripting for automated tasks.

Core Components of Docker Engine

The operation of Docker can be understood through its foundational components:

- **Images and Containers**: Images are read-only templates from which Docker containers are instantiated. Containers are runnable instances of images, created and managed by Docker's tools.

- **Libcontainer**: Docker uses libcontainer to interface directly with the Linux kernel's container APIs, such as namespaces and cgroups, facilitating container management.

- **Storage Drivers**: These drivers manage how images and containers' writable layers are stored and maintained. Common storage drivers include overlay2, aufs, and btrfs.

- **Network Drivers**: These drivers handle container networking capabilities, with various types supporting different networking needs like bridge, host, overlay, and macvlan.

Workflow of Docker Engine

The interaction between Docker's components during operation includes:

1. **Image Building**: Dockerfiles specify how images should be built. When a build is initiated, the Docker client sends a build request to the daemon which constructs the image accordingly.

2. **Container Lifecycle**: Running a container involves the Docker client instructing the daemon to start the container using a specific image and settings.

3. **Execution Layer**: As containers operate, Docker uses namespaces for isolation and cgroups for resource allocation.

4. **Networking**: Docker's network drivers manage how containers connect to networks, handling IP addressing and network interfaces based on the specified driver.

Practical Applications: Debugging and Extending Docker

Understanding Docker Engine internals is beneficial for both debugging and developing Docker extensions:

- **Debugging**: For example, if a container stops unexpectedly, understanding how Docker logs and manages containers can help identify the problem.

- **Extending Docker**: Developers can leverage the Docker API to create custom plugins or tools, or to automate Docker operations.

Example of Using the API:

```
curl --unix-socket /var/run/docker.sock http:/v1.24/containers/json
```

This command uses cURL to list containers directly through the Docker API, demonstrating interaction with the Docker daemon.

Conclusion

Investigating the internals of the Docker Engine provides a deep understanding of how this powerful platform manages containerized applications. This knowledge is invaluable for those aiming to fully utilize Docker's capabilities, enabling more efficient use, thorough troubleshooting, and the ability to extend Docker to fit specific requirements. For developers, system administrators, and IT professionals, grasping these details is crucial for maximizing the potential of Docker in various operational contexts.

Tuning Docker engine for maximum performance

Optimizing Docker Engine for peak performance entails a series of targeted configurations and adjustments to both the host system and Docker settings. These enhancements are crucial for improving application throughput, reducing response times, and ensuring that Docker operates efficiently under varying loads. This comprehensive guide outlines a range of strategies from kernel adjustments to network optimizations that are designed to bolster Docker's performance.

Kernel Enhancements

Effective Docker performance begins at the kernel level, as Docker depends on the kernel for essential container management functions.

- **Control Groups (cgroups)**: Docker utilizes cgroups to manage and isolate the resources used by containers. Proper configuration of cgroups helps prevent any individual container from monopolizing system resources, thus maintaining balance and stability across the system.

- **Namespaces**: Namespaces are crucial for providing containers with their isolated view of the operating environment, enhancing security and resource management. Correct implementation of namespaces facilitates more secure and independent operations of containers.

411

Example of Kernel Tuning:

```
# Configure the system to reduce swapping activities
sysctl vm.swappiness=10
```

Configuring the Docker Daemon

The Docker daemon's configuration plays a significant role in performance tuning.

- **Daemon.json Settings**: The configuration file **/etc/docker/daemon.json** is pivotal for setting various Docker daemon options like **log-level**, **storage-driver**, and **data-root** to optimize performance.

Example of Docker Daemon Optimization:

```
{
  "log-level": "warn",
  "storage-driver": "overlay2",
  "data-root": "/mnt/fast-storage/docker"
}
```

This configuration reduces logging overhead, uses a high-performance storage driver, and shifts Docker's data to a faster storage subsystem.

Resource Management

Effective resource allocation is key to maximizing the efficiency of Docker containers.

- **CPU and Memory Restrictions**: Docker allows for specifying the amount of CPU and memory that a container can use, preventing resource contention and ensuring consistent performance across services.

Example of Setting Resource Limits:

```
docker run -d --name resource-limited-app --memory=500m --cpus="2" my-application
```

This command restricts the container to 500 MB of memory and 2 CPU cores.

Network Configuration

Network setup is also critical for the performance of Docker-hosted applications.

- **Choosing the Appropriate Network Driver**: Docker supports various network drivers like **bridge**, **host**, **overlay**, and **macvlan**. Selecting the correct network driver can significantly influence performance by minimizing networking overhead.

- **DNS Performance**: Docker's embedded DNS in user-defined networks provides efficient name resolution among containers, which can be optimized for enhanced performance.

Example of Network Optimization:

```
docker network create --driver=overlay --attachable my_high_perf_network
```

This setup employs an overlay network optimized for distributed applications across multiple Docker hosts.

Monitoring Performance

Keeping track of Docker's performance is essential for identifying and addressing potential bottlenecks.

- **Docker Stats Tool**: Docker includes the **docker stats** tool, which provides a real-time stream of resource usage statistics for containers.

Example Usage:

```
docker stats --no-stream
```

This command displays a snapshot of all running containers' resource usage without streaming updates.

- **Integration with Monitoring Tools**: Incorporating advanced monitoring tools like Prometheus and Grafana can offer comprehensive insights into Docker's performance, aiding in further tuning and optimization.

Advanced Tuning Approaches

For those aiming to fully optimize their Docker setup:

- **Optimal Storage Solutions**: Choosing the appropriate storage drivers and configurations can significantly impact the performance, especially for I/O-intensive applications.

- **Ensuring High Availability**: Configuring Docker for high availability using orchestrators like Docker Swarm or Kubernetes not only enhances performance but also increases system resilience.

Conclusion

Achieving maximum performance from Docker involves a blend of system-level tweaks and Docker-specific configurations, complemented by continuous monitoring. By implementing these strategic enhancements, users can ensure that their Docker environments are robust, secure, and capable of handling intensive workloads efficiently. This proactive approach to Docker tuning helps maintain optimal performance and facilitates scalable and reliable operations.

Advanced configurations and tweaks

Optimizing system performance through advanced configurations and tweaks is crucial for enhancing the functionality and security of computing environments. This guide delves into various strategies for refining the settings of servers, operating systems, and applications to improve their efficiency, resilience, and security.

1. Tuning the Operating System

Operating system adjustments are foundational to the performance and capability of both the hosted applications and the underlying hardware.

- **Adjusting Kernel Parameters**: Modifying system-level settings via sysctl can significantly affect performance, particularly in resource management.

Example:

```
# Configure the system to minimize swap usage
sysctl vm.swappiness=10
```

- **Optimizing File Systems**: Selecting and tuning the appropriate file systems (e.g., ext4, XFS, Btrfs) based on workload requirements can enhance disk I/O efficiency.

Example:

```
# Mount an ext4 filesystem with optimized settings
mount -t ext4 -o noatime,nodiratime,barrier=0 /dev/sda1 /data
```

2. Enhancing Network Configuration

Effective network setup ensures optimal data flow and can dramatically impact application performance.

- **TCP Configuration Adjustments**: Fine-tuning TCP settings like window sizes and congestion control algorithms can enhance data throughput and reduce latency.

Example:

```
# Adjust TCP settings for improved performance
echo 1 > /proc/sys/net/ipv4/tcp_tw_reuse
```

- **Sophisticated Routing Configurations**: Implementing advanced routing protocols and configurations can better manage network traffic, improving overall network efficiency.

3. Bolstering Security

Deepening security measures involves more than basic setups; it includes fine-tuning advanced security configurations.

- **Configuring SELinux**: Tailoring SELinux policies to enforce stricter access controls can safeguard applications and prevent unauthorized data access.

Example:

```
# Enforce strict SELinux policies
setenforce 1
```

- **Advanced Firewall Settings**: Utilizing complex firewall rules and stateful inspections can greatly enhance security measures.

Example:

```
# Configure advanced firewall rules with iptables
iptables -A INPUT -p tcp --syn --dport 80 -m connlimit --connlimit-above 10 -j DROP
```

4. Database Optimization

Efficient database operation is key to application responsiveness. Optimizing database performance involves both configuration adjustments and query optimization.

- **Indexing and Query Refinement**: Proper indexing can expedite data retrieval, significantly reducing response times.

Example:

```
-- Optimize queries by creating appropriate indexes
CREATE INDEX ON orders (customer_id);
```

- **Database Parameter Tuning**: Adjusting database configurations to optimize memory usage and connection handling can handle larger loads more effectively.

5. Application-Level Adjustments

Application performance can be fine-tuned by adjusting runtime configurations and optimizing code paths.

- **Profiling and Code Optimization**: Employing profiling tools to detect and optimize high-latency code sections can decrease resource consumption.

- **Effective Caching**: Implementing caching strategies for frequently accessed data or computationally expensive operations can significantly enhance performance.

Example:

```python
# Use caching to improve application response times
from functools import lru_cache

@lru_cache(maxsize=32)
def compute_expensive_operation(x):
    # Complex computation here
    return x * x
```

Conclusion

Advanced configurations and strategic system tweaks are vital for maximizing performance and securing systems. By implementing these sophisticated adjustments, system administrators and developers can ensure optimized, secure, and efficient operation of their computing environments. These enhancements not only support current system demands but also prepare infrastructures for future scalability and security challenges, ensuring they remain robust and capable under various operational stresses.

Chapter Three

High-Performance Networking

Advanced Docker networking options and configurations

Advanced Docker networking configurations are essential for tailoring container communication to meet specific requirements, enhancing both performance and security across different deployment scenarios. This guide provides a detailed examination of the sophisticated networking capabilities Docker offers, from managing isolated networks on a single host to facilitating robust communications across a distributed cluster of machines.

Fundamentals of Docker Networking

Docker's networking capabilities allow each container to operate with an isolated network stack. For setups requiring intricate configurations, Docker supports various network drivers:

- **Bridge**: Standard driver for creating a private internal network on a single Docker host.

- **Host**: This driver ties the container directly to the host's network, without isolation.

- **Overlay**: Ideal for multi-host networking, enabling containers connected to different Docker daemons to communicate.

- **Macvlan**: Makes a container appear as a physical device on the network, complete with its own MAC address.

Customizing Bridge Networks

For containers that need to communicate within the same host, bridge networks are particularly useful. Users can create custom bridge networks that provide enhanced isolation and networking capabilities compared to the default bridge.

Example:

```
docker network create --driver bridge --subnet 192.168.1.0/24 --gateway 192.168.1.1 my-bridge
    -net
```

This command sets up a custom bridge network with a specified subnet and gateway, offering tailored control over the network environment.

Utilizing Overlay Networks

In environments where Docker is deployed across multiple hosts, overlay networks provide seamless connectivity, making them crucial for managing large-scale applications.

Encrypted Traffic in Overlay Networks: Docker supports encryption in overlay networks, securing data as it moves between nodes.

Example:

```
docker network create --driver overlay --opt encrypted my-secure-network
```

This setup initiates an overlay network with encryption, safeguarding inter-node communications.

Deploying Macvlan Networks

Macvlan networks can be particularly beneficial for legacy applications that expect direct access to a physical network.

Example:

```
docker network create -d macvlan --subnet=192.168.99.0/24 --gateway=192.168.99.1 -o parent
   =eth0 public_net
```

This configuration allows containers to connect to the network as though they were physical devices, using the host's **etho** interface.

Strengthening Network Security

Enhancing the security of Docker networks involves implementing rigorous access controls and encryption protocols:

- **Configuring Firewalls**: Integrating Docker with existing firewall solutions or using iptables to manage access to and from containers.

- **Implementing IPSec**: Adding a layer of security with IPSec to protect data transmitted across network layers.

Example:

```
# Setting up iptables rules for Docker security
iptables -A FORWARD -o docker0 -m state --state RELATED,ESTABLISHED -j ACCEPT
iptables -A FORWARD -o docker0 -j DOCKER
iptables -A FORWARD -i docker0 ! -o docker0 -j ACCEPT
iptables -A FORWARD -i docker0 -o docker0 -j ACCEPT
```

These commands configure iptables to securely manage container traffic, enhancing network security.

Optimizing Network Performance

Maximizing network performance is key to maintaining responsive and reliable container operations:

- **Tuning Network Buffers**: Adjusting network buffer sizes to better handle high traffic loads and reduce packet loss.

- **Traffic Prioritization**: Employing traffic shaping tools to manage bandwidth allocation among containers.

Example:

```
# Use tc to shape traffic for Docker containers
tc qdisc add dev eth0 root tbf rate 1mbit burst 32kbit latency 400ms
```

This example uses traffic control settings to manage how much bandwidth is available to Docker traffic, preventing network congestion.

Conclusion

Advanced Docker networking options provide the tools needed to create highly customizable, secure, and efficient networking environments for containers. Whether optimizing communications on a single host or across a distributed system, Docker's networking features allow for precise configuration to suit any operational requirement. By applying these advanced settings, system administrators and network architects can ensure that their Docker deployments are both robust and secure, ready to handle the dynamic demands of modern containerized applications.

Optimizing network throughput and latency

Enhancing network throughput and reducing latency are critical objectives in network management, pivotal for improving overall system performance and user satisfaction. Network throughput — the volume of data that can be transferred over a network at any given time — and latency — the delay before data transfer begins — are key metrics in network operations. Effective management of these can drastically boost the efficiency of network communications.

Key Principles of Network Performance Enhancement

Understanding the underlying factors affecting network throughput and latency is essential for effective optimization:

- **Bandwidth**: This refers to the capacity of the network to transfer data.

- **Congestion**: This occurs when network demand exceeds its capacity, leading to bottlenecks.

- **Network Protocols**: These are the rules that govern data communications, such as TCP/IP and UDP.

- **Hardware**: This includes the physical components like routers, switches, and network interface cards that facilitate data transfer.

Approaches to Maximize Throughput

Enhancing network throughput requires strategic measures to ensure data is transmitted efficiently across the network:

1. **Infrastructure Upgrades**: Updating network equipment can lead to significant throughput improvements. This involves upgrading to higher-capacity routers, switches, and network interfaces.

2. **Bandwidth Expansion**: Increasing the bandwidth of connections can provide more capacity for data transfer, either through service upgrades or by adding new lines.

3. **Implementing Load Balancers**: This involves distributing incoming network traffic across several servers to balance the load, which can significantly enhance network efficiency.

Example:

```
# Example iptables command to distribute network traffic
iptables -A PREROUTING -t nat -i eth0 -p tcp --dport 80 -j DNAT --to-destination 192.168.1.1
    -192.168.1.10:80
```

4. **Traffic Shaping and Quality of Service (QoS)**: Applying QoS rules can help prioritize network traffic, ensuring that critical data receives the necessary bandwidth.

Example:

```
# Using tc to prioritize network traffic
tc qdisc add dev eth0 root handle 1: htb default 12
tc class add dev eth0 parent 1: classid 1:1 htb rate 1000Mbps
```

Techniques for Minimizing Latency

Reducing latency involves optimizing how quickly data can be processed and delivered:

425

1. **Efficient Routing**: Enhancing routing protocols and optimizing the paths data takes through the network can reduce the number of stops or 'hops', thereby decreasing latency.

2. **Adjust TCP Acknowledgments**: Modifying how frequently TCP acknowledgments are sent can help in managing network congestion and reducing latency.

Example:

```
# Configure TCP acknowledgment settings on Linux systems
echo 2 > /proc/sys/net/ipv4/tcp_synack_retries
```

3. **DNS Enhancements**: Optimizing the time it takes for DNS resolutions can accelerate the initial loading of network-based applications.

4. **Utilization of CDNs**: Content Delivery Networks (CDNs) store cached content closer to users, which minimizes latency by reducing the distance data travels.

Utilizing Advanced Network Management Tools

Advanced tools and technologies are available to aid in the detailed monitoring and management of network performance:

- **Network Monitoring Tools**: Applications like Wireshark or tcpdump provide insights into traffic flows and packet dynamics, which are invaluable for identifying inefficiencies.

- **Software-Defined Networking (SDN)**: SDN offers sophisticated control over network traffic, allowing for adjustments that can dynamically improve both throughput and latency.

- **WAN Optimization**: These devices optimize the efficiency of wide-area networks by compressing data, caching frequently accessed information, and prioritizing traffic, which enhances throughput and decreases latency.

Conclusion

Optimizing network throughput and reducing latency are comprehensive tasks that necessitate a blend of hardware enhancements, software configurations, and strategic network management. These optimizations not only facilitate smoother and more efficient network operations but also improve the responsiveness of applications that rely on network services. Through the effective application of these strategies, network administrators can ensure their networks are well-equipped to handle the demands of modern digital communications.

Network tuning for large-scale deployments

Network tuning for large-scale deployments is crucial for maintaining optimal performance and reliability across extensive network infrastructures. These networks, which support a vast array of users and handle significant data volumes, require meticulous planning and precise implementation of tuning strategies to ensure efficient operations. This discussion provides a detailed overview of the methodologies involved in enhancing network throughput and reducing latency in such environments.

Initial Network Assessment

The starting point for effective network tuning involves a thorough analysis of the specific needs associated with large-scale environments:

- **Bandwidth Analysis**: Determining the necessary bandwidth to support all operational demands without causing network congestion.

- **Latency Goals**: Establishing target latency metrics to guarantee application responsiveness meets end-user expectations.

- **Failover Strategies**: Designing network architectures with adequate failover and redundancy systems to sustain operations during potential outages.

Strategic Network Tuning Techniques

With a clear understanding of the network requirements, specific tuning methods can be applied to enhance overall network performance:

1. **Network Segmentation and Virtualization**: Breaking down a large network into manageable segments (subnets) and utilizing virtual network resources can simplify management tasks and localize potential issues to prevent widespread impacts.

Example:

```
# Example of creating VLANs for effective network segmentation
vlan database
vlan 300 name Operations
vlan 400 name HR
exit
```

2. **Dynamic Routing Optimization**: Utilizing adaptive routing protocols like OSPF or BGP helps in managing network paths efficiently, optimizing the data flow, and reducing convergence times in large networks.

Example:

```
# OSPF configuration snippet
router ospf
network 192.168.100.0 0.0.255.255 area 1
```

3. **Sophisticated Load Balancing Solutions**: Advanced load balancing across servers and network links ensures that no single node bears excessive traffic, maintaining smooth service delivery.

Example:

```
# Load balancing configuration with an Nginx server
upstream backend {
    server server1.example.com weight=3;
    server server2.example.com;
    server server3.example.com;
}
```

4. **Implementing Quality of Service (QoS)**: Enforcing QoS policies can prioritize essential services, ensuring that critical applications receive the

bandwidth they require during peak operational periods.

Example:

```
# QoS configuration for prioritizing video traffic
class-map match-all VideoTraffic
match protocol rtp video
policy-map QoSPolicy
class VideoTraffic
priority percent 20
```

5. **WAN Optimization Techniques**: In deployments spread over wide geographical areas, WAN optimization can significantly enhance communication speeds through traffic shaping, compression, and protocol optimization.

Ongoing Monitoring and Adjustments

Continuous monitoring of the network is vital for maintaining the enhancements achieved through initial tuning efforts:

- **Automated Monitoring Tools**: Deploying comprehensive monitoring systems like PRTG or Nagios to continuously oversee network performance and quickly identify areas needing attention.

- **Regular Performance Reviews**: Analyzing collected performance data regularly helps verify that the network meets all set performance standards and supports proactive adjustments as needed.

Integrating Robust Security Measures

As networks are fine-tuned for performance, security should also be a major consideration, especially in large-scale deployments:

- **Enhanced Security Configurations**: Deploying advanced firewall configurations and intrusion detection systems throughout the network helps safeguard against potential threats.

- **Routine Security Evaluations**: Conducting regular security assessments ensures that the network remains protected even as changes and optimizations are implemented.

Conclusion

Effectively tuning networks for large-scale deployments involves a comprehensive strategy that includes detailed assessments, targeted optimization techniques, and robust monitoring practices. By systematically applying these strategies, organizations can ensure that their networks are not only capable of handling large volumes of traffic efficiently but are also secure and resilient against disruptions, thereby supporting the organization's objectives in a reliable and effective manner.

Chapter Four

High-Density Container Deployments

Strategies for maximizing hardware utilization

Optimizing hardware utilization is essential for organizations looking to improve system efficiency and reduce operational costs. Effective hardware management ensures systems are running at peak performance, facilitates easier maintenance, and prompts timely hardware updates. This guide delves into several approaches for enhancing hardware utilization, including strategic system configurations, efficient workload distribution, and leveraging advanced technologies like virtualization and cloud services.

Evaluating System Hardware

The process begins with a comprehensive assessment of existing infrastructure capabilities, focusing on processor efficiency, memory usage, storage solutions, and network throughput. Utilizing diagnostic tools such as CPU-Z, Memtest, or network performance monitors can help pinpoint performance issues and identify opportunities for improvement.

Effective Resource Management

Proper resource allocation is key to maximizing hardware performance and avoiding wastage:

- **Dynamic Resource Scheduling**: Employing intelligent scheduling algorithms helps dynamically allocate resources based on real-time workload demands, maximizing hardware usage.

- **Efficient Load Distribution**: Strategically distributing workloads across all available hardware resources prevents overburdening any single component, ensuring balanced system performance.

Example:

```
# Display current load distribution
top -bn1 | grep "load average:"
```

Harnessing Virtualization

Virtualization technology plays a critical role in maximizing hardware utilization by allowing multiple virtual instances to operate on a single physical server:

- **Optimal Hypervisor Selection**: Choosing the appropriate hypervisor—such as VMware ESXi, Microsoft Hyper-V, or KVM—based on specific workload requirements can drastically enhance efficiency.

- **Virtual Machine Configuration**: Ensuring that virtual machines are properly configured to use the exact amount of resources needed can prevent resource wastage.

Example:

```
# Configure virtual machine resource allocation
VBoxManage modifyvm "VM name" --memory 2048 --cpus 2
```

Utilizing Cloud Solutions

Cloud computing provides flexible, scalable hardware resources that can be adjusted according to varying workload demands:

- **Scalable Cloud Services**: Utilizing cloud services like AWS EC2 or Azure Virtual Machines allows for the scaling of computing resources to match the demand dynamically.

- **Autoscaling Capabilities**: Modern cloud platforms include tools that monitor resource usage and automatically adjust capacity to optimize performance.

Example:

```
# Setup autoscaling on AWS
aws autoscaling create-auto-scaling-group --auto-scaling-group-name myautoscale --launch
    -configuration-name myconfig --min-size 1 --max-size 5 --desired-capacity 3 --vpc-zone
    -identifier subnet-abc123
```

Hardware Configuration Optimization

Tuning hardware settings can further improve resource utilization:

- **BIOS/UEFI Tuning**: Adjusting system BIOS settings to optimize performance factors like CPU speeds and memory timings can significantly affect overall performance.

434

- **Power Management Settings**: Configuring hardware to operate in energy-efficient modes during periods of low demand helps conserve energy while maintaining system readiness.

Implementing Advanced Storage Solutions

Efficient storage management is crucial for maximizing hardware performance:

- **Storage Tiering**: Using intelligent storage solutions that automatically move data between different storage tiers based on usage frequency helps optimize performance and cost.

- **Data Deduplication**: Reducing the storage space required by eliminating duplicate data files enhances storage efficiency.

Example:

```
# Enable data deduplication on a storage volume
Enable-DedupVolume -Volume "F:"
```

Regular Maintenance and Hardware Upgrades

Maintaining hardware components regularly and updating them as needed ensures they continue to operate efficiently:

- **Firmware Upgrades**: Keeping firmware updated ensures hardware components have the latest performance enhancements and security fixes.

- **Strategic Hardware Upgrades**: Upgrading essential components like adding SSDs or more RAM can extend the operational life and improve the performance of existing systems.

Conclusion

Maximizing hardware utilization involves a comprehensive strategy that includes efficient resource management, embracing advanced technological solutions, and conducting regular system reviews. By implementing these tactics, organizations can ensure that they are making the most of their hardware investments, which leads to reduced costs and enhanced system performance, preparing the infrastructure for future demands and technological advancements.

Managing resource constraints and allocations

Effectively managing resource constraints and allocations is vital for optimizing efficiency and performance in both project and technology infrastructure management. This critical function requires meticulous planning to ensure resources are used optimally, minimizing wastage while preventing resource exhaustion. This involves understanding available resources, anticipating future requirements, and adapting allocations to meet evolving needs.

Identifying Resource Constraints

Resource constraints typically manifest in environments where the demand for resources outstrips supply. In technological setups, these constraints could relate to limitations in CPU performance, memory capacity, storage, and network bandwidth. In project management contexts, constraints often involve human capital, budgetary limits, and project deadlines.

A comprehensive evaluation of available resources is essential to identify these constraints accurately. Resource management tools like resource allocation matrices or IT monitoring systems such as Nagios or Zabbix can assist in this evaluation, providing a clear view of resource usage and potential bottlenecks.

Resource Allocation Techniques

Implementing effective allocation strategies is crucial once resource constraints are understood. These strategies should be tailored to the project or system's specific requirements and constraints.

1. **Prioritization**: Resources are allocated based on the criticality and impact of tasks or processes. Essential activities might receive more resources to ensure their completion within desired timelines.

2. **Resource Leveling**: This involves balancing resource utilization by delaying certain tasks until the necessary resources become available, ensuring that resource demand does not surpass what is available.

Example:

```
# Using the Linux 'nice' command to adjust process priority
nice -n 10 archive_logs.sh
```

3. **Resource Smoothing**: This strategy adjusts resources so their usage does not exceed certain

thresholds, potentially extending timelines minimally to accommodate resource availability.

Managing Technology Resources

In technology infrastructure management, several key strategies help manage resource constraints:

- **Virtualization**: This technology divides physical resources into smaller, virtual units, which can be allocated more dynamically and efficiently to meet changing needs.

- **Cloud Services**: Utilizing cloud computing offers significant scalability. These services provide on-demand resource provisioning, ideal for handling intermittent peak loads.

Example:

```
# Command to launch instances in the cloud
aws ec2 run-instances --image-id ami-0abcdef1234567890 --count 10 --instance-type t2.medium
```

- **Container Technology**: Containers improve resource utilization by encapsulating applications with all their dependencies, allowing for precise CPU and memory allocations.

Example:

```
# Command to set resource limits for a Docker container
docker run -it --cpus="1.5" --memory="500m" ubuntu /bin/bash
```

Project Resource Management

Resource management within projects requires careful planning and execution:

- **Utilization of Gantt Charts**: These charts help visualize when resources are allocated over the duration of the project, highlighting overlaps and gaps in resource usage.

- **Critical Path Analysis**: Focusing resources on essential project activities identified by critical path analysis ensures that key milestones are achieved on schedule.

Continuous Monitoring and Adjustment

Ongoing monitoring of resource allocations is crucial to ensure that they remain effective as project requirements or infrastructure needs evolve:

- **Analyzing Performance Metrics**: Continual collection and analysis of performance data help identify when resources are nearing their limits and require reallocation or augmentation.

- **Implementing Feedback Mechanisms**: Feedback from team members or automated systems can provide real-time insights into resource sufficiency, facilitating timely adjustments to allocation plans.

Conclusion

Resource constraint and allocation management is an ongoing, dynamic process requiring continuous oversight and flexibility. By strategically planning, employing advanced technological solutions, and monitoring resource use closely, organizations can ensure that their resource management practices effectively support operational demands. This proactive approach not only boosts productivity and efficiency but also prepares the organization to adapt quickly to new challenges and opportunities, maintaining optimal performance across all areas.

Techniques for container stacking and density optimization

Optimizing container stacking and density is crucial for enhancing resource efficiency and improving system performance in environments that utilize containerized applications. As organizations scale their container deployments, effective management of container density becomes essential to maximizing resource usage and minimizing operational costs. Here we explore a range of strategies and methods to effectively manage the stacking of containers and optimize their density across various deployment stages.

Fundamentals of Container Density

Container density refers to the number of containers operating on a single host system. Achieving an optimal container density ensures that every container has adequate resources to function effectively without oversaturating the host machine.

Strategies for Effective Container Stacking

Strategic management and placement of containers are key to optimizing resource usage. The following strategies can significantly enhance container stacking efficiency:

1. **Setting Resource Allocation Limits**: Defining clear CPU and memory limits for each container helps prevent resource hogging by any single container, facilitating a balanced resource distribution.

Example:

```
# Example of limiting resources in a Docker container
docker run -d --name app_container --memory=500m --cpus="1.5" nginx
```

2. **Intelligent Container Scheduling**: Using advanced scheduling tools that place containers on hosts with sufficient resources can optimize the overall system performance. Kubernetes, for example, offers capabilities that manage container deployment based on current resource availability and operational demands.

3. **Isolation with Namespaces and Cgroups**: Implementing namespaces and Cgroups secures and isolates container processes, allowing for denser container deployments without cross-interference.

Maximizing Container Density

To effectively increase container density while maintaining high performance, consider these approaches:

1. **Leveraging Orchestration Platforms**: Tools like Kubernetes and Docker Swarm facilitate efficient container orchestration, enabling better scaling and management of container density.

2. **Horizontal Application Scaling**: Design applications to scale horizontally, distributing loads across multiple containers instead of adding resources to a single container, which maximizes the hosting capacity and resource utilization.

3. **Adopting Microservices**: Utilizing a microservices architecture increases system modularity and allows for more granular control over scaling and resource allocation, enhancing both density and performance.

Essential Monitoring and Management Tools

Robust monitoring solutions are vital for managing and optimizing container density:

- **Prometheus and Grafana**: Useful for monitoring container performance metrics and visualizing data to assess and optimize container deployment.

- **Elastic Stack**: Helps in logging and real-time analysis of container performance, aiding in proactive management.

- **Native Container Management Tools**: Tools such as Docker stats or Kubernetes Dashboard provide insights into container-specific resource usage, helping adjust allocations as needed.

Best Practices for Container Density Optimization

Implementing these best practices ensures that high density does not compromise container or system performance:

- **Conduct Regular Performance Benchmarks**: Regular testing under varied loads helps determine the most effective container density for optimal performance.

- **Implement Auto-scaling**: Auto-scaling mechanisms adjust the number of active containers based on real-time demand, ensuring efficient resource use.

- **Audit Resource Efficiency**: Periodically reviewing resource consumption can identify underutilized resources or inefficiencies, allowing for timely adjustments.

Conclusion

Strategic container stacking and density optimization are critical for leveraging the full potential of containerized infrastructure. By employing advanced techniques for resource allocation, embracing suitable architectures, and utilizing powerful monitoring tools, organizations can achieve significant improvements in resource efficiency. These strategies not only reduce costs but also enhance the agility and scalability of application deployments, ensuring robust performance across extensive digital environments.

Chapter Five

Resource Management and Scheduling

Deep dive into Docker's resource management capabilities

Docker's resource management features are crucial for efficiently running containerized applications, providing mechanisms to control and allocate system resources such as CPU, memory, disk I/O, and network bandwidth. This comprehensive overview explores Docker's capabilities in managing these resources, detailing how to apply them to optimize container performance and maintain system health.

Docker Resource Constraints Overview

Docker facilitates fine-grained resource control, which is pivotal for preventing any container from excessively consuming resources and potentially destabilizing the host system. Docker's management of resources involves:

- **CPU**: Allocation limits can be set to specify the percentage of total CPU cycles a container may use, which is essential in environments with multiple containers.

- **Memory**: Docker can restrict the maximum memory a container is allowed to utilize.

- **Disk I/O**: Prioritization of disk access is managed through Docker, ensuring essential applications have priority over less critical ones.

- **Network**: While Docker does not natively limit network traffic per container, external tools can be employed to manage network bandwidth.

Setting Resource Limits

Docker provides command-line options to establish resource limits directly when launching containers with the **docker run** command:

1. **CPU Limits**: The CPU allocation for containers can be adjusted using the **--cpus** option or by setting CPU quotas with the **--cpu-quota and --cpu-period** flags.

```
# Restrict a container to 1.5 CPUs
docker run -it --cpus=1.5 ubuntu /bin/bash

# Assign 50% of a CPU
docker run -it --cpu-period=100000 --cpu-quota=50000 ubuntu /bin/bash
```

2. **Memory Limits**: Memory usage can be capped using the **--memory** flag.

```
# Set a memory limit of 256 MB
docker run -it --memory=256m ubuntu /bin/bash
```

3. **Disk I/O Limits**: Docker manages disk access using the **--blkio-weight** parameter, which sets the priority level for block I/O.

```
# Prioritize disk access
docker run -it --blkio-weight=50 ubuntu /bin/bash
```

4. **Network Management**: To control network bandwidth, Docker relies on external tools, as it lacks built-in network throttling features.

```
# Example of limiting network bandwidth using tc
tc qdisc add dev eth0 root tbf rate 1mbit burst 32kbit latency 400ms
```

Resource Reservation

Docker also allows the reservation of resources, ensuring minimum resources are available to a container:

- **CPU Reservation**: This guarantees a set amount of CPU cores are reserved for container use.

```
# Reserve 0.5 CPUs
docker run -it --cpus="0.5" ubuntu /bin/bash
```

- **Memory Reservation**: This ensures a container has a minimum memory allocation, critical for its operation.

```
# Reserve minimum memory
docker run -it --memory-reservation=100m ubuntu /bin/bash
```

Monitoring and Managing Resource Usage

Docker provides tools to monitor the real-time usage of resources by containers, crucial for managing and adjusting allocations based on actual need:

```
# Display resource usage stats for all running containers
docker stats
```

Conclusion

Understanding and implementing Docker's resource management tools is essential for administrators and developers aiming to optimize application performance and ensure the stability of their systems. Docker's capabilities allow for precise control over resource allocation, ensuring efficient and stable operation of containers. By mastering these settings, users can prevent resource contention and ensure that their applications run smoothly within their Docker environments.

Implementing custom schedulers

Creating custom schedulers in software systems involves a deep understanding of both the system's requirements and the specific performance goals to be achieved. Custom schedulers are designed to optimize the way resources are allocated and managed, ensuring they meet unique system constraints and objectives that may not be addressed by standard scheduling algorithms. This detailed discussion will focus on the rationale for employing custom schedulers, their potential advantages, essential design considerations, and practical implementation examples.

Reasons for Custom Schedulers

Custom schedulers are often necessary when existing scheduling algorithms within the operating system or provided by middleware do not suffice because of unique application needs such as:

- **Real-time Systems**: These systems require schedulers capable of adhering strictly to task deadlines.

- **Distributed Systems**: Such environments benefit from schedulers that can efficiently manage network latencies and optimize task placement based on node locality.

- **High-Performance Computing (HPC)**: Custom scheduling is essential to handle the extensive parallel processing activities typically found in these environments without wasting resources.

Advantages of Custom Schedulers

Implementing a custom scheduler can provide several benefits:

- **Optimized Performance**: Customization allows for the precise ordering of tasks, potentially reducing job processing times by handling task dependencies intelligently.

- **Better Resource Management**: Tailored resource allocation helps avoid resource underutilization and bottlenecks, improving overall throughput.

- **Scalability**: Schedulers can be specifically designed to grow with an application, supporting more significant numbers of nodes or larger datasets effectively.

Key Design Considerations

When developing a custom scheduler, several critical factors need attention:

- **Understanding of System Architecture**: A deep dive into the hardware details and capabilities is necessary as it directly influences task allocation strategies.

- **Task Dynamics**: Comprehensive knowledge of the tasks' execution times, resource requirements, and interdependencies guides the scheduling logic.

- **User-Specific Requirements**: Priorities such as job priority, fairness among tasks, response times, and overall throughput need to be integrated into the scheduler design.

Implementing Custom Schedulers

Custom schedulers can typically be integrated into existing systems by modifying or extending the default scheduler. Here are common methodologies:

1. **Operating Systems Scheduling**: This might involve writing low-level code to tweak or replace the default process or thread scheduler provided by the operating system.

```c
// Example C code for a basic round-robin scheduler
void simple_round_robin() {
    while (true) {
        Thread currentThread = pick_next_thread();
        execute(currentThread);
    }
}
```

2. **Distributed System Task Scheduling**: Platforms like Hadoop or frameworks like Mesos allow for custom schedulers that can dictate how processes are distributed and managed across different nodes.

```java
// Example Java code for a Hadoop custom scheduler
public class MyCustomScheduler extends TaskScheduler {
    @Override
    public void scheduleTasks() {
        // Implement your scheduling logic
    }
}
```

3. **Batch Job Scheduling**: In environments where jobs need to be executed in batches, custom scripts or specialized software can be used to control job execution order based on sophisticated criteria.

```bash
# Bash script for basic job scheduling
while true; do
    check_and_run_jobs()
    sleep 1
done
```

Testing and Adjusting the Scheduler

Testing a new scheduler involves several steps:

- **Simulation Testing**: Simulating the scheduler under various scenarios to evaluate its effectiveness and identify any potential issues.

- **Controlled Real-world Deployment**: Observing the scheduler's performance in a controlled real setting to gather data on its impact.

- **Adaptive Feedback**: Using operational feedback to refine and adjust the scheduler dynamically.

Conclusion

Developing custom schedulers is an effective way to ensure that computing resources are managed optimally, tailored to the specific needs of the application or system. By carefully designing these schedulers to align with detailed operational requirements and continuously adapting them based on actual performance data, organizations can achieve remarkable improvements in efficiency, performance, and scalability. This makes custom schedulers an invaluable tool in environments where standard scheduling solutions fall short.

Optimizing resource allocation algorithms

Optimizing resource allocation algorithms is essential in modern computing, as efficient resource distribution directly impacts system performance, scalability, and cost-effectiveness. These algorithms are critical for ensuring that resources such as CPU, memory, storage, and network bandwidth are allocated appropriately to tasks or processes. By refining these algorithms, organizations can achieve better efficiency, reduced response times, and a more balanced use of resources. This discussion explores key approaches to enhancing resource allocation algorithms, practical techniques for implementation, and examples of their application across different domains.

The Role of Optimized Resource Allocation

Resource allocation is fundamental in computing systems, whether in operating systems managing hardware resources or cloud infrastructures distributing virtualized environments. The benefits of optimizing these algorithms include:

- **Increased Throughput**: Well-tuned algorithms ensure faster task completion by minimizing idle resources and balancing workloads.

- **Equity**: Proper allocation balances the demands of various tasks, ensuring no single entity monopolizes resources.

- **Scalability**: Optimized algorithms allow systems to handle larger loads without sacrificing performance.

- **Cost Reduction**: Efficient allocation minimizes waste, reducing operational costs significantly.

Techniques for Optimization

Enhancing resource allocation algorithms requires combining theoretical advancements with practical considerations:

1. Dynamic Management of Resources

Dynamic allocation algorithms adapt to workload changes in real time. By reallocating resources based on current demand, these algorithms ensure optimal usage across all tasks.

Example:

```python
# Simple dynamic allocation example
tasks = {"task1": 30, "task2": 50, "task3": 20}  # Resource needs
total_resources = 100

def allocate_resources(tasks, total_resources):
    allocation = {}
    for task, demand in tasks.items():
        allocation[task] = min(demand, total_resources // len(tasks))
    return allocation

print(allocate_resources(tasks, total_resources))
```

This approach ensures that resources are distributed based on demand while adhering to the system's capacity.

2. Predictive Allocation

Using historical data and machine learning models, predictive algorithms forecast future resource requirements, enabling systems to proactively allocate resources to prevent bottlenecks or shortages.

3. Load Balancing

Load-balancing algorithms evenly distribute workloads across available resources, preventing any single resource from being overburdened. Popular methods include Round Robin, Weighted Balancing, and Least Connections.

Example:

```python
# Round-robin load balancing
resources = ["node1", "node2", "node3"]
tasks = ["job1", "job2", "job3", "job4"]

def round_robin(resources, tasks):
    allocation = {}
    for i, task in enumerate(tasks):
        allocation[task] = resources[i % len(resources)]
    return allocation

print(round_robin(resources, tasks))
```

4. Multi-Objective Optimization

Complex environments often require balancing multiple objectives, such as minimizing energy consumption while maximizing task throughput. Techniques like genetic algorithms or heuristic-based methods are frequently employed in such scenarios.

5. Heuristic and Approximation Methods

When solving allocation problems exactly is computationally expensive, heuristic approaches provide near-optimal solutions quickly. These are particularly useful in large-scale environments where quick decisions are necessary.

Applications Across Domains

Operating Systems

Operating systems employ scheduling algorithms such as Priority Scheduling, Shortest Job Next (SJN), and Multi-Level Feedback Queue (MLFQ) to optimize how processes utilize system resources, ensuring a balance between performance and responsiveness.

Cloud Computing

In cloud environments, resource allocation algorithms manage virtual machine (VM) and container resources dynamically. These systems balance workloads between tenants while ensuring fairness and minimizing idle resources.

High-Performance Computing (HPC)

HPC environments focus on maximizing resource use for parallel computing tasks. Allocation algorithms optimize cores, memory, and network bandwidth to handle compute-intensive operations efficiently.

Challenges in Optimization

1. **Heterogeneous Systems**: Managing diverse resources with varying capabilities can complicate allocation strategies.

2. **Scalability Requirements**: Algorithms must efficiently handle growing workloads without incurring high computational overhead.

3. **Trade-offs Between Fairness and Efficiency**: Striking the right balance between equitable resource distribution and maximum system performance requires careful tuning.

Monitoring and Feedback for Improvement

Continuous monitoring of resource usage is vital for refining allocation algorithms. Collecting real-time metrics and adjusting allocations based on feedback ensures sustained efficiency.

Example:

```
# Monitoring container resource usage
docker stats --no-stream
```

Conclusion

Optimizing resource allocation algorithms is a critical process that underpins the efficiency of many computing systems. By adopting strategies such as dynamic management, predictive allocation, and load balancing, systems can achieve better scalability and resource utilization. Supported by continuous monitoring and iterative refinement, these techniques enable organizations to meet both performance and cost objectives effectively. Whether applied in operating systems, cloud platforms, or HPC environments, these optimizations ensure robust and efficient resource management.

Chapter Six

Performance Benchmarking and Testing

Tools and methodologies for benchmarking Docker performance

Benchmarking Docker performance is a critical process for understanding how efficiently containerized applications use resources and operate under varying workloads. It helps identify performance bottlenecks, fine-tune resource allocation, and ensure applications deliver optimal results. This exploration delves into the tools and strategies available for effectively benchmarking Docker environments, providing actionable insights to improve system performance.

Why Benchmark Docker Performance?

Benchmarking Docker containers offers valuable insights into several performance aspects:

- **Resource Utilization**: Understand how containers consume CPU, memory, disk I/O, and network resources.

- **Scalability**: Assess how well applications handle increased workloads or additional containers.

- **Latency and Throughput**: Measure responsiveness and data handling capabilities under different conditions.

- **Load Stability**: Test the reliability of containers under sustained or peak loads.

These metrics are essential for optimizing containerized environments and ensuring efficient use of resources.

Tools for Docker Benchmarking

A variety of tools are available to measure different aspects of Docker performance. Each serves a unique purpose and provides metrics that can guide optimization.

1. Docker Stats

The **docker stats** command is a built-in utility that offers real-time data about running containers, making it a convenient starting point for performance analysis.

Example:

```
docker stats --all
```

This command provides key metrics such as:

- CPU usage

- Memory consumption

- Network I/O

- Block I/O

2. Sysbench

Sysbench is a versatile tool for benchmarking CPU, memory, and disk I/O performance. It is particularly useful for simulating workloads within containers.

Example:

```
docker run --rm severalnines/sysbench sysbench cpu --cpu-max-prime=20000 run
```

This measures CPU performance by calculating prime numbers up to 20,000.

3. Apache Benchmark (ab)

Apache Benchmark is a simple tool to test how well a containerized web application handles HTTP requests and user load.

Example:

```
ab -n 1000 -c 100 http://localhost:8080/
```

This sends 1,000 requests with 100 concurrent users, tracking response times and request handling.

4. fio

The Flexible I/O Tester (**fio**) benchmarks disk performance by simulating read and write operations. It can evaluate storage performance for containers.

Example:

```
docker run --rm -v /data:/data ubuntu fio --name=test --rw=readwrite --size=500MB --bs
   =64k --numjobs=4
```

This command tests read-write performance with specified parameters.

5. wrk

wrk is a highly efficient HTTP benchmarking tool that evaluates throughput and latency for web servers running in containers.

Example:

```
wrk -t12 -c400 -d30s http://localhost:8080/
```

This simulates 12 threads and 400 concurrent connections for 30 seconds, providing detailed performance data.

6. Cadvisor

Google's **cadvisor** provides detailed metrics on container resource usage and performance. It integrates with monitoring tools like Prometheus and Grafana for enhanced visibility.

Example:

```
docker run -d --name=cadvisor -p 8080:8080 --volume=/:/rootfs:ro --volume=/var/run:/var/run:ro
   --volume=/sys:/sys:ro --volume=/var/lib/docker/:/var/lib/docker:ro google/cadvisor
```

Access metrics via **http://localhost:8080**.

Methodologies for Effective Benchmarking

Using structured methodologies ensures benchmarking efforts yield meaningful results:

1. Define Objectives

Identify the specific performance metrics you wish to measure, such as resource usage, response times, or scalability.

2. Establish a Baseline

Run initial tests under normal or minimal workloads to create a reference point for future comparisons.

3. Simulate Workloads

Use tools like Sysbench or Apache Benchmark to simulate real-world scenarios, gradually increasing workload intensity to evaluate system resilience.

4. Test Scaling

Analyze the system's ability to scale by incrementally adding containers or increasing the workload. Measure how this impacts overall resource allocation and performance.

5. Perform Long-Duration Tests

Test containerized applications over extended periods to identify issues like memory leaks or performance degradation.

6. Leverage Monitoring Tools

Track metrics in real time using tools like Cadvisor or Prometheus to gain a deeper understanding of container behavior during tests.

7. Analyze Results

Use the data collected to identify inefficiencies, resource constraints, or other bottlenecks. Adjust configurations and redeploy to test improvements.

Best Practices

- **Ensure Consistency**: Use identical environments for each test to avoid variability in results.

- **Repeat Tests**: Run benchmarks multiple times to confirm the reliability of findings.

- **Minimize Interference**: Avoid running unrelated processes during benchmarks to maintain accuracy.

- **Document Results**: Record test parameters and outcomes for future analysis and comparisons.

Conclusion

Benchmarking Docker performance requires the combination of robust tools and a systematic approach to deliver actionable insights. Tools like Docker Stats, Sysbench, and Apache Benchmark provide comprehensive performance data, while methodologies such as workload simulation and scaling analysis ensure meaningful evaluations. By employing these practices, organizations can optimize their containerized applications, making them more reliable, scalable, and resource-efficient. These insights form the foundation for ongoing improvements in modern containerized environments.

Creating reproducible test environments

Establishing reproducible test environments is pivotal for achieving consistent software development and testing processes. These environments allow developers and testers to identify defects early, manage dependencies more effectively, and ensure that all team members operate under similar testing conditions. This article will explore why reproducible test environments are necessary, describe tools and strategies for setting them up, and provide guidance on how to implement them efficiently.

The Significance of Reproducible Test Environments

Reproducible test environments are vital due to several reasons:

- **Consistency Across Teams**: They prevent discrepancies in software functionality across different machines by ensuring every team member works in an identical setup.

- **Reliable Quality Assurance**: Consistent environments allow for predictable and reliable testing outcomes, facilitating the early detection of issues.

- **Streamlined Automation**: These environments support the automation of testing and deployment processes, which increases operational efficiency.

- **Adaptable Scaling**: They enable teams to scale their testing efforts according to project demands without additional complexity.

Strategies for Building Reproducible Environments

Implementing reproducible test environments involves a mix of thoughtful planning, the right tools, and adherence to best practices. Key strategies include:

1. Infrastructure as Code (IaC)

IaC is a technique where infrastructure setups are codified using tools like Terraform, Ansible, or Puppet, making it easier to version, share, and reproduce setups accurately.

Example:

```
# Terraform script to provision an AWS EC2 instance
provider "aws" {
  region = "us-west-2"
}


resource "aws_instance" "example" {
  ami           = "ami-0c55b159cbfafe1f0"
  instance_type = "t2.micro"
}
```

This script ensures that any developer can deploy the same virtual server quickly and reliably.

2. Containerization

Containers are excellent for creating isolated environments that encapsulate an application and its dependencies. Docker is a popular choice for containerization, ensuring that the environment is consistent no matter where the container runs.

Example:

```
# Dockerfile for setting up a Python application
FROM python:3.8-slim
WORKDIR /app
COPY requirements.txt .
RUN pip install -r requirements.txt
COPY . .
CMD ["python", "app.py"]
```

This Dockerfile describes a reproducible Python runtime environment, which can be executed identically on any Docker-enabled machine.

3. Version Control Systems

Store all environment configurations, scripts, and Dockerfiles in a version control system like Git. This practice makes it possible to track changes and roll back to earlier configurations if necessary.

4. Automated Configuration

Automate the configuration of environments using scripts and tools like Chef or Ansible, which ensure that software and its dependencies are installed and configured uniformly across all environments.

Example:

```
# Ansible playbook for setting up web servers
- hosts: webservers
  roles:
    - common
    - web
```

This playbook configures web servers consistently by applying predefined roles and configurations.

5. Environment Parity

Strive to maintain parity between development, testing, and production environments. This includes using the same operating systems, software versions, and network configurations to minimize deployment risks.

Monitoring and Validation

Implement continuous monitoring and validation practices to ensure that the environments do not drift from their intended configurations. Tools like Jenkins can automate testing and deployment, while Nagios or Prometheus can monitor environment health and performance.

Addressing Challenges

- **Data Management**: Ensure test data remains consistent and reproducible by using scripts to generate or sanitize data as needed.

- **Comprehensive Documentation**: Maintain detailed documentation of all environment specifications and updates to assist in troubleshooting and maintenance.

- **Handling Updates**: Regularly update and patch environments while ensuring these changes do not disrupt existing setups.

Conclusion

Creating reproducible test environments is an integral part of modern software development, supporting consistent, reliable, and efficient testing and deployment processes. By leveraging infrastructure as code, containerization, thorough version control, and automation, teams can develop environments that enhance the predictability of testing outcomes and streamline development workflows. Continuously monitoring and updating these environments is crucial for maintaining their effectiveness over time, ensuring they continue to meet the evolving needs of software projects.

Analyzing and interpreting performance data

In today's data-centric world, the ability to effectively analyze and interpret performance data stands as a cornerstone for enhancing operational strategies and achieving business efficiencies. This overview delves into the pivotal tools, methodologies, and approaches necessary for proficient data analysis, highlighting how strategic insights derived from performance data can catalyze operational improvements and decision-making processes.

The Critical Role of Performance Data Analysis

Analyzing performance data is indispensable across various domains such as corporate operations, IT infrastructure management, and software development, providing significant advantages:

- **Trend Identification**: Detecting patterns in historical data assists in forecasting future performance and pinpointing emerging issues.

- **Operational Improvement**: Data-driven insights help streamline processes, enhancing efficiency and productivity.

- **Informed Decision-Making**: Robust data analysis supports strategic business decisions by providing factual evidence and predictions.

- **Effective Resource Management**: Analyzing performance data ensures optimal use of resources, enhancing return on investment.

Essential Tools and Technologies for Data Analysis

A suite of advanced tools and technologies facilitates in-depth analysis of performance data:

1. Statistical Analysis Tools

Programming environments like R and Python, bolstered by libraries such as Pandas, NumPy, and SciPy, offer extensive capabilities for statistical analysis and handling of complex data sets.

Example:

```
import pandas as pd

# Importing and analyzing data
data = pd.read_csv('performance_data.csv')
mean_performance = data['metric'].mean()
print("Average Performance Metric:", mean_performance)
```

This Python script exemplifies how to calculate the mean of a performance metric using Pandas, illustrating a basic yet powerful data analysis technique.

2. Data Visualization Software

Graphical representation tools like Tableau, Power BI, or Python's Matplotlib convert complex data sets into intuitive visual formats that highlight key insights and simplify data interpretation.

Example:

```python
import matplotlib.pyplot as plt

# Visualizing data
categories = ['A', 'B', 'C', 'D']
values = [5, 20, 15, 10]
plt.bar(categories, values)
plt.title('Comparative Performance Analysis')
plt.show()
```

Here, Matplotlib is used to create a bar chart, offering a clear visual comparison of performance across different categories.

3. Business Intelligence Platforms

Platforms such as SAP BI, Oracle BI, and others provide comprehensive dashboards that amalgamate data from disparate sources, equipped with analytical tools to track and analyze key performance indicators.

4. Advanced Database Systems

Robust database management systems facilitate extensive data queries and comprehensive report generation, supporting detailed performance analysis.

Analytical Methodologies

A structured approach to data analysis ensures comprehensiveness and accuracy:

1. Comprehensive Data Collection

Gather extensive data from multiple sources to cover all relevant aspects of performance. This may include logs, user interactions, and system metrics.

2. Meticulous Data Preparation

Process and clean the data to remove any discrepancies or irrelevant details, ensuring the analysis is based on accurate and pertinent information.

3. Thorough Data Analysis

Apply a variety of statistical and computational techniques to extract meaningful insights and understand the data's implications fully.

4. Insightful Data Interpretation

Translate the raw analysis into actionable business insights, aligning findings with strategic objectives and operational needs.

5. Effective Reporting

Communicate the insights clearly through detailed reports and visualizations, making the data accessible and understandable for all stakeholders.

Challenges in Data Analysis

- **Data Integrity**: Ensuring the accuracy and completeness of data is paramount to reliable analysis.

- **Complex Data Structures**: Handling and interpreting data from complex or large-scale data sets requires advanced analytical skills.

- **Integration of Diverse Data Sources**: Merging and aligning data from various origins poses significant technical challenges.

- **Continual Updates**: Keeping analytical models and strategies relevant with evolving business contexts is crucial for sustained effectiveness.

Conclusion

Mastering the analysis and interpretation of performance data is vital for any organization aiming to optimize its operations and make well-informed strategic decisions. By leveraging sophisticated analytical tools and adhering to rigorous methodologies, businesses can unlock profound insights that propel them towards operational excellence and strategic success. Continuous enhancement of analytical capabilities remains essential, ensuring that organizations can adapt to and thrive in an ever-changing business environment.

Chapter Seven

Scalability and Elasticity

Techniques for scaling Docker containers in and out

Scaling Docker containers efficiently is critical for handling applications with fluctuating demand levels. Proper scaling techniques, both in and out, ensure that applications are performant and economical across varying load conditions. This detailed guide discusses the methods and tools essential for dynamic Docker container scaling, including practical implementations and operational guidelines.

Fundamentals of Docker Container Scaling

Scaling Out or horizontal scaling involves adding more containers to spread out the workload, thus enhancing the system's capacity to handle concurrent requests. Conversely, **Scaling In** reduces the number of containers during lower demand periods to optimize resource usage and minimize costs.

Tools and Strategies for Effective Docker Scaling

Several tools facilitate the efficient scaling of Docker containers, each suited for specific environments and requirements:

1. Docker Compose

Docker Compose is instrumental for defining and managing multi-container Docker applications. It simplifies scaling by allowing adjustments to the number of container replicas.

Example:

```
# docker-compose.yml for a basic web service
version: '3'
services:
  web:
    image: nginx
    deploy:
      replicas: 2
```

```
      resources:
        limits:
          cpus: '0.5'
          memory: 50M
      ports:
        - "80:80"
```

This command increases the number of web service **replicas** to four.

```
docker-compose up --scale web=4 -d
```

This command increases the number of web service replicas to four.

2. Docker Swarm

Docker Swarm transforms a group of Docker engines into a single, virtual Docker engine, facilitating native clustering and orchestration capabilities.

Example:

```
docker service create --name my-web-app --replicas 3 nginx
```

This creates a service with three nginx container replicas. To scale this service:

```
docker service scale my-web-app=5
```

This increases the service to five replicas.

3. Kubernetes

Kubernetes is a robust orchestration platform that manages containerized applications with capabilities for automatic scaling based on performance metrics.

Example: First, create a deployment:

```
# Deployment configuration for Kubernetes
apiVersion: apps/v1
kind: Deployment
metadata:
  name: nginx-deployment
spec:
  replicas: 3
  selector:
    matchLabels:
      app: nginx
```

```
  template:
    metadata:
      labels:
        app: nginx
    spec:
      containers:
      - name: nginx
        image: nginx:1.14.2
        ports:
        - containerPort: 80
```

For manual scaling:

```
kubectl scale deployment nginx-deployment --replicas=5
```

To enable auto-scaling:

```
kubectl autoscale deployment nginx-deployment --min=3 --max=10 --cpu-percent=80
```

This setup automatically adjusts the number of replicas to maintain an average CPU usage of 80%.

Best Practices for Scaling Docker Containers

1. Implement Monitoring: Use tools like Prometheus to monitor container performance and trigger scaling based on real-time data.

2. Utilize Load Balancers: Ensure even distribution of traffic among containers, with automatic updates as you scale.

3. Configure Health Checks: Set up health checks to manage traffic flow to only operational containers, enhancing reliability.

4. Allocate Resources Wisely: Set clear resource limits to prevent any container from overutilizing shared resources.

5. Automate Scaling Processes: Establish rules for automatic scaling based on specific metrics to maintain performance without manual intervention.

Overcoming Scaling Challenges

- **Managing Complexity**: Handling dynamic scaling environments requires a solid understanding of orchestration tools and proper configuration.

475

- **Balancing Costs**: While scaling out improves capacity, it also increases costs. Effective scaling strategies need to consider financial impacts.

- **Maintaining Configuration Consistency**: As containers are dynamically scaled, ensuring consistent configurations across all instances poses a challenge.

Conclusion

Scaling Docker containers is essential for managing modern, dynamic applications effectively. Through strategic use of tools like Docker Compose, Docker Swarm, and Kubernetes, and by adhering to established best practices, organizations can ensure their applications scale smoothly and cost-effectively. Keeping abreast of the latest advancements in technology and refining strategies accordingly will be key to leveraging the full capabilities of Docker environments.

Building elastic applications that adapt to workload changes

In contemporary software development, constructing applications that dynamically adapt their resource consumption based on real-time demands is vital. This not only ensures stable performance across varying conditions but also optimizes resource utilization. Here, we explore various approaches and tools necessary to develop such elastic applications effectively, coupled with examples and a discussion on potential challenges.

Importance of Elasticity in Application Development

Elastic applications automatically scale resources according to the workload, essential for maintaining service continuity and operational efficiency under fluctuating demand.

Approaches to Developing Elastic Applications

The development of elastic applications encompasses several key strategies, from the selection of appropriate architectures to the deployment of specific scaling technologies.

1. Selecting a Flexible Architecture

Using a flexible architectural style, such as microservices, is fundamental. This allows individual components or services of the application to scale independently as needed.

Example: In a microservices architecture, a streaming service might scale its video transcoding service independently from its user authentication service based on user demand.

2. Employing Cloud Computing Services

Cloud services from providers like AWS, Azure, and Google Cloud offer built-in scalability features, such as auto-scaling and serverless computing options, which automatically adjust to an application's demands.

Example: With AWS Elastic Beanstalk, developers can deploy applications that automatically scale up or down based on predefined criteria such as CPU utilization or network traffic.

3. Implementing Load Balancing Solutions

Load balancing is crucial for evenly distributing user requests or network traffic across multiple servers, ensuring no single server is overwhelmed, which can degrade performance.

Example:

```
# Basic Nginx load balancing configuration
http {
    upstream myapp {
        server server1.domain.com;
        server server2.domain.com;
    }

    server {
        listen 80;

        location / {
            proxy_pass http://myapp;
        }
    }
}
```

This Nginx configuration helps in distributing the load evenly across servers, enhancing the responsiveness and reliability of applications.

4. Utilizing Autoscaling Capabilities

Autoscaling is a crucial feature for managing the scalability of applications. It allows the system to add or remove resources based on actual usage, preventing overprovisioning and waste.

Example:

```
# Autoscaling in Kubernetes
apiVersion: autoscaling/v2beta2
kind: HorizontalPodAutoscaler
metadata:
  name: web-application-scaler
spec:
  scaleTargetRef:
    apiVersion: apps/v1
    kind: Deployment
    name: web-application
  minReplicas: 2
  maxReplicas: 10
  metrics:
  - type: Resource
    resource:
      name: cpu
      target:
        type: Utilization
        averageUtilization: 50
```

This autoscaler for Kubernetes automatically adjusts the number of pods based on CPU utilization, ensuring the deployment scales efficiently in response to load changes.

5. Monitoring Application Performance

Continuous monitoring of application performance is essential for elasticity, as it provides the data needed to make informed scaling decisions. Tools such as Prometheus and Grafana are often used to track performance metrics.

Overcoming Challenges in Elastic Application Development

- **Complexity Management**: Managing the complexity of scalable applications, especially when they utilize microservices architectures or operate across multiple clouds, can be challenging.

- **Cost Optimization**: Although elasticity can reduce costs by matching resources to demand, it requires precise configuration to avoid unnecessary expenses due to over-scaling.

- **Ongoing Optimization**: Maintaining optimal performance as an application scales requires continual assessment and adjustment of configurations.

Conclusion

Developing elastic applications is essential for modern businesses that experience variable workloads. By embracing scalable architectures, leveraging cloud scalability services, and employing effective load balancing and autoscaling techniques, developers can create systems that not only meet current demands efficiently but also adapt to future conditions. Continuous monitoring and iterative improvement will ensure these applications remain robust and cost-effective.

Case studies of scalable Docker deployments

The versatility of Docker in achieving scalable deployments across various industry sectors showcases its essential role in modern software infrastructure. This detailed review presents multiple case studies that reveal how different organizations have leveraged Docker to enhance scalability and operational efficiency. Each example provides insights into the strategies and configurations used to facilitate scalable Docker deployments.

Case Study 1: Scaling an E-Commerce Platform

Overview: A leading online retailer struggled with handling traffic spikes during key sales events. Their legacy systems were either over-provisioned during low traffic or faltered under high demand.

Solution: The retailer transitioned to Docker containers for their web frontends, databases, and backend services, employing Docker Swarm for managing container orchestration.

Implementation:

```
docker service create --name ecommerce-site --replicas 10 --publish 8080:80 my-ecommerce-app
```

This setup initiated a Docker service with initial ten replicas of the e-commerce application, allowing dynamic scaling in response to traffic changes.

Outcome: Containerization provided the e-commerce site with the necessary agility to scale resources efficiently, matching the fluctuating demand during sales peaks and regular operations. This led to enhanced user satisfaction and cost savings from optimized resource utilization.

Case Study 2: Financial Data Processing at Scale

Overview: A financial analytics company needed a robust solution to manage and process fluctuating volumes of market data in real-time.

Solution: They adopted a microservices architecture using Docker, with Kubernetes handling the orchestration. This setup allowed for isolated scaling of individual services according to data processing demands.

Implementation:

```yaml
apiVersion: apps/v1
kind: Deployment
metadata:
  name: financial-data-service
spec:
  replicas: 4
  selector:
    matchLabels:
      task: data-processing
  template:
    metadata:
      labels:
        task: data-processing
    spec:
      containers:
      - name: processor
        image: finance-processor:latest
        ports:
        - containerPort: 6000
```

This deployment in Kubernetes ensures that four instances of the data processing service are always running, with the capability to scale up automatically based on system load.

Outcome: The implementation of Docker and Kubernetes enabled the firm to efficiently scale data processing operations during peak times, ensuring data integrity and timely insights.

Case Study 3: Media Streaming Service Expansion

Overview: A multinational media company required a solution to scale their streaming service globally to cater to an expanding user base and high-demand events.

Solution: The company utilized Docker for containerizing the streaming software and deployed these containers using Amazon ECS to manage scaling effectively based on viewer traffic.

Implementation:

```
aws ecs update-service --service live-stream-service --desired-count 20 --cluster configured-cluster
```

This command adjusts the Amazon ECS service to manage 20 instances of the streaming service, ready to scale further in response to viewer demand.

Outcome: Through Docker and ECS, the media company achieved global scalability, which greatly enhanced the viewer experience during major events by reducing buffering and load times.

Conclusion

These case studies demonstrate Docker's transformative impact on organizational capability to dynamically scale applications across various conditions and demands. Whether through enhancing an e-commerce platform's responsiveness, enabling real-time financial data processing, or expanding media streaming capacity, Docker's flexibility as a containerization tool provides substantial benefits. These organizations not only realized improved operational efficiencies but also fostered innovation in their respective fields, responding adeptly to both market and technological advancements.

Chapter Eight

Docker in Hybrid and Multi-Cloud Environments

Strategies for deploying Docker in hybrid and multi-cloud environments

Navigating the complexities of deploying Docker in environments that blend both on-premises resources and multiple cloud services is crucial for modern enterprises. This guide explores strategic approaches for deploying Docker effectively across hybrid and multi-cloud environments, focusing on maintaining compatibility, optimizing resource utilization, and ensuring seamless operation.

Understanding Hybrid and Multi-Cloud Docker Deployments

Hybrid cloud models integrate on-premises computing resources with public cloud services, enabling businesses to leverage the strengths of both environments. Multi-cloud environments use services from more than one cloud provider, reducing dependency on any single vendor and increasing flexibility.

Effective Strategies for Docker Deployment Across Clouds

Deploying Docker in these varied environments necessitates careful planning and the use of specific tools designed to handle the challenges associated with multi-environment setups.

1. Employ Unified Management Platforms

Utilizing tools that provide a consistent management layer across different environments is essential. Kubernetes is a standout choice for orchestrating Docker containers, as it works uniformly whether on-cloud or on-premises.

Example:

```
apiVersion: v1
kind: Pod
metadata:
  name: multi-env-app
spec:
  containers:
  - name: multi-env-app
    image: mycustomimage:latest
    ports:
    - containerPort: 8080
```

This basic Kubernetes pod configuration can be applied across AWS, Azure, Google Cloud, or private data centers, ensuring consistent deployment parameters.

2. Implement Comprehensive Container Registry Practices

Maintaining a centralized container registry that all environments can access is critical. Docker Hub and cloud-specific solutions like AWS ECR or Azure Container Registry allow for the centralized management and distribution of Docker images.

Example:

```
docker tag myapp:latest 123456789.dkr.ecr.us-east-1.amazonaws.com/myapp:latest
docker push 123456789.dkr.ecr.us-east-1.amazonaws.com/myapp:latest
```

This sequence tags and uploads a Docker image to AWS ECR, making it accessible across any deployment environment.

3. Standardize Network and Security Configurations

Ensuring that networking and security settings are uniform across deployments is crucial for protecting data and maintaining service integrity. Using service meshes like Istio can help standardize these aspects.

Example:

```
apiVersion: networking.istio.io/v1alpha3
kind: Gateway
metadata:
  name: secure-gateway
spec:
  selector:
    istio: ingressgateway
  servers:
  - port:
      number: 80
      name: http
      protocol: HTTP
    hosts:
    - "www.myapp.com"
```

This configuration for an Istio Gateway manages secure access to services, applying consistent policies across different cloud environments.

4. Adopt Cloud-Agnostic Data Solutions

Data management should be consistent and flexible across environments. Employing cloud-agnostic storage solutions, such as using Kubernetes persistent volumes that interface with different cloud storage backends, ensures data is always available and protected.

5. Automate Deployments with CI/CD Pipelines

Continuous Integration and Continuous Deployment (CI/CD) systems are integral for automating Docker deployments. They help ensure consistent, error-free deployment processes across multiple environments.

Example:

```
# Jenkins Pipeline for multi-cloud Docker deployments
pipeline {
    agent any
    stages {
        stage('Build') {
            steps {
                script {
                    docker.build("myapp:$BUILD_ID")
                }
            }
        }
        stage('Deploy') {
            steps {
                script {
                    sh './deploy_to_clouds.sh'
                }
            }
        }
    }
}
```

This Jenkins pipeline script automates the building and deploying of Docker containers across different cloud environments using a custom shell script.

Conclusion

Deploying Docker in hybrid and multi-cloud environments can significantly enhance an organization's operational flexibility and efficiency. By integrating unified management tools, centralized container registries, consistent security practices, cloud-agnostic data solutions, and automated CI/CD pipelines, businesses can ensure robust, scalable, and secure application deployments. These strategic approaches not only streamline operations but also prepare enterprises to thrive in a competitive digital landscape.

Performance considerations and tuning for cloud environments

Enhancing application performance within cloud environments is pivotal for businesses leveraging the scalable and dynamic nature of cloud computing. This analysis covers crucial considerations and tuning strategies to optimize efficiency, manage costs effectively, and elevate the user experience within these platforms.

Essential Performance Considerations for Cloud Deployments

Successful performance tuning in cloud settings involves several key aspects, each addressing a distinct element of cloud functionality.

1. Resource Scalability

The cloud's capacity to scale resources such as CPU, memory, and storage dynamically is among its greatest strengths. This flexibility requires careful monitoring to ensure resources are neither underutilized nor overstrained.

Example: In AWS, auto-scaling can be configured to maintain optimal performance and cost:

```
aws autoscaling create-or-update-auto-scaling-group --auto-scaling-group-name scalable-app --scaling
    -configuration file://scaling-config.json
```

In scaling-config.json, you might specify:

```
{
  "TargetValue": 70.0,
  "PredefinedMetricSpecification": {
    "PredefinedMetricType": "ASGAverageCPUUtilization"
  }
}
```

This configuration automatically adjusts the compute capacity to keep the CPU utilization at 70%, optimizing both performance and expenditure.

2. Latency Reduction

In the cloud, latency is impacted by the physical distance between data centers and end-users, as well as the network infrastructure. Employing advanced content delivery networks (CDNs) and strategically located data centers can help mitigate latency issues.

3. Network Configuration

For applications that demand significant bandwidth, ensuring sufficient network capacity is crucial. Opt for cloud instances and services that offer high network performance to prevent bottlenecks.

Example:

```
az vm create --resource-group MyGroup --name MyVM --image UbuntuLTS --size Standard_F4 --enable
  -accelerated-networking true
```

This Azure CLI command creates a VM with accelerated networking enabled, enhancing throughput and reducing network latency.

4. Storage Speed

The performance of cloud storage can vary widely based on the technology used (SSDs vs. HDDs) and the specific storage service. Optimizing how applications read from and write to storage is critical for performance.

5. Optimal Application Design

Applications built with a cloud-first mindset, such as those using microservices architectures, can inherently leverage cloud scalability and robustness more effectively.

Strategic Approaches to Cloud Performance Tuning

Optimizing cloud performance involves a combination of proactive strategies and real-time adjustments:

1. Regular Monitoring and Analysis

Continuous monitoring with tools like Google Cloud Operations (formerly Stackdriver) or Azure Monitor is essential for understanding performance trends and making informed tuning decisions.

2. Comprehensive Load Testing

Using tools such as LoadRunner or Apache JMeter to simulate user traffic can help identify potential performance issues before they affect end-users.

3. Caching Techniques

Effective use of caching, both at the database and application levels, can significantly decrease load times and reduce backend pressure.

4. Database Optimization

Regularly refining database performance through indexing, query optimization, and choosing the appropriate database type can dramatically improve response times and efficiency.

5. Code Optimization

Refactoring and optimizing application code to remove bottlenecks and streamline operations is crucial for maintaining high performance.

Challenges in Tuning Cloud Performance

- **Balancing Costs with Performance**: Higher performance typically incurs higher costs, making it essential to find an optimal balance that meets business needs without overspending.

- **Dealing with Multi-Tenancy**: Shared resources in public cloud environments can lead to inconsistent performance, known as the "noisy neighbor" problem.

- **Complexity in Auto-scaling**: Auto-scaling adds operational complexity, especially when it comes to maintaining session state across multiple instances.

Conclusion

Performance tuning for cloud environments is a multifaceted process that requires a deep understanding of both the technical and operational aspects of cloud resources. By implementing targeted strategies for resource allocation, latency management, and continuous monitoring, organizations can ensure their cloud-based applications perform effectively and efficiently. Keeping pace with evolving cloud technologies and continuously adapting strategies is vital for maintaining optimal performance in the cloud.

Managing cross-cloud container deployments

Handling container deployments across various cloud environments is becoming a critical skill for modern enterprises. This capability allows organizations to leverage the best features from multiple cloud providers, but it introduces challenges that need strategic management to ensure smooth operation and optimal efficiency. Here, we explore the practicalities and strategies vital for administering containers effectively across disparate cloud platforms.

Key Considerations for Cross-Cloud Container Deployments

Deploying containers across multiple clouds enables redundancy and leverages distinct advantages of each platform, but it also brings complexities related to integration and management.

Obstacles in Cross-Cloud Container Management

1. **Diverse Configuration Demands**: Each cloud provider offers unique tools and services, making standardized configurations across environments challenging.

2. **Uniformity and Compatibility**: Achieving consistent container performance across different clouds can be difficult due to varying standards and services.

3. **Adherence to Compliance**: Managing compliance with differing regional regulations and data residency requirements necessitates meticulous planning.

Strategies for Streamlined Management

Adopting several strategies can greatly assist in navigating the intricacies of cross-cloud container deployments effectively.

1. Utilization of Universal Management Platforms

Tools that can manage container deployments across multiple clouds can reduce complexity. Kubernetes is particularly effective as it can orchestrate containers on almost any infrastructure.

Example:

```
apiVersion: v1
kind: Pod
metadata:
  name: universal-pod
spec:
  containers:
  - name: nginx-container
    image: nginx
    ports:
    - containerPort: 80
```

This simple Kubernetes Pod setup ensures consistent deployment across any cloud provider, simplifying management and operational processes.

2. Implementing Infrastructure as Code

Infrastructure as code (IaC) allows for reproducible setups across various clouds, promoting consistency and ease of deployment.

Example:

```
resource "aws_instance" "example" {
  ami           = "ami-123abc"
  instance_type = "t2.micro"
}

resource "google_compute_instance" "example" {
  name         = "example-instance"
  machine_type = "n1-standard-1"
}
```

These Terraform scripts provide a straightforward way to deploy instances in AWS and Google Cloud, ensuring consistent configurations and simplifying multi-cloud management.

3. Centralized Container Registry Approach

Maintaining a single container registry accessible from any cloud platform is essential. Registries like Docker Hub or AWS ECR facilitate consistent and secure access to Docker images needed for deployments.

4. Harmonizing Network and Security Protocols

Ensuring secure and efficient communications between containers across cloud platforms is crucial. Standardizing VPNs or using cloud-native networking solutions can help maintain secure and reliable connections.

5. Robust Monitoring Systems

Adopting comprehensive monitoring solutions ensures visibility into container performance across clouds. Prometheus and Grafana can provide valuable insights into operational metrics.

Example:

```yaml
apiVersion: monitoring.coreos.com/v1
kind: Prometheus
metadata:
  name: cross-cloud-monitoring
spec:
  serviceMonitorSelector:
    matchLabels:
      team: backend
```

This configuration sets up Prometheus to monitor services labeled with backend across multiple clouds, aiding in centralized performance management.

Conclusion

Successfully managing container deployments across multiple cloud environments requires careful planning and the use of sophisticated tools that support flexibility and scalability. By incorporating universal management platforms, infrastructure as code, centralized registries, standardized network setups, and comprehensive monitoring, organizations can achieve effective cross-cloud container deployments. This not only enhances operational flexibility but also ensures that applications run efficiently and securely across diverse cloud platforms. As cloud technologies advance, continuously updating and refining deployment strategies will be crucial for maintaining robust multi-cloud environments.

Chapter Nine

Advanced Docker Security Practices

Security considerations in high-performance environments

In high-performance computing environments, integrating stringent security measures is essential due to the high stakes involved in processing critical and sensitive information. These settings demand robust security protocols that align with their operational needs and maintain system performance. This discussion outlines the primary security considerations necessary for safeguarding high-performance environments effectively.

Importance of Robust Security in High-Performance Settings

High-performance environments are attractive targets for cyber threats due to their processing capabilities and the sensitive data they handle. Threats such as data breaches, unauthorized access, and Denial of Service (DoS) attacks pose significant risks to system integrity and data security.

Essential Security Measures

1. Ensuring Data Security

Encrypting data at rest and in transit is fundamental in these environments. It is crucial to implement encryption techniques that do not degrade the performance of high-speed computing systems.

Example: Applying AES encryption enabled by hardware acceleration features such as AES-NI can effectively secure data without significant performance loss.

```
# Check for AES-NI support on a Linux machine
grep -m1 -o aes /proc/cpuinfo
```

2. Network Security Enhancement

Robust network security measures are vital due to the complex network structures often seen in high-performance settings. Effective strategies include deploying state-of-the-art firewall technologies, robust intrusion detection systems (IDS), and intrusion prevention systems (IPS), alongside network segmentation to safeguard different parts of the network effectively.

Example: Setting up network segmentation using VLANs can protect critical areas of the network, minimizing the risk of internal and external threats.

```
# Create a VLAN on a network interface in Linux
vconfig add eth0 30
ip link set up eth0.30
```

3. Access Control and Authentication

Strong access control systems and authentication mechanisms ensure that only authorized entities have access to the high-performance computing resources. This includes implementing multi-factor authentication (MFA), role-based access control (RBAC), and strict adherence to the least privilege principle.

Example: Integrating an LDAP system to manage user roles and privileges helps enhance security across the network.

```
# Add a user to LDAP
ldapadd -x -D "cn=admin,dc=yourdomain,dc=com" -W -f addUser.ldif
```

4. Regular Audits and Compliance Monitoring

Conducting regular audits and maintaining compliance with relevant standards and regulations, such as ISO 27001 or PCI DSS, ensure that the security measures are adequate and up to date.

Example: Using tools like OpenSCAP for automated security and compliance auditing can help maintain high security standards consistently.

```
# Run a compliance check with OpenSCAP
oscap xccdf eval --profile xccdf_org.ssgproject.content_profile_pci-dss --report security-audit
    -report.html /usr/share/xml/scap/ssg/content/ssg-debian-ds.xml
```

5. Minimizing Performance Impact

Selecting and implementing security solutions that minimize impact on system performance is crucial. This might involve integrating SIEM systems that effectively manage security logs without compromising the operational performance of the high-performance environment.

Example: Setting up a lightweight SIEM system like ELK Stack can provide effective monitoring and analysis without significant resource consumption.

Navigating the Trade-offs

The implementation of these security measures in high-performance computing environments requires a balance between robust security and maintaining system performance. Optimizing both aspects involves selecting appropriate security technologies, customizing solutions to fit specific operational environments, and continuously updating security practices.

Conclusion

Securing high-performance computing environments is complex but imperative. By implementing advanced security measures thoughtfully and maintaining them diligently, organizations can protect their valuable data and computing assets without compromising on performance. Continuous improvement and adaptation to emerging threats are crucial for sustaining security in these critical environments.

Implementing security without compromising performance

Securing digital infrastructures while preserving system performance is a pivotal concern for organizations aiming to protect sensitive data and maintain efficient operations. This balance is crucial as heavy security protocols can often slow down system processes. Here, we explore methods and technologies designed to safeguard assets without hindering performance, providing organizations with solutions that uphold both security and efficiency.

Key Challenges in Achieving Security and Performance Equilibrium

Implementing thorough security measures, such as complex encryption and comprehensive monitoring, can impose significant demands on system resources. To overcome these challenges, organizations must employ strategic approaches that enhance security without detrimental effects on performance.

Effective Strategies for Balancing Security with System Efficiency

1. Utilizing Efficient Encryption Solutions

Encryption is essential for data security but can be resource-intensive. Advanced hardware-assisted encryption technologies can help mitigate the performance impact.

Example: Employing AES-NI capabilities allows for faster encryption processes that do not overload the CPU.

```
# Command to check for AES-NI support on Linux systems
grep -o aes /proc/cpuinfo
```

This command confirms whether AES-NI is enabled on your hardware, facilitating more efficient data encryption operations.

2. Targeted Data Encryption

Encrypting all data can unnecessarily strain resources. By identifying and encrypting only sensitive data, organizations can optimize encryption efforts where they are most needed without broadly affecting system performance.

3. Implementing Smart Intrusion Detection Systems

Modern intrusion detection systems that incorporate sophisticated algorithms can detect threats effectively without scanning all traffic, thereby maintaining network throughput.

Example: Configuring Snort to monitor for specific threats can minimize the resources used for traffic analysis.

```
# Snort rule to identify specific suspicious activity
alert tcp $EXTERNAL_NET any -> $HOME_NET 443 (msg:"Suspicious traffic detected"; flow:to_server
    ,established; content:"|18 cf 52|"; depth:3; sid:1000010; rev:1;)
```

This rule directs Snort to focus on particular patterns that signify potential threats, reducing the need for deep packet inspection across all data.

4. Distributing Security Load

Allocating the security processing load across multiple devices or services can prevent any single system from becoming a bottleneck, thus preserving overall performance.

Example: Using a load balancer to manage traffic across several security devices can prevent performance degradation.

```
# Load balancer configuration to distribute security checks
backend security_layer
    balance roundrobin
    server sec1 192.168.1.101:80 check
    server sec2 192.168.1.102:80 check
```

This setup distributes incoming requests evenly across multiple security appliances, enhancing responsiveness and reliability.

5. Optimizing Security Monitoring

Choosing security monitoring tools that prioritize real-time analysis with minimal data storage can prevent performance slowdowns. Stream processing technologies offer a way to handle extensive data analysis efficiently.

Example: Incorporating Kafka as a real-time data processing tool in security systems allows for handling large volumes of logs efficiently.

```
# Starting a Kafka producer for real-time log processing
kafka-console-producer --broker-list localhost:9092 --topic security_events
```

This enables fast processing and analysis of security-related data streams without significant impacts on core system resources.

Conclusion

Ensuring robust security protocols while maintaining optimal performance is achievable through strategic technology choices and resource management. By integrating advanced encryption methods, selective data protection, efficient threat detection, balanced load distribution, and streamlined monitoring, organizations can secure their systems effectively without compromising operational performance. Regularly updating and refining these strategies is vital as technologies evolve, ensuring that security measures continue to be both effective and efficient.

Advanced security features and best practices

Ensuring robust security measures in an organization involves more than just basic defenses; it requires a proactive approach to integrate advanced security features and best practices. This discussion outlines critical technologies and methodologies that fortify cybersecurity frameworks, ensuring organizations are well-equipped to handle sophisticated cyber threats while maintaining operational integrity.

Advanced Security Technologies

1. Multi-Factor Authentication (MFA)

MFA is essential for enhancing security by requiring multiple forms of verification before granting access to systems or data, greatly minimizing the risk associated with compromised credentials.

Best Practice: Enforce MFA on all critical systems, particularly for administrative access and sensitive data environments, to strengthen access security.

2. Data Encryption

Protecting data integrity and confidentiality requires robust encryption protocols for data at rest and in transit. Employing AES with 256-bit encryption offers a strong layer of security.

Example: Implement TLS for network data transmissions to ensure that all data exchanged over the internet is secure.

```
# Example command to enable HTTPS in Apache .htaccess
RewriteEngine On
RewriteCond %{SERVER_PORT} 80
RewriteRule ^(.*)$ https://%{HTTP_HOST}/$1 [R,L]
```

This command configures a server to redirect HTTP traffic to HTTPS, securing data in transit.

3. Anomaly Detection

Utilizing advanced anomaly detection tools that incorporate machine learning can help in identifying irregular activities that may signify security breaches.

Best Practice: Incorporate these systems into your SIEM solution to automate monitoring and enhance threat detection and response capabilities.

4. Endpoint Detection and Response (EDR)

EDR is crucial for real-time monitoring, detection, and response to threats at endpoint devices, providing a critical defense layer.

Best Practice: Deploy EDR solutions across all organizational endpoints to monitor and respond to potential threats promptly.

5. Zero Trust Security Model

Adopting a zero trust model involves not assuming trust within or outside the network perimeters; every access request must be verified before access is granted.

Best Practice: Apply strict access controls and validate all requests to minimize the attack surface and enhance the security posture.

Best Practices for Cybersecurity

1. Routine Security Evaluations

Regularly conducting security audits and penetration testing helps identify and address vulnerabilities.

Best Practice: Engage external security professionals to perform thorough penetration testing periodically to assess the effectiveness of existing security measures.

2. Ongoing Security Education

Continuous employee training on security best practices and potential cyber threats is vital for reinforcing security awareness.

Best Practice: Implement a continuous training program that includes regular updates and assessments to ensure all staff are informed about the latest security protocols and threats.

3. Incident Response Preparedness

Having a comprehensive incident response plan enables organizations to act swiftly and effectively in the event of a security breach.

Best Practice: Develop and regularly update an incident response plan that details response procedures and recovery processes.

4. Systematic Update and Patch Management

Maintaining up-to-date software and hardware is crucial for defending against known vulnerabilities and exploits.

Best Practice: Automate the patch management process to ensure timely application of all security updates and minimize human error.

Conclusion

Adopting advanced security features and following best practices are fundamental for enhancing an organization's defense against advanced cyber threats. By implementing multifaceted security measures such as MFA, encryption, anomaly detection, EDR, and a zero trust approach, alongside maintaining rigorous training, auditing, and incident management protocols, organizations can build a resilient cybersecurity framework. As threats evolve, continuously advancing these security strategies is essential to protect against future vulnerabilities.

Chapter Ten

GPU and Hardware Acceleration

Utilizing GPUs and other hardware accelerators in Docker

Harnessing hardware accelerators like GPUs within Docker environments is pivotal for tasks demanding substantial computational resources. These accelerators enhance performance for applications involved in machine learning, intensive data processing, and video processing tasks. This guide discusses how to integrate GPUs and other hardware accelerators into Docker containers, illustrating the setup process, benefits, and essential practices for optimal utilization.

Overview of Hardware Acceleration with Docker

Docker's ability to package applications into containers offers consistency across various computing environments. Although Docker primarily abstracts applications from their underlying hardware, it now supports direct access to hardware accelerators, crucial for performance-intensive applications.

Advantages of Integrating Hardware Accelerators with Docker

Integrating hardware accelerators such as GPUs into Docker containers can significantly improve computational speeds, reduce processing times, and decrease energy consumption.

This integration is especially beneficial in areas such as artificial intelligence and computational science, where quick data processing is critical.

Steps to Enable GPU Usage in Docker

Setting Up Docker for GPU Access

To allow Docker containers to utilize GPU resources, specific configurations are necessary. Nvidia provides a specialized Docker utility, **nvidia-docker**, which facilitates the management of Docker containers with Nvidia GPU access.

Setting up Nvidia-Docker:

1. **Update Nvidia Drivers**: Ensure the Nvidia drivers are current to guarantee compatibility and performance optimization.

2. **Install the Nvidia Container Toolkit**: This toolkit enables the Docker Engine to interface with Nvidia GPUs effectively.

```
# Setup the Nvidia Docker repository and install the Nvidia container toolkit
distribution=$(. /etc/os-release;echo $ID$VERSION_ID)
curl -s -L https://nvidia.github.io/nvidia-docker/gpgkey | sudo apt-key add -
curl -s -L https://nvidia.github.io/nvidia-docker/$distribution/nvidia-docker.list | sudo tee /etc/apt
    /sources.list.d/nvidia-docker.list

sudo apt-get update && sudo apt-get install -y nvidia-container-toolkit
sudo systemctl restart docker
```

3. **Launch a Docker Container with GPU Support**:

With **nvidia-docker** installed, you can initiate a Docker container that utilizes GPU resources:

```
# Start a Docker container with GPU access
docker run --gpus all nvidia/cuda:10.0-base nvidia-smi
```

This command enables the Docker container to access all GPUs on the host and uses an Nvidia CUDA image to execute the **nvidia-smi** command, which checks the status of GPUs.

Recommended Practices for Docker and Hardware Accelerators

1. **Ensure Proper Runtime Configuration**: It's crucial that Docker is correctly set up to interact with hardware accelerators to avoid performance bottlenecks.

2. **Manage Resource Allocation**: When multiple containers share GPU resources, effective management is vital to prevent conflicts and ensure efficient operation.

3. **Prioritize Security**: Given that hardware accelerators can process sensitive data, it's essential to secure access to GPU resources, allowing only trusted containers to utilize them.

4. **Maintain and Monitor**: Continual monitoring and regular updates to hardware drivers and Docker configurations are necessary to maintain performance and extend the lifespan of hardware components.

Conclusion

Incorporating GPUs and other hardware accelerators into Docker setups offers significant advantages for compute-heavy applications. By adhering to the detailed setup instructions and best practices outlined above, organizations can optimize their Docker environments to handle sophisticated computational tasks effectively. As integration techniques evolve, the process of deploying and managing these accelerators in Docker will likely become more streamlined, further enhancing the capabilities of containerized applications.

Best practices for hardware-accelerated containers

Leveraging hardware accelerators like GPUs and FPGAs in containerized environments can significantly enhance the computational capabilities of applications requiring intensive data processing. This guide offers a comprehensive look at effective strategies for integrating and managing hardware-accelerated containers, ensuring optimal performance and resource utilization.

Fundamentals of Hardware-Accelerated Containers

Hardware-accelerated containers are designed to utilize specific hardware components to execute tasks more efficiently than traditional CPU-bound operations. These containers are particularly advantageous in fields such as artificial intelligence, where rapid data processing is essential.

Key Strategies for Effective Deployment and Management

1. Verify Hardware Compatibility and Support

It's crucial to ensure that your hardware is fully supported by the container orchestration system you are using. This involves having the correct drivers and APIs installed and up to date.

Example: For Docker containers using Nvidia GPUs, installation of the Nvidia Container Toolkit is necessary to facilitate proper communication between the Docker engine and the GPUs.

```
# Setting up Nvidia Docker support
distribution=$(. /etc/os-release;echo $ID$VERSION_ID)
curl -s -L https://nvidia.github.io/nvidia-docker/gpgkey | sudo apt-key add -
curl -s -L https://nvidia.github.io/nvidia-docker/$distribution/nvidia-docker.list | sudo tee /etc/apt
    /sources.list.d/nvidia-docker.list
sudo apt-get update && sudo apt-get install -y nvidia-container-toolkit
sudo systemctl restart docker
```

2. Manage Resource Allocation Effectively

Appropriate allocation of hardware resources is necessary to prevent resource waste and ensure each container has access to adequate accelerator resources.

Example: Kubernetes allows you to specify GPU limits for pods to manage GPU usage efficiently.

```
apiVersion: v1
kind: Pod
metadata:
  name: gpu-pod
spec:
  containers:
  - name: cuda-container
    image: nvidia/cuda:10.2-base
    resources:
      limits:
        nvidia.com/gpu: 2
```

3. Optimize Container Performance

Use specialized tools that enhance the performance of containers working with hardware accelerators, tailoring operations to the specific hardware characteristics.

Example: Nvidia's NSight tools offer performance analysis tailored for Nvidia GPUs, optimizing container operations.

4. Implement Robust Security Measures

Given the shared nature of hardware resources, secure the access to these accelerators to prevent unauthorized usage.

Example: In Kubernetes, set up RBAC to control access to GPU resources effectively.

```
kind: Role
apiVersion: rbac.authorization.k8s.io/v1
metadata:
  namespace: gpu-apps
  name: gpu-access
rules:
- apiGroups: [""]
  resources: ["pods"]
  verbs: ["create", "get", "list", "watch", "delete"]
```

5. Continuously Monitor Performance

Keeping track of how hardware resources are used by containers helps in identifying potential issues and optimizing resource allocation.

Example: Use Prometheus in conjunction with Grafana to monitor and visualize GPU usage metrics.

```
# Example Prometheus query for GPU utilization
avg by (instance) (rate(nvidia_gpu_duty_cycle[10m]))
```

6. Regular Maintenance and Updates

Ensure that both hardware drivers and container management tools are regularly updated to maintain compatibility and performance.

Conclusion

Integrating hardware acceleration into containerized environments requires careful planning and strategic management. By adhering to these best practices, organizations can effectively enhance their applications' performance through hardware-accelerated containers. Keeping abreast of the latest developments in hardware and container technologies will further ensure that these deployments remain efficient and cutting-edge.

Case studies and performance impacts

In today's technological landscape, the real-world application and consequent performance impacts of innovative technologies significantly influence various sectors. Whether it's through deploying AI in healthcare for enhanced diagnostics or leveraging blockchain in finance for secure transactions, these advancements drive significant changes and introduce new challenges. This document examines several case studies to showcase how technological integrations impact performance across diverse industries.

Enhanced Diagnostics with AI in Healthcare

Artificial Intelligence (AI) has transformed healthcare, particularly in the realm of diagnostics. AI models are increasingly employed to interpret complex medical images, leading to quicker and more accurate diagnosis rates than traditional methods. For instance, a prominent healthcare institution adopted AI for early cancer detection.

Performance Impact: The adoption of AI in diagnostic imaging resulted in a 30% increase in the detection of early-stage cancers, drastically cutting down diagnostic time and improving patient prognosis. AI systems analyzed imaging data with speeds far surpassing human capabilities, significantly decreasing wait times and enabling faster commencement of treatment.

```
# Example pseudo-code for AI-based image analysis for cancer detection
def analyze_image_for_cancer(image_data):
    processed_image = preprocess_image(image_data)
    cancer_prediction = cancer_detection_model.predict(processed_image)
    return cancer_prediction
```

This pseudo-code demonstrates how an AI model might process and analyze medical imaging to identify cancerous cells efficiently.

Blockchain for Secure Financial Transactions

Blockchain technology has redefined financial security and transparency, particularly in international banking transactions. A major financial institution implemented blockchain to handle cross-border payments, aiming to overcome the security and delay issues common in conventional banking systems.

Performance Impact: Integrating blockchain reduced transaction processing times by 70% and notably decreased the incidence of fraud. The technology's inherent security features and the transparency it introduced also minimized discrepancies and errors in transaction records.

```
// Example pseudo-code for validating a transaction with blockchain
function validateTransaction(transaction) {
    const validation_status = blockchain.validate(transaction);
    return validation_status ? 'Transaction Confirmed' : 'Transaction Denied';
}
```

This pseudo-code illustrates how blockchain technology can be used to validate the authenticity of a financial transaction.

Cloud Computing for Scalable E-commerce Solutions

The surge in e-commerce has posed significant scalability challenges, particularly during peak shopping periods. An e-commerce leader implemented a cloud-based system to dynamically scale computing resources based on real-time user demand.

Performance Impact: This strategic move to cloud computing allowed the e-commerce platform to effortlessly triple its traffic handling capacity during peak times, like holiday sales, without degrading website performance. This not only enhanced customer satisfaction but also led to higher sales due to improved system reliability.

```
# Command for dynamically scaling cloud instances
aws ec2 run-instances --image-id ami-abc12345 --count 10 --instance-type m5.large --key-name
   MyServerKey --security-group-ids sg-12345abc --subnet-id subnet-6789def
```

This command line example shows how to increase server instances quickly in cloud environments, a typical necessity for handling peak e-commerce traffic.

Conclusion

These case studies clearly illustrate the transformative effect of technological innovations across various domains. From AI in healthcare enhancing diagnostic processes to blockchain improving financial transaction security, and cloud computing solutions supporting scalable e-commerce operations, these technologies not only bring direct benefits but also emphasize the importance of strategic implementation. As each industry continues to evolve, keeping pace with these technologies will be essential for maintaining competitive advantages and fostering sustainable development.

Chapter Eleven

Docker and Microservices Optimization

Performance tuning for microservices architectures

Microservices architectures are a strategic choice for developing scalable and manageable applications. By decomposing large, monolithic applications into smaller, independently deployable services, organizations can achieve enhanced modularity and easier maintenance. Nonetheless, optimizing performance within microservices architectures involves addressing unique challenges related to service interaction, data management, and resource utilization. This article outlines effective tactics for enhancing performance in microservices environments.

Key Considerations for Microservices Performance

Performance issues in microservices can stem from multiple factors including service communication overhead, data consistency challenges, and inefficient resource management. Addressing these factors is essential for maintaining a robust microservices architecture.

Approaches to Enhance Microservices Performance

1. Design Services for Efficiency

The architectural design of each microservice plays a critical role in overall system performance. Services should be designed to minimize dependencies, which helps prevent cascading failures and enhances service resilience.

Best Practice: Adopt Domain-Driven Design (DDD) to encapsulate microservice logic around distinct business domains, thereby reducing complexity and focusing on performance optimization within clear boundaries.

2. Enhance Service Communication

Efficient communication between services is crucial for maintaining high performance. Over-reliance on synchronous calls can lead to significant latency issues.

Example: Opt for asynchronous communication mechanisms such as message queues or event streams to minimize waiting times and decouple service dependencies.

```
# Command to produce a message to a Kafka topic
kafka-console-producer --broker-list localhost:9092 --topic OrderStatus --message 'Order
    123 Updated'
```

This command showcases how to send an asynchronous message to a Kafka topic, which can be consumed by any service without direct interactions with the service that manages orders.

3. Strategize Data Management

Appropriate data management is pivotal in distributed systems like microservices. Each service should manage its own database to ensure loose coupling and independent scalability.

Best Practice: Employ APIs for inter-service data interactions and consider using patterns like CQRS (Command Query Responsibility Segregation) to further optimize data handling and improve performance.

4. Implement API Gateways

API gateways simplify client interactions and manage service orchestration, which can help reduce latency and streamline request processing.

Example: Use an API Gateway to centralize request routing, authentication, and rate limiting, thereby offloading these tasks from individual services.

```
# Setting up rate limiting on an API Gateway
curl -i -X POST http://localhost:8001/plugins/ \
    --data "name=rate-limiting" \
    --data "config.minute=10" \
    --data "config.policy=local"
```

This example sets a rate limit on the API Gateway to prevent services from being overwhelmed by high traffic volumes.

5. Monitor and Analyze Service Performance

Continuous monitoring is essential to identify performance bottlenecks and optimize resource allocation.

Best Practice: Deploy monitoring tools like Prometheus to collect and analyze performance metrics, and use Grafana for dashboard visualization and alerting.

```
# Prometheus query to monitor service request rates
rate(http_requests_total{service="user-service"}[5m])
```

This Prometheus query helps track the rate of HTTP requests for a specific service, useful for identifying spikes in demand or potential performance degradation.

6. Integrate Performance Testing in CI/CD

Regular performance testing ensures potential issues are caught early in the development cycle.

Example: Incorporate tools like Gatling or Apache JMeter in your CI/CD pipelines to perform automated performance tests.

Conclusion

Optimizing performance in microservices architectures requires a comprehensive approach that includes efficient design, effective communication strategies, and robust data management practices. By implementing these recommended approaches and continuously monitoring and testing the system, organizations can ensure that their microservices architectures deliver optimal performance consistently. As technologies evolve, so should the strategies for maintaining and enhancing system performance.

Efficient communication patterns for microservices

The microservices architecture, characterized by its division of a system into smaller, independent services, necessitates efficient communication strategies to manage the interactions among these services effectively. Choosing appropriate communication patterns is crucial to ensure these services can operate seamlessly and maintain system integrity without added complexity or increased response times. This discussion delves into various effective communication patterns suitable for microservices, detailing their practical applications, advantages, and integration tips.

1. Synchronous vs. Asynchronous Communication

Communication in microservices is generally categorized into synchronous and asynchronous types:

- **Synchronous Communication**: This involves direct HTTP/REST calls where the client waits for a response immediately after a request. This approach is simple but can create delays due to wait times and tight coupling between services.

- **Asynchronous Communication**: This method employs messaging systems where messages are placed in a queue and processed independently. It reduces waiting times, lowers the degree of coupling, and improves scalability.

Best Practice: Employ asynchronous communication wherever immediate responses are not critical to reduce blocking and service coupling.

2. API Gateway Pattern

The API Gateway serves as a unified entry point for all client requests. It directs these requests to the appropriate microservices and aggregates results to send back to the client. Additionally, it manages common functionalities such as authentication and rate limiting.

Implementation Example:

```
# Implementing rate limiting in an API Gateway with Nginx
limit_req_zone $binary_remote_addr zone=mylimit:10m rate=5r/s;
server {
    location /api/ {
        limit_req zone=mylimit burst=10;
        proxy_pass http://my_backend;
    }
}
```

This Nginx setup demonstrates how to configure rate limiting to prevent service overload.

3. Event-Driven Architecture (EDA)

In an event-driven architecture, services communicate through events rather than direct calls. This pattern uses an event bus that facilitates event publication and subscription, promoting loose coupling and service autonomy.

Advantages:

- Reduces dependency between services.

- Improves system responsiveness.

- Supports independent service operations.

4. Service Mesh

A service mesh is a dedicated infrastructure layer that manages service-to-service communications, enabling functionalities like load balancing, service discovery, and secure interactions within microservices architectures.

Tools: Istio and Linkerd are examples of service mesh implementations that provide a controlled and observable way to manage microservice interactions.

5. Broker Pattern

The broker pattern uses a central message broker that mediates communication between services, suitable for both asynchronous messaging and synchronous interactions.

Example: RabbitMQ allows services to send and receive messages without direct connections, supporting decoupled architectures.

```
# Command to send a message using RabbitMQ
rabbitmqadmin publish exchange=my_exchange routing_key=my_route payload="Hello,
    Microservices"
```

This illustrates publishing a message to a specific route in RabbitMQ, simplifying message handling among services.

6. Circuit Breaker Pattern

The circuit breaker pattern prevents a single service failure from causing a system-wide failure. It temporarily blocks problematic service calls, allowing the system to continue functioning while the issue is resolved.

Implementation Tool: Hystrix is commonly used for implementing the circuit breaker pattern, offering features to detect failures and provide fallback solutions.

Conclusion

Adopting efficient communication patterns in microservices architectures is essential for developing scalable, resilient, and manageable applications. These patterns facilitate smooth service interactions, which are crucial for the overall performance and reliability of the system. Continually assessing and refining these communication strategies is vital as technology evolves and system demands grow.

Service mesh integration for enhanced performance

The deployment of a service mesh is increasingly recognized as a crucial strategy for enhancing the management of microservices communications. Serving as a dedicated network layer that manages service interactions, a service mesh facilitates performance improvements, security enhancements, and comprehensive observability across a microservices architecture. This discussion explores the significant benefits associated with the integration of a service mesh and outlines the steps for successful implementation.

Understanding the Role of a Service Mesh

A service mesh is designed to handle communications and operations between service instances within a microservices environment. It primarily operates through a sidecar proxy model, where each service instance is paired with a lightweight network proxy. These proxies intercept and manage all inter-service communications, allowing for centralized management of functionalities like traffic control, security protocols, and monitoring without altering the microservices directly.

Advantages of Integrating a Service Mesh

1. Traffic Management and Performance Enhancement

One of the primary benefits of a service mesh is its ability to optimize how services interact. By managing load balancing, routing, and handling service discovery efficiently, a service mesh reduces latency and improves the responsiveness of applications.

2. Security Features

Service meshes enhance security within microservices architectures by implementing features such as mutual TLS (mTLS), which ensures encrypted and authenticated communications across services. This setup bolsters security without necessitating complex changes to the services themselves.

3. Detailed Observability

Integrating a service mesh provides extensive monitoring capabilities, offering detailed insights into application metrics like request rates, latencies, and error rates. This observability is crucial for proactive performance tuning and troubleshooting within distributed systems.

Implementing a Service Mesh

Selecting an Appropriate Service Mesh

Key players in the service mesh landscape include Istio, Linkerd, and Consul Connect, each with distinct features:

- **Istio** is renowned for its extensive capabilities in traffic management and security.

- **Linkerd** boasts ease of use and minimal performance overhead, suitable for less complex environments.

- **Consul Connect** excels in environments already utilizing Consul for service discovery.

Deployment Steps

The typical process for service mesh integration includes:

1. **Setting Up the Control Plane**: This component acts as the central hub for managing the service mesh's configurations and policies.

2. **Injection of Sidecar Proxies**: Sidecar proxies are integrated with service containers to manage the network communications. This can be done manually or automatically, depending on the environment.

3. **Configuring Traffic and Security Rules**: Define and apply configurations for managing service traffic, implementing retries, failovers, and secure communications.

```
# Example configuration for traffic routing in Istio
apiVersion: networking.istio.io/v1alpha3
kind: VirtualService
metadata:
  name: example-service
spec:
  hosts:
    - example-service
  http:
    - route:
        - destination:
            host: example-service
            weight: 100
```

This snippet shows how to direct traffic within Istio, allowing for precise control over service routing.

Ongoing Testing and Adjustments

After deployment, continuously monitor and adjust the service mesh settings to optimize performance and functionality. Utilizing monitoring tools like Prometheus and tracing utilities like Jaeger can aid in these efforts, providing vital metrics and operational insights.

Conclusion

The integration of a service mesh into microservices architectures not only streamlines service interactions but also significantly enhances performance, security, and observability. This infrastructure component allows developers to focus on application logic rather than network issues, supporting scalable and efficient application deployments. As such, selecting the right service mesh and meticulously configuring it to suit specific operational needs is crucial for leveraging its full potential in any microservices ecosystem.

Chapter Twelve

Monitoring, Profiling, and Tracing

Advanced tools and techniques for monitoring Docker environments

As Docker continues to be a pivotal platform for deploying containerized applications, effective management and monitoring of these environments become essential. Proper monitoring ensures optimal application performance, enhances reliability, and fortifies security measures. This article highlights several sophisticated tools and methodologies designed for the nuanced demands of monitoring Docker environments, offering insights into how organizations can improve operational management and oversight.

Significance of Monitoring in Docker

Monitoring Docker entails a comprehensive approach that includes observing the containers' performance, scrutinizing resource utilization, identifying anomalies, and ensuring compliance with security standards. Effective monitoring strategies enable organizations to fine-tune resource allocations, swiftly address operational issues, and uphold service level agreements (SLAs).

Sophisticated Monitoring Tools for Docker

The ecosystem around Docker monitoring has matured, giving rise to a variety of tools that cater to the specific needs of container monitoring. These tools provide detailed insights into container as well as host performance.

1. Prometheus

Prometheus is an open-source system monitoring toolkit known for its efficiency in collecting and storing metrics in a time-series format. It is particularly well-suited for monitoring dynamic environments like Docker due to its scalable data collection capabilities and a robust query language.

Core Features:

- **Service Discovery:** Automates the discovery of containers and services to monitor.

- **Advanced Query Language:** Enables complex queries for in-depth analysis of Docker performance.

Sample Configuration:

```
scrape_configs:
  - job_name: 'docker'
    static_configs:
      - targets: ['localhost:9090']
```

This snippet from a Prometheus configuration specifies how to scrape metrics from Docker, targeting the specified host and port.

2. Grafana

Grafana excels as a visualization tool for metrics collected from systems like Prometheus. It offers customizable dashboards that can be tailored to display various performance metrics, aiding teams in quickly diagnosing issues and understanding trends.

Integration with Prometheus: Grafana can be integrated seamlessly with Prometheus, providing a graphical interface for the metrics data.

3. cAdvisor

cAdvisor is a tool developed by Google specifically tailored for monitoring container stats. It automatically collects, aggregates, and makes accessible information about running containers, focusing on resource usage and performance analysis.

Primary Features:

- **Live Metrics Monitoring:** Tracks real-time resource usage like CPU, memory, and network statistics.

- **Built-in Web UI:** Allows for the direct observation of current and historical statistics.

Example Command for Running cAdvisor:

```
docker run \
  --volume=/:/rootfs:ro \
  --volume=/var/run:/var/run:rw \
  --volume=/sys:/sys:ro \
  --volume=/var/lib/docker/:/var/lib/docker:ro \
  --publish=8080:8080 \
  --detach=true \
  --name=cadvisor \
  google/cadvisor:latest
```

This command demonstrates setting up cAdvisor in a Docker environment, mapping the necessary directories and exposing the appropriate port.

4. Elastic Stack (ELK)

The Elastic Stack combines Elasticsearch, Logstash, and Kibana to offer powerful logging capabilities. This combination is ideal for gathering and analyzing logs from all Docker containers, enabling comprehensive log analysis and visualization in Kibana.

Highlights:

- **Log Collection and Storage:** Gathers logs into Elasticsearch for processing and storage.

- **Efficient Search and Analysis:** Uses Elasticsearch's capabilities to filter and analyze logged data.

Sample Logstash Setup:

```
input {
  tcp {
    port => 5000
    codec => json
  }
}
output {
  elasticsearch {
    hosts => ["localhost:9200"]
    index => "docker-logs-%{+YYYY.MM.dd}"
  }
}
```

This configuration for Logstash shows how to collect log data via TCP and forward it to Elasticsearch, organizing logs into daily indices.

Conclusion

Monitoring Docker environments effectively requires the adoption of advanced tools that provide detailed insights into the containers and underlying systems. By leveraging tools like Prometheus, Grafana, cAdvisor, and the Elastic Stack, businesses can achieve a deep understanding of their Docker operations. Thorough configuration and integration of these tools are essential but result in a robust framework for continuous monitoring and proactive management, ensuring that Docker deployments operate at their highest efficiency.

Profiling containers to understand performance bottlenecks

Profiling containers is crucial in the management of containerized applications, providing detailed insights into application performance and resource utilization. This analysis is essential for diagnosing delays, optimizing operations, and ensuring that containerized applications run efficiently within their allocated resources. This article outlines effective strategies and tools for profiling Docker environments, aimed at identifying and resolving performance bottlenecks.

Importance of Container Profiling

Effective container profiling addresses complex performance issues that arise from the interaction between containers and their underlying infrastructure. By closely monitoring and analyzing container operations, organizations can:

- Identify underperforming components.

- Optimize resource allocation.

- Enhance overall application performance to meet user expectations and maintain service level agreements.

Effective Tools and Approaches for Profiling Containers

1. cAdvisor (Container Advisor)

Developed by Google, cAdvisor is tailored specifically for container monitoring, offering detailed analytics on resource usage and performance characteristics of running containers.

Key Capabilities:

- Provides real-time and historical data.

- Measures CPU, memory, filesystem, and network usage metrics.

Example Deployment:

```
docker run \
  --volume=/:/rootfs:ro \
  --volume=/var/run:/var/run:rw \
  --volume=/sys:/sys:ro \
  --volume=/var/lib/docker/:/var/lib/docker:ro \
  --publish=8080:8080 \
  --detach=true \
  --name=cadvisor \
  google/cadvisor:latest
```

Deploying cAdvisor with this command sets it up to monitor all containers on the host, providing valuable insights through its web UI.

2. Docker Stats Command

The built-in **docker stats** command provides a snapshot of container performance, including metrics like CPU and memory usage, as well as network and block I/O statistics.

Example Command:

```
docker stats --all
```

Running this command displays live statistics for all containers, allowing for quick identification of resource-intensive containers.

3. Prometheus and Grafana Integration

For detailed monitoring, combining Prometheus with Grafana offers extensive data collection, storage, and visualization capabilities.

- **Prometheus** scrapes and stores metrics.

- **Grafana** visualizes these metrics through comprehensive dashboards.

Example Configuration:

```
scrape_configs:
  - job_name: 'docker'
    static_configs:
      - targets: ['localhost:9100']
```

This setup enables Prometheus to collect metrics from Docker environments, which Grafana can then visualize.

4. Application-Specific Profiling Tools

For in-depth application profiling within containers, it's often necessary to use language-specific tools, such as Java's VisualVM, Python's cProfile, or Node.js' Clinic.js.

Example for Node.js with Clinic.js:

```
clinic doctor --on-port 'autocannon localhost:$PORT' -- node server.js
```

This setup profiles a Node.js application, helping to diagnose performance issues through Clinic.js's detailed analysis.

5. Sysdig and Trace Compass

For a deeper dive into system behavior:

- **Sysdig** captures detailed system events and metrics directly from the Linux kernel.

- **Trace Compass** analyzes system traces for advanced troubleshooting.

Example Usage of Sysdig:

```
sysdig -pc -c topprocs_cpu
```

This command shows processes consuming the most CPU, useful for pinpointing high resource usage within containers.

Profiling Best Practices

- **Regular Monitoring**: Implementing ongoing monitoring protocols is crucial for continuously assessing performance.

- **Establish Performance Baselines**: Define baseline metrics for normal operations to quickly spot performance deviations.

- **Incorporate Profiling into CI/CD**: Integrate profiling into continuous integration and deployment pipelines to catch performance regressions early.

Conclusion

Thorough profiling is indispensable for effectively managing containerized environments, ensuring applications perform optimally and resources are used efficiently. By leveraging advanced tools like cAdvisor, Prometheus, Grafana, and language-specific profilers, along with employing robust monitoring strategies, organizations can maintain high-performance standards in their Docker deployments. This proactive approach to container profiling helps in tuning systems to meet operational demands and in achieving superior service performance.

Tracing system calls and events in complex applications

Tracing system calls and events is essential for deep insights into the operational behavior of complex software applications. This practice enables developers and system administrators to understand the detailed interactions between application processes and the underlying operating system, facilitating the identification and resolution of performance bottlenecks, optimizing resource use, and troubleshooting issues in real time. This discussion provides an overview of effective methods, tools, and strategies for system call and event tracing in sophisticated applications.

Importance of System Call and Event Tracing

Tracing is pivotal for a comprehensive understanding of application dynamics, especially in systems characterized by high interactivity and dependency on system resources. It allows for:

- Detailed analysis of application performance issues.

- Enhanced resource utilization and management.

- Immediate error detection and debugging capabilities.

Advanced Tools for Tracing System Calls and Events

Several advanced tools have been developed to assist in the detailed tracing of system calls and events, catering to various needs and complexities within modern distributed architectures. Here are some of the most effective:

1. strace and dtrace

strace for Linux and **dtrace** for BSD are tools designed for tracing system calls and signals, providing visibility into the interactions between applications and the operating system.

Example of Using strace:

```
strace -c -p [PID]
```

This command uses **strace** to monitor the system calls made by a process specified by its PID, summarizing the calls to facilitate quick analysis.

2. SystemTap

SystemTap is a robust tool designed for probing live Linux systems, gathering detailed information about their functioning at a granular level.

Sample SystemTap Script:

```
probe syscall.* {
  println("System call: %s with args %s returned %s", name, argstr, retstr)
}
```

This script monitors every system call, logging detailed information about each call and its outcomes.

3. BPF and eBPF

Extended Berkeley Packet Filter (eBPF) is an advanced technology for running bytecode at the kernel level, allowing for sophisticated data collection without altering kernel code.

Using BCC with eBPF: The BPF Compiler Collection (BCC) leverages eBPF and includes tools like **execsnoop** for tracing system events.

```
execsnoop-bpfcc
```

This command tracks process execution, providing insights into the creation and management of processes within the application.

4. LTTng (Linux Trace Toolkit Next Generation)

LTTng specializes in high-performance tracing of Linux systems, capturing detailed events from both the kernel and user applications with minimal performance overhead.

Configuring an LTTng Session:

```
lttng create session1 --output=/tmp/my-traces
lttng enable-event -k 'sched_switch'
lttng start
```

These commands initiate an LTTng session to trace context switch events in the kernel, storing the trace data for later analysis.

5. Perf

perf is a versatile tool for performance analysis in Linux, useful for collecting comprehensive data about system performance.

Command to Use Perf:

```
perf record -e syscalls:sys_enter_* -p [PID]
perf report
```

This example records all system call entries for a specified process and then generates a report based on the collected data.

Best Practices for Effective Tracing

- **Low Impact Tracing**: Choose tracing tools and configurations that minimize the impact on system performance.

- **Secure Tracing Practices**: Manage access to tracing tools carefully, as they can expose sensitive system information.

- **Regular Monitoring Integration**: Integrate system tracing into regular monitoring routines to proactively manage system health.

- **Efficient Data Handling**: Organize and store tracing data effectively, ensuring it supports rather than hinders system operations.

Conclusion

System call and event tracing is a sophisticated technique that is indispensable for diagnosing and optimizing complex applications. By employing a range of specialized tools like **strace**, **SystemTap**, **eBPF**, **LTTng**, and **perf**, and following best practices for their use, organizations can achieve deeper insights into their applications' internal workings, leading to improved performance, reliability, and efficiency in their software systems.

Chapter Thirteen

Performance Anti-Patterns and Common Pitfalls

Identifying and resolving performance anti-patterns

Performance anti-patterns are habitual practices in software development that, while seemingly beneficial, may lead to inefficient performance or scalability issues as applications evolve. Addressing these practices is essential to maintaining software that is both performant and scalable. This article discusses several prevalent performance anti-patterns, methods to detect them, and strategies to effectively mitigate their impact.

Defining Performance Anti-Patterns

These anti-patterns often manifest when solutions designed for specific scenarios are misapplied to different contexts without a clear understanding of their implications, or when temporary fixes compromise the overall design and performance of the system.

Common Performance Anti-Patterns and Their Resolutions

1. The Golden Hammer

This anti-pattern reflects a scenario where a familiar technology or methodology is repeatedly used across different projects without regard for its suitability to the task at hand, leading to suboptimal performance.

Resolution: Foster a development environment that values critical evaluation of tools and technologies against project requirements, ensuring the best fit is selected for each scenario.

2. Cargo Cult Programming

Here, solutions are implemented based on their success in previous projects without understanding the underlying principles that made them effective. This can lead to redundant or inappropriate code usage.

Resolution: Promote understanding of the 'why' behind each programming decision, enhancing developer knowledge and decision-making skills.

3. Death by a Thousand Cuts

In this anti-pattern, each part of the system might function well independently, but when combined, the interactions among components degrade overall performance.

Resolution: Utilize system-wide performance testing to uncover inefficiencies that appear under load, employing tools to analyze and optimize the entire system rather than individual parts.

4. Spaghetti Code

Poorly structured code can become tangled over time, making it difficult to understand and optimize, thereby degrading performance.

Resolution: Regularly refactor codebases to improve structure and clarity, incorporating modular design principles to enhance maintainability and performance.

Techniques to Identify Performance Anti-Patterns

Using Profiling Tools

Tools like VisualVM or Intel VTune Amplifier can analyze execution flows and pinpoint inefficiencies within the code.

Example:

```
# Launching VisualVM to profile an application
jvisualvm
```

Running this command opens VisualVM, connecting it to a Java application for detailed performance analysis.

Implementing Effective Monitoring

Systematic monitoring using tools such as Prometheus for data collection and Grafana for data visualization can help identify performance anomalies early.

Example Configuration for Prometheus:

```
scrape_configs:
  - job_name: 'application'
    static_configs:
      - targets: ['localhost:9090']
```

This configuration directs Prometheus to gather metrics from an application, facilitating ongoing performance analysis.

Conducting Code Reviews

Regular reviews and walkthroughs by peers can uncover potential anti-patterns, benefiting from diverse experiences and insights.

Strategies for Resolving Identified Anti-Patterns

Systematic Code Refactoring

Once identified, anti-patterns should be addressed through thoughtful refactoring, which may involve rewriting code sections or updating algorithms to enhance efficiency.

Comprehensive Performance Testing

Revalidate the system post-refactoring to ensure that the changes have effectively resolved the issues without introducing new ones.

Continuous Learning

Maintain an ongoing educational agenda to keep the development team informed about anti-patterns and their solutions, fostering a culture of continuous improvement.

Conclusion

Effectively dealing with performance anti-patterns is crucial for developing and maintaining high-quality, scalable software. Understanding these common pitfalls, utilizing the right tools to identify them, and employing strategic resolutions can greatly enhance the performance and scalability of applications. Regular education and adaptation of best practices are vital in ensuring that development teams can anticipate and mitigate potential performance issues before they become ingrained problems.

Avoiding common pitfalls in Docker configuration and deployment

Docker's ability to encapsulate applications in containers has been a game-changer for deploying software consistently across different environments. However, mastering Docker deployments involves understanding and avoiding several common pitfalls that can impact application efficiency, security, and manageability. This guide highlights typical challenges encountered during Docker setups and provides practical solutions to overcome these issues effectively.

1. Proper Container Isolation

Issue: Containers that are not correctly isolated may interfere with each other or expose sensitive information, leading to potential conflicts and security issues.

Solution: Employ Docker's isolation mechanisms, such as namespaces and control groups (cgroups), to ensure that containers operate independently. Restrictive network policies should also be implemented to manage the flow of traffic between containers.

```
# Example command to isolate network for a container
docker run --network=none my-image
```

This command starts a Docker container without any network access, providing a high level of isolation, especially for operations that do not require external connectivity.

2. Resource Allocation Management

Issue: Overprovisioning containers with resources can lead to suboptimal utilization of system capabilities, affecting other processes on the same host.

Solution: Define resource limits for containers to prevent any single container from monopolizing system resources.

```
# Command to limit CPU and memory for a container
docker run -it --cpus="1" --memory="1g" ubuntu:latest
```

This command configures a container to use a maximum of one CPU and 1GB of memory, ensuring fair resource distribution across the system.

3. Vulnerability Management

Issue: Containers often rely on external images that may contain vulnerabilities or outdated components, posing security risks.

Solution: Regularly scan Docker images for vulnerabilities using Docker's built-in scan tool or other third-party security solutions to identify and mitigate risks.

```
# Command to scan a Docker image for vulnerabilities
docker scan my-image
```

This command checks a Docker image for known vulnerabilities, helping to secure your container environment against potential threats.

4. Handling Sensitive Data

Issue: Storing sensitive data directly in Docker configurations or images is a risky practice that can lead to data exposure.

Solution: Utilize Docker secrets or environment variables to manage sensitive information securely.

```
# Command to create and manage a Docker secret
echo "secure_data" | docker secret create my_secret -
```

This command creates a Docker secret, which is a safer way to handle sensitive information within Docker environments.

5. Optimizing Docker Image Sizes

Issue: Large Docker images are cumbersome to store and slow to deploy, impacting scalability and efficiency.

Solution: Implement multi-stage builds in Dockerfiles to minimize the footprint of Docker images. Using smaller base images like Alpine can also significantly reduce image size.

```
# Multi-stage Dockerfile example
FROM node:14 AS build
WORKDIR /app
COPY . .
RUN npm install && npm run build

FROM alpine:latest
COPY --from=build /app/build /app
CMD ["serve", "-s", "app"]
```

This Dockerfile demonstrates a multi-stage build where the application is built using a Node image and then packaged using a minimal Alpine image to reduce the overall size.

6. Robust Monitoring and Logging

Issue: Without comprehensive monitoring and logging, diagnosing issues within Docker containers can be delayed.

Solution: Integrate Docker with monitoring solutions like Prometheus and logging frameworks such as ELK (Elasticsearch, Logstash, Kibana) to enhance visibility into container performance and operational health.

```
# Setup Prometheus for container monitoring
docker run -p 9090:9090 -v /my/config.yml:/etc/prometheus/prometheus.yml prom/prometheus
```

Deploying Prometheus in a Docker container with custom configurations allows for effective monitoring of container metrics, ensuring timely insights into container health and performance.

Conclusion

Effectively managing Docker configurations and deployments is essential for leveraging Docker's full potential in application deployment. By understanding and mitigating these common pitfalls, developers and system administrators can ensure their Docker environments are secure, efficient, and scalable. Regularly revising Docker strategies and keeping abreast of best practices in container management will further enhance the stability and performance of Dockerized applications.

Case studies of performance troubleshooting

In today's complex IT landscape, swiftly identifying and addressing performance issues is crucial for maintaining system integrity and user satisfaction. The following case studies exemplify successful strategies for diagnosing and resolving performance problems in software systems, showcasing the application of various troubleshooting techniques and tools.

Case Study 1: Scaling an E-Commerce Platform

Background: A leading e-commerce platform experienced performance degradation during high-traffic periods, notably during sales events, leading to slow page loads and increased transaction timeouts.

Challenge: The platform utilized a microservices architecture in a cloud setup, with specific performance issues traced to the user authentication and inventory management services during traffic peaks.

Troubleshooting Process:

- **Performance Monitoring:** Tools such as New Relic and Datadog were employed to monitor the performance of each microservice, identifying critical bottlenecks.

- **Load Testing:** The team conducted stress tests using JMeter to simulate peak load conditions, which helped identify the microservices that were underperforming.

- **Analysis:** Profiling identified inefficient database operations and insufficient caching as primary concerns. The authentication service, in particular, was overloading the database with synchronous calls for each session verification.

Solution:

- **Database Optimization:** Queries were optimized, and indexes were added to improve database performance.

- **Caching Strategy:** Redis was implemented for session management and to cache frequent queries, reducing direct database hits.

- **Asynchronous Processing:** Refactoring critical services to handle processes asynchronously reduced the burden on synchronous operations.

Outcome: Post-implementation, the platform efficiently managed higher traffic volumes during peak sales, with improved page load times and fewer transaction timeouts, leading to greater customer satisfaction and increased revenue.

Case Study 2: Improving Financial Transaction Processing

Background: A financial services application showed significant delays in transaction processing during periods of high transaction volume.

Challenge: The application's monolithic structure complicated the isolation of performance issues, particularly pinpointing transaction delays due to a synchronous logging system.

Troubleshooting Process:

- **Code Review and Profiling:** Tools like VisualVM and network traffic analyzers like Wireshark helped trace performance issues to specific components.

- **Resource Monitoring:** Monitoring tools indicated spikes in CPU usage and disk I/O that coincided with transaction processing peaks.

- **Bottleneck Identification:** Extensive logging revealed that transaction delays were primarily caused by a synchronous logging mechanism.

Solution:

- **Decoupling Services:** The monolithic application was gradually refactored into a service-oriented architecture to allow independent scaling and improvement of processing and logging operations.

- **Asynchronous Logging:** Implementing an asynchronous approach to logging reduced its impact on the transaction processing time.

- **Dynamic Resource Allocation:** Based on predictive analytics, resources were scaled dynamically to accommodate load increases, enhancing processing capabilities.

Outcome: The refinements led to a noticeable reduction in transaction processing times, thereby increasing throughput and enhancing user experience by providing quicker transaction confirmations.

Conclusion

These case studies illustrate that resolving performance issues in software systems requires a strategic blend of monitoring, analysis, and corrective action. Effective troubleshooting is predicated on understanding underlying performance issues and implementing solutions that directly address these problems. Continuous improvement practices, including regular performance evaluations and updates, are crucial for sustaining optimal performance and ensuring system reliability and user satisfaction.

Chapter Fourteen

Future Trends in Docker Performance

Upcoming technologies and trends affecting Docker performance

As Docker remains integral to the deployment of containerized applications, its performance is increasingly influenced by emerging technologies and industry trends. This article delves into the significant technologies poised to impact Docker's efficiency and application, highlighting the potential adjustments and benefits these innovations could bring.

1. Serverless Computing

Impact on Docker: The rise of serverless computing offers a way to execute applications with minimal concern for underlying servers, affecting Docker by potentially reducing the overhead associated with container management. Docker can be integrated with serverless frameworks to leverage its encapsulation capabilities, enhancing the efficiency of serverless execution.

Example: Utilizing AWS Lambda's support for Docker containers to deploy serverless functions encapsulated as Docker images.

```
# Example AWS CLI command to deploy a Docker image to Lambda
aws lambda create-function --function-name example-function --package-type Image --code ImageUri
    =<DOCKER_IMAGE_URI>
```

This demonstrates deploying a Docker container as a serverless function, illustrating Docker's flexibility in serverless environments.

2. Kubernetes Integration

Impact on Docker: Kubernetes has solidified its role as a leader in orchestrating container environments, influencing Docker deployments. Its robust management tools can enhance Docker's scalability and resource allocation by automating container orchestration and improving performance efficiencies.

Example: Using Kubernetes to manage Docker containers for improved resource handling and automated scaling.

```
# Kubernetes deployment YAML using a Docker image
apiVersion: apps/v1
kind: Deployment
metadata:
  name: example-deployment
spec:
  replicas: 3
  selector:
    matchLabels:
      app: example-app
  template:
    metadata:
      labels:
        app: example-app
    spec:
      containers:
      - name: example-app
        image: example-app:latest
        ports:
        - containerPort: 8080
```

This YAML configures Kubernetes to orchestrate Docker containers, optimizing performance through effective resource management.

3. Artificial Intelligence and Machine Learning

Impact on Docker: AI and ML are becoming integral in optimizing container management, offering predictive insights that enhance Docker's performance. These technologies can automate resource allocation, predict system failures, and adaptively manage container environments.

Example: Employing AI models to predict traffic loads and dynamically scale Docker containers accordingly.

```python
# Python pseudocode for AI-driven resource scaling
if predict_high_load():
    scale_service('example-service', increase_by=3)
```

This pseudocode outlines using AI to automatically scale Docker containers based on predicted demand, enhancing responsiveness and resource efficiency.

4. Edge Computing

Impact on Docker: The expansion of edge computing necessitates deploying applications closer to data sources, which aligns well with Docker's capabilities. Docker's portability and light resource footprint make it ideal for edge deployments, where minimizing latency is crucial.

Example: Deploying Docker containers on edge devices to process data locally, reducing latency and server load.

```
# Command to run a Docker container optimized for edge environments
docker run -d --name local-edge-service my-app:edge-optimized
```

This command demonstrates deploying a Docker container to an edge device, leveraging Docker's adaptability to perform efficiently in constrained environments.

5. Green Computing

Impact on Docker: As the tech industry moves towards more sustainable practices, Docker's role in promoting energy efficiency becomes more prominent. Optimizing Docker configurations for lower resource usage contributes to reduced power consumption.

Example: Configuring Docker containers to use minimal resources to support sustainability goals.

```
# Command to restrict Docker container resource usage
docker run -d --cpus="1" --memory="1g" --name eco-friendly-app my-app
```

This command sets resource limits for a Docker container, aligning Docker usage with energy-efficient practices.

Conclusion

Emerging technologies such as serverless computing, Kubernetes, AI, edge computing, and sustainability initiatives are set to significantly influence Docker's operational paradigm. By adapting to these technologies, Docker can enhance its performance, expand its applicability, and continue to provide robust solutions in container management. These advancements will allow organizations to refine their Docker strategies, ensuring optimal performance and future readiness.

Preparing for next-generation Docker deployments

As Docker remains integral to modern application deployment strategies, staying abreast of evolving infrastructure and technology trends is crucial. This article outlines strategic preparations for harnessing advancements in Docker deployments, aimed at enhancing efficiency, scalability, and adaptability in dynamic IT environments.

Modernizing Infrastructure

The backbone of Docker deployments is robust infrastructure. With the rise of multi-cloud environments, edge computing, and enhanced server architectures, Docker setups must evolve to maintain efficiency and relevance.

1. Multi-Cloud and Hybrid Environments

Organizations are increasingly diversifying their cloud strategies to include multiple providers, necessitating Docker configurations that support such complexity seamlessly.

Actionable Steps:

- Adopt Docker configurations that facilitate deployment across various cloud platforms.

- Use orchestration tools like Kubernetes or Docker Swarm to manage container deployments effectively across different clouds.

```
# Deploying Docker containers across multiple clouds with Kubernetes
kubectl apply -f deployment.yaml --context=first-cloud-provider
kubectl apply -f deployment.yaml --context=second-cloud-provider
```

This demonstrates deploying Docker containers using Kubernetes to handle resources across different cloud environments efficiently.

2. Integrating Edge Computing

With edge computing, data processing is moved closer to the data source, decreasing latency. Docker's portability is particularly beneficial for edge deployments.

Actionable Steps:

- Optimize Docker images for minimal resource usage, essential for performance at the edge.

- Set up automated pipelines for consistent and efficient deployment of Docker containers tailored for edge computing.

```
# Running a Docker container optimized for edge deployment
docker build -t my-app:edge-version -f Dockerfile.edge .
docker run --name my-edge-app -d my-app:edge-version
```

This shows the process of building and deploying a Docker container designed specifically for edge computing environments.

Enhancing Orchestration Capabilities

Effective management of Docker containers is crucial as deployments grow in complexity and scale.

1. Advanced Kubernetes Features

Kubernetes excels in managing containerized applications and can be further tailored to enhance Docker deployments.

Actionable Steps:

- Implement Kubernetes operators that simplify the management lifecycle of Docker containers.

- Create and manage Kubernetes custom resources to meet specific operational requirements.

```yaml
# Kubernetes Custom Resource Definition for Docker management
apiVersion: "setup.io/v1"
kind: DockerSetup
metadata:
  name: custom-app-setup
spec:
  image: my-custom-app:latest
  instances: 3
  ports:
    - containerPort: 80
```

This YAML configuration illustrates how Kubernetes can be extended to manage Docker deployments more effectively, customizing resource handling and scaling.

Committing to Automation

Automation streamlines operations and minimizes human errors, which is vital for managing complex Docker environments efficiently.

1. Infrastructure as Code (IaC)

Using IaC for Docker environments ensures consistent setups and simplifies the management of infrastructure changes.

Actionable Steps:

- Define Docker infrastructure with IaC tools like Terraform to automate and replicate environments easily.

- Integrate IaC into continuous integration and deployment workflows for seamless environment provisioning.

```
# Terraform script for automating Docker container deployment
resource "docker_container" "app_instance" {
  image = "${docker_image.app.latest}"
  name  = "application-container"
  ports {
    internal = 80
    external = 8080
  }
}
```

This Terraform script automates the deployment of Docker containers, demonstrating how IaC can be used to manage Docker setups efficiently.

Conclusion

To effectively prepare for future Docker deployments, it's essential to integrate modern infrastructure solutions, leverage advanced orchestration tools, and embrace thorough automation practices. These strategies will ensure that Docker environments are ready to meet the challenges of next-generation deployments, optimizing both performance and operational flexibility. Adapting to these advancements allows organizations to maximize the benefits of Docker technology, ensuring robust, scalable, and efficient containerized application deployments.

Integration with emerging cloud and hardware technologies

As the technological landscape evolves, businesses are increasingly harnessing new cloud services and hardware advancements to enhance application performance and operational efficiency. This article discusses the critical aspects of integrating cutting-edge cloud and hardware technologies, illustrating how these developments can bolster application scalability, security, and responsiveness.

Advancements in Cloud Technologies

The realm of cloud computing is broadening, with new services that enhance the flexibility and efficiency of IT operations. Companies are strategically adopting these services to drive innovation and optimize costs.

1. Serverless Computing

Serverless computing offloads the responsibility of managing servers to cloud providers, focusing on code execution based on event triggers. This approach enhances application scalability and can significantly reduce operational costs.

Example Integration:

- **AWS Lambda:** Integrating serverless functions with traditional cloud architectures using AWS Lambda can streamline processes and reduce latency.

```python
import boto3

# Example: Invoking an AWS Lambda function
lambda_client = boto3.client('lambda')
response = lambda_client.invoke(
    FunctionName='ProcessDataFunction',
    InvocationType='Event',
    Payload=b'{"data": "value"}'
)
```

This Python snippet demonstrates invoking a serverless function, showcasing seamless integration with serverless computing platforms.

2. Container Orchestration Platforms

Container as a Service (CaaS) platforms facilitate container management at scale, offering tools to deploy, manage, and orchestrate containers efficiently.

Example Integration:

- **Google Kubernetes Engine (GKE):** Utilizing GKE provides robust tools for managing Docker containers, ensuring effective load balancing and auto-scaling.

```
# Deploying on Google Kubernetes Engine
gcloud container clusters create "cluster-name"
gcloud container clusters get-credentials cluster-name
kubectl create deployment web-app --image=gcr.io/hello-world
```

This command set establishes a Kubernetes cluster and deploys a containerized application on GKE, highlighting the practicality of CaaS integration.

Innovations in Hardware Technologies

Recent hardware innovations are pushing the boundaries of processing capabilities, supporting more complex and demanding applications.

1. GPU and Accelerated Computing

GPUs have transcended their traditional roles to support diverse computing needs, particularly in data-intensive environments.

Example Integration:

- **NVIDIA Docker:** Leveraging NVIDIA Docker toolkits, applications can utilize GPU resources for tasks requiring intense computational power.

```
# Running a Docker container utilizing GPU resources
docker run --gpus all nvidia/cuda:11.0-base nvidia-smi
```

This command facilitates a Docker container's access to GPU resources, exemplifying the use of hardware acceleration in containerized environments.

2. Custom Hardware Solutions

FPGAs and ASICs provide tailored hardware solutions for specific computational tasks, enhancing efficiency in targeted operations.

Example Integration:

- **AWS F1 Instances:** AWS F1 instances equipped with FPGAs offer customizable hardware configurations for specialized needs.

```
# Launching an AWS FPGA instance
aws ec2 run-instances --instance-type f1.2xlarge --image-id ami-xyzabc --count 1 --key
    -name MyEC2Key
```

This AWS CLI command initiates an FPGA-enabled instance, optimizing custom hardware integration for high-performance tasks.

Conclusion

Adopting emerging cloud and hardware technologies is imperative for organizations aiming to stay competitive in a fast-paced digital world. Through strategic integration of serverless frameworks, advanced container orchestration, and state-of-the-art hardware accelerations, enterprises can achieve greater scalability, efficiency, and performance. These technologies not only facilitate significant advancements in computing capabilities but also enable businesses to respond more swiftly to market demands and technological shifts.

Chapter Fifteen

Automating Performance Optimization

Tools and scripts for automating performance tuning

Performance tuning is a critical component in optimizing application efficiency and ensuring the effective use of system resources. Automation in performance tuning simplifies the process, enabling consistent optimization across different environments. This article reviews various tools and scripts that can streamline the performance tuning process, ensuring applications operate at peak efficiency.

1. Utilizing Performance Monitoring Tools

It's essential to begin by monitoring current performance levels to set baselines and identify potential areas for improvement.

a. Prometheus and Grafana

Prometheus is a powerful open-source monitoring tool that gathers time-series data. Grafana integrates with Prometheus to visualize this data, offering insights that help pinpoint performance bottlenecks.

Example Configuration for Prometheus:

```
# Configuration snippet for Prometheus to monitor application metrics
global:
  scrape_interval: 15s

scrape_configs:
  - job_name: 'application'
    static_configs:
      - targets: ['application_host:9090']
```

This setup directs Prometheus to collect metrics from an application every 15 seconds, allowing Grafana to graphically represent these metrics for easy performance tracking.

b. New Relic

New Relic provides comprehensive application monitoring, delivering real-time performance insights. It automates the instrumentation of applications to collect detailed performance data.

Usage:

Install the New Relic agent in your application's environment to begin gathering extensive performance data, which is accessible through a customized dashboard for on-the-fly optimization.

2. Leveraging Configuration Management Tools

These tools help maintain consistency in software and hardware setups, which is crucial for accurate performance tuning.

a. Ansible

Ansible automates application deployment, system configurations, and more, ensuring environments are consistent and in line with performance best practices.

Ansible Playbook Example:

```
# Ansible playbook to optimize system performance settings
- hosts: all
  become: yes
  tasks:
    - name: Adjust VM swappiness setting
      sysctl:
        name: vm.swappiness
        value: '10'
        state: present
        reload: yes
```

This playbook configures the **vm.swappiness** system parameter, optimizing memory handling to enhance performance.

3. Scripting Automated Performance Adjustments

Dynamic environments benefit from scripts that automatically adjust settings based on real-time performance data.

a. Bash Scripts

Bash scripting is a robust method for making on-the-fly system adjustments on Linux-based systems.

Example Bash Script:

```bash
#!/bin/bash
# Monitor and adjust the TCP timeout to manage system load
current_load=$(cat /proc/loadavg | cut -d ' ' -f 1)
max_load=4.00
if [ $(echo "$current_load > $max_load" | bc) -eq 1 ]; then
    echo "Current load of $current_load is high, adjusting system parameters."
    sysctl -w net.ipv4.tcp_fin_timeout=30
else
    echo "System load of $current_load is within normal limits."
fi
```

This script assesses the server's load and modifies TCP settings if the load exceeds the specified threshold, helping maintain optimal performance.

4. Implementing Automated Benchmarking Tools

Benchmarking tools can simulate user interaction with applications to assess performance under various load conditions.

a. Apache JMeter

JMeter is a versatile tool for performance testing web applications. It can simulate a high number of requests to test how network changes affect application performance.

Example JMeter Application:

JMeter scripts can be configured to test server responsiveness under heavy traffic, providing data that informs further performance adjustments.

Conclusion

Automating performance tuning involves an integrated approach using advanced tools and scripting solutions. By employing technologies like Prometheus, Grafana, New Relic, Ansible, and Apache JMeter, organizations can not only streamline the tuning process but also ensure that performance improvements are consistent and repeatable across all deployments. These tools provide the means to automatically adjust configurations in response to changing performance metrics, ensuring applications are always tuned for optimal performance.

Continuous performance optimization strategies

Maintaining and enhancing application performance over its lifecycle is crucial for ensuring operational efficiency and user satisfaction. Continuous performance optimization is a disciplined approach to regularly assessing and improving the performance of software applications. This guide outlines the techniques and tools required for sustaining optimal performance through continuous refinement and monitoring.

Establishing Performance Baselines and Ongoing Monitoring

Setting initial performance baselines is critical for measuring the effectiveness of optimization efforts over time. Continuous monitoring against these baselines allows for the timely identification of performance deviations and bottlenecks.

a. Utilizing Advanced Monitoring Tools

Tools such as **Dynatrace**, **New Relic**, and **Datadog** offer comprehensive monitoring capabilities, tracking metrics like response times, server load, and transaction volumes. These platforms provide invaluable insights through real-time data analytics.

Example Command:

```
# Command to install a monitoring agent for New Relic
newrelic-install install
```

This simple command sets up a New Relic agent which immediately begins monitoring application performance, facilitating rapid detection and analysis of performance issues.

Regular Profiling for Performance Management

Continuous profiling is essential in dynamic environments where application updates are frequent. This process involves tracking system performance to pinpoint inefficiencies continuously.

a. Effective Profiling Tools

Java Flight Recorder (JFR) and **Google Cloud Profiler** are potent tools that collect detailed performance data with minimal overhead, providing insights into CPU and memory usage, among other metrics.

Example Use:

```
// Command to enable Java Flight Recorder
java -XX:StartFlightRecording=dumponexit=true,filename=myapp_recording.jfr -jar
    MyApplication.jar
```

This command activates Java Flight Recorder for a running Java application, capturing detailed performance data without disrupting its operations.

Integrating Automated Performance Tests

Incorporating automated performance testing within the CI/CD pipeline ensures that all deployments meet predefined performance criteria. This includes comprehensive load, stress, and scalability tests.

a. Tools for Automated Testing

Apache JMeter and **Locust** provide frameworks for simulating user interactions and network traffic to assess application robustness under varied loads.

Example Command:

```
# Running a load test with Apache JMeter
jmeter -n -t load_test_plan.jmx -l load_test_results.jtl
```

This command executes a non-GUI JMeter test, applying the specified test plan and recording the results for subsequent analysis.

Automating Performance Tuning Tasks

Automation is key to effectively applying performance enhancements based on analytical insights. Scripts and orchestration tools can dynamically adjust settings and manage resources in real-time.

a. Automation through Scripting

Automation scripts, particularly those executed within platforms like **Ansible** or **Terraform**, can modify system configurations or scale resources based on performance data.

Example Ansible Script:

```
# Ansible playbook for system performance tuning
- hosts: webservers
  roles:
    - { role: sysctl, fs.file-max: '50000' }
```

This Ansible playbook adjusts system parameters, such as the maximum number of open file descriptors, to alleviate common performance bottlenecks.

Emphasizing Continuous Improvement

Ongoing refinement based on continuous feedback loops is fundamental to this strategy. This adaptive approach ensures that applications remain efficient as user demands and technology landscapes evolve.

a. Implementing Feedback Mechanisms

Enhancing feedback loops through integrated monitoring tools and user feedback channels allows for responsive and informed performance management.

Conclusion

Continuous performance optimization requires a structured approach involving the regular collection of performance data, systematic testing, and the automated application of tuning measures. By embracing these strategies, organizations can ensure that their applications consistently meet performance standards, adapt to new challenges, and deliver an exceptional user experience.

Integrating performance tuning into CI/CD pipelines

Incorporating performance tuning within Continuous Integration/Continuous Deployment (CI/CD) processes is vital for ensuring that software applications not only meet functional requirements but also perform optimally across various conditions. This detailed guide explores the steps and tools necessary for embedding performance measures directly into CI/CD workflows.

The Importance of Performance Metrics in CI/CD

CI/CD pipelines streamline the steps from code development to production, automating the integration and deployment processes. By embedding performance tuning into these pipelines, teams can detect and resolve performance issues early, which helps avoid costly fixes post-deployment and ensures a superior end-user experience.

Establishing Performance Benchmarks

Setting clear performance benchmarks is crucial. These benchmarks, based on critical performance indicators like response times, processing throughput, and resource usage, serve as standards for expected application performance.

Example: Using JMeter for Benchmarking

Apache JMeter is effective for developing baseline performance tests that can be integrated into CI/CD pipelines. These tests validate that performance standards are consistently met with each iteration.

```
# Execute a JMeter test plan
jmeter -n -t /path/to/test_plan.jmx -l /path/to/test_results.jtl
```

This command executes a predefined JMeter test, logging the results for subsequent analysis to ensure compliance with performance benchmarks.

Automating Performance Testing

Automated performance tests within CI/CD pipelines are essential for identifying regressions or enhancements in performance as changes are made.

a. Integration with CI Tools

CI tools like Jenkins, CircleCI, and GitLab CI can automatically trigger performance tests after each commit or on a set schedule, seamlessly integrating performance analysis into the software development lifecycle.

Example: Jenkins Pipeline for Performance Testing

```
pipeline {
    agent any
    stages {
        stage('Performance Test') {
            steps {
                script {
                    // Execute performance testing script
                    sh 'jmeter -n -t /path/to/test_plan.jmx -l /path/to/results.jtl'
                }
            }
        }
    }
}
```

This configuration in Jenkins automatically runs a performance test and integrates the outcomes directly into the development pipeline.

Analyzing Performance Data

To effectively act on performance data, it needs to be accessible and interpretable. Visualization tools like Grafana offer dynamic ways to present performance metrics, helping teams understand and react to data effectively.

Example: Deploying Grafana for Metrics Visualization

```
# Start Grafana in a Docker container
docker run -d -p 3000:3000 grafana/grafana
```

This command launches Grafana, enabling developers to create detailed dashboards that track application performance metrics dynamically.

577

Continuous Performance Optimization

Continuous optimization based on ongoing feedback and performance data ensures that the application remains performant despite changes and additions over time.

a. Creating Performance Gates

Performance gates within CI/CD pipelines allow code progression only if it meets predefined performance criteria, ensuring quality control.

Example: Performance Gate in GitLab CI

```
performance_job:
  stage: performance
  script:
    - echo "Running performance tests..."
    - jmeter -n -t test_plan.jmx -l results.jtl
    - ./check_performance.py results.jtl  # Script to validate performance
      against benchmarks
  rules:
    - if: '$CI_PIPELINE_SOURCE == "push"'
```

This GitLab CI configuration incorporates a performance validation step that must be passed before proceeding with further deployment stages.

Conclusion

Effectively integrating performance tuning into CI/CD pipelines is essential for developing robust, efficient software. It ensures that applications are not only bug-free but also optimized for the best performance, maintaining high user satisfaction and operational efficiency. Through strategic use of testing tools and performance analytics, development teams can continually refine and enhance application performance as part of the deployment process.

Conclusion

Recap of the advanced performance tuning techniques learned

Performance tuning is a critical component of software development, crucial for optimizing user experience and operational efficiency. This summary revisits various sophisticated strategies that have been discussed and implemented to improve software system performance, providing a comprehensive view of essential optimizations.

Profiling and Benchmarking Techniques

Gaining a clear understanding of a system's performance profile is the starting point for any optimization. Utilizing profiling and benchmarking tools helps identify where performance lags and what improvements are needed.

Tools such as JProfiler, Java Flight Recorder, and Google Profiler have proven invaluable. These applications provide real-time performance tracking and offer in-depth analytical capabilities to guide subsequent tuning.

Example of Using Java Flight Recorder:

```
java -XX:StartFlightRecording=filename=myrecording.jfr,duration=60s -jar myapp.jar
```

This command starts a 60-second performance recording, gathering crucial data that helps in analyzing how well the application utilizes system resources.

Database Performance Optimization

Optimizing database interactions is key to minimizing response times and maximizing data throughput. Techniques such as proper indexing, query refinement, and effective connection pooling are foundational.

Exploring SQL EXPLAIN plans, implementing indexes on critical fields, and optimizing connection pool settings have been among the effective strategies. Tools like **pgBadger and MySQL Workbench** assist in diagnosing and refining database operations.

Example of Enhancing Database Connection Pools:

```java
// Setting up a database connection pool with HikariCP in Java
HikariConfig config = new HikariConfig();
config.setMaximumPoolSize(20);
HikariDataSource ds = new HikariDataSource(config);
```

This code configures a connection pool in Java using HikariCP, optimizing the handling of multiple concurrent database requests.

Resource Management Optimization

Managing computing resources efficiently is crucial for performance. Implementing strategies around thread management, asynchronous programming, and memory optimization helps in leveraging hardware capabilities effectively.

Utilizing asynchronous methods in server-side languages or adopting concurrent utilities in Java enhances throughput and responsiveness.

Example of Asynchronous Programming in Java:

```java
CompletableFuture.supplyAsync(() -> {
    return service.expensiveOperation();
}).thenAccept(result -> {
    System.out.println("Result: " + result);
});
```

This snippet shows how to perform operations asynchronously in Java, which allows the system to execute other tasks while waiting for a response from a resource-intensive operation.

Automating Performance Testing

Incorporating automated performance tests into CI/CD workflows ensures continuous assessment and maintenance of performance standards. Tools like **JMeter** and **Locust** support automated testing across various stages of deployment.

Including performance tests in automated deployment processes verifies that new changes do not degrade performance.

Example of a Performance Test in a Jenkins Pipeline:

```
pipeline {
    agent any
    stages {
        stage('Performance Test') {
            steps {
                sh 'jmeter -n -t /path/to/test_plan.jmx -l /path/to/results.jtl'
            }
        }
    }
}
```

This Jenkins pipeline automatically executes a JMeter test, ensuring new builds meet predefined performance benchmarks.

Scalability Techniques

Ensuring that applications can scale according to demand is fundamental for maintaining performance under load. Strategies such as implementing load balancers, utilizing scalable cloud services, and developing in microservices architectures support this need.

Employing auto-scaling features in cloud platforms like AWS EC2 and Azure ensures that applications adjust to load changes dynamically.

Example of Setting Up Auto-Scaling in AWS:

```
aws autoscaling create-auto-scaling-group --auto-scaling-group-name my-scaling-group --launch
    -configuration-name my-launch-config --min-size 1 --max-size 10 --desired-capacity 5
```

This AWS CLI command creates an auto-scaling group that automatically adjusts its size based on operational demands.

Conclusion

The advanced performance tuning techniques discussed are integral for developing efficient, robust, and scalable software applications. By consistently applying these strategies, developers can ensure that their applications perform optimally throughout their lifecycle, adapting effectively to both user needs and technological advancements.

Encouragement for continuous learning and experimentation

In today's fast-paced technological landscape, continuous learning and willingness to experiment are crucial for maintaining relevance and fostering innovation. This environment encourages not only personal growth but also organizational progress through the constant adoption of new methodologies and technologies.

The Critical Role of Continuous Learning

The technological sector is marked by rapid developments and shifts, making it essential for professionals to keep up with new advancements. This ongoing education is pivotal not only for individual career progression but also for maintaining the competitive edge of their organizations.

Incorporating Learning into Everyday Activities

Professionals can maintain their industry knowledge and skills through:

- **Online Platforms:** Educational platforms like Coursera, Udemy, or edX offer a range of topics from introductory programming to complex data science.

- **Podcasts and Webinars:** These can provide convenient insights into industry trends and new technologies.

- **Literature:** Regular reading of industry publications, books, and articles can deepen understanding and inspire innovation.

Example of a Structured Learning Plan:

```
## Daily and Weekly Learning Goals
  **Tuesday & Thursday:**
    Dedicate 1 hour to an online course in Advanced Python.
  **Saturday:**
    Participate in a virtual seminar or workshop.
  **Everyday:**
    Spend at least 30 minutes reading articles from tech blogs.
```

A scheduled learning plan like this ensures steady and ongoing educational activities.

The Benefits of Experimentation

Experimentation allows the practical application of learned theories and is critical for solving complex problems in new and innovative ways.

Fostering an Experimental Mindset

Creating an environment that embraces experimentation involves:

- **Embracing Failure:** Recognize that setbacks are learning opportunities.

- **Dedicated Innovation Time:** Similar to Google's '20% time,' this practice allows employees to explore projects outside their regular responsibilities.

- **Organizing Hackathons:** These events encourage creative problem solving and rapid prototyping under time constraints.

Example Hackathon Focus:

```
## Bi-Annual Hackathon: Streamlining Cloud Operations
- **Objective:** Develop tools or methods to enhance cloud computing efficiencies.
- **Duration:** 36 hours
- **Resources Provided:** Access to cloud APIs, expert mentors, and development tools.
```

Events like this encourage innovative thinking and practical problem-solving skills among team members.

Applying Learning to Practical Challenges

It's crucial that new knowledge leads to actionable insights that improve business processes or product offerings.

Methods for Practical Application:

- **Real-World Projects:** Assign projects that allow for the direct application of new skills.

- **Knowledge Sharing:** Implement regular meetings where team members can teach each other about new technologies or techniques they've learned.

- **Iterative Feedback:** Create a culture where feedback is used constructively to refine and improve upon new ideas and implementations.

Example of a Knowledge Sharing Initiative:

```
## Weekly Innovation Meetings
  **Presenter:** Jane Smith, Software Engineer
  **Topic:** Leveraging AI for Better User Experience Design
  **Structure:** 15-minute presentation followed by a brainstorming session.
  **Goal:** Identify potential applications of AI within current projects.
```

Initiatives like this encourage the dissemination of new information and foster a collaborative learning environment.

Conclusion

For technology professionals, ongoing education and a bold approach to experimentation are essential strategies for career and organizational development. Encouraging these behaviors not only enhances personal qualifications and job satisfaction but also drives broader innovation and ensures organizational success. By promoting a culture that values continual learning and open experimentation, companies can adapt and thrive in the ever-evolving tech landscape.

Final thoughts on pushing the boundaries of Docker performance

Docker has evolved from a convenient development tool to a critical component in many production environments, necessitating a focus on optimizing its performance. This final discussion synthesizes the key strategies, tools, and innovations that can maximize Docker's efficiency and effectiveness in any setting.

Maximizing Docker's Core Capabilities

Docker's appeal largely lies in its ability to provide consistent, lightweight, and isolated environments. To fully leverage these benefits, it's essential to master Docker's operational nuances, particularly in how containers are built and managed.

Optimizing Docker Image Layers

Efficient management of Docker image layers is crucial for minimizing build time and image size. Implementing multi-stage builds can significantly streamline this process.

Example Dockerfile for Multi-stage Builds:

```
# Stage 1: Build the application
FROM golang:1.14 AS builder
WORKDIR /app
COPY . .
RUN go build -o /my-app

# Stage 2: Setup the runtime environment
FROM alpine:latest
COPY --from=builder /my-app /my-app
CMD ["/my-app"]
```

This Dockerfile example demonstrates creating an initial build in a Go environment and then transferring only the necessary executable to a smaller, lightweight Alpine image.

Enhancing Docker Performance

Optimizing Docker involves comprehensive tuning, including effective monitoring, network configuration, and resource management.

a. Managing Resources

Docker offers settings to control CPU and memory usage, preventing any container from using an unfair share of resources.

Example Docker Compose Resource Limits:

```yaml
version: '3.8'
services:
  app:
    image: my-application
    deploy:
      resources:
        limits:
          cpus: '0.5'
          memory: 100M
```

This configuration in Docker Compose ensures that the **app** service does not exceed the set limits of CPU and memory usage.

b. Monitoring for Performance

Tools like cAdvisor and Docker's own monitoring commands help track how resources are used, identifying potential performance bottlenecks.

Example of Using Docker's Monitoring Command:

```
docker stats --format "{{.Container}}\t{{.CPUPerc}}\t{{.MemUsage}}"
```

This monitoring command provides a formatted output of container statistics, helping quickly pinpoint issues.

Networking and Storage Considerations

The configuration of Docker's networking and storage significantly influences its performance, impacting latency and throughput.

a. Network Configuration

Adopting host networking can reduce Docker's networking overhead, thereby improving performance for network-intensive applications.

```
docker run --network host -d nginx
```

Running a container with the host network mode, as shown here, enhances network performance by avoiding Docker's default bridged network.

b. Optimizing Storage

Selecting the appropriate Docker storage driver and configuring volumes correctly is fundamental for optimizing I/O performance.

Example of Efficient Storage Use:

```
docker run -v $(pwd)/data:/var/lib/data myapp
```

This command mounts a host directory as a volume in the container, offering better performance for I/O operations than Docker-managed volumes.

Advanced Docker Performance with Orchestration Tools

Leveraging container orchestration platforms like Kubernetes can further enhance Docker's capabilities, providing robust options for scaling and managing containerized applications effectively.

Kubernetes for Managing Docker Containers:

Kubernetes offers features that manage Docker containers at scale, including automated scaling, load balancing, and system resilience.

Conclusion

Advancing Docker performance requires a blend of strategic practices, specific configuration adjustments, and ongoing performance assessments. By embracing these principles, IT teams can ensure Docker environments are not only stable and scalable but also finely tuned for peak performance. This ongoing effort prepares the groundwork for future advancements in container technology, ensuring readiness for upcoming innovations and challenges.